Crime and Social Control in a Changing China

Crime and Social Control in a Changing China

大變革時期中國社會的犯罪與社會控制

EDITED BY JIANHONG LIU,
LENING ZHANG, AND STEVEN F. MESSNER

主編: 劉建宏
副主編: 張樂寧
　　　　司帝文.麥司納

Contributions in Criminology and Penology, Number 53

GREENWOOD PRESS
Westport, Connecticut • London

Library of Congress Cataloging-in-Publication Data

Crime and social control in a changing China / edited by Jianhong Liu, Lening Zhang, and
    Steven F. Messner.
        p.   cm.—(Contributions in criminology and penology, ISSN 0732–4464 ; no. 53)
        Added t.p. title: Da bian ge shi qi Zhongguo she hui de fan zui yu she hui kong zhi.
        Includes index.
        ISBN 0–313–31652–X (alk. paper)
        1. Crime—China.   2. Criminology—China.   3. Criminal justice, Administration of—
    China.   4. Social change—China.   5. Social control—China.   I. Title: Da bian ge shi qi
    Zhongguo she hui de fan zui yu she hui kong zhi.   II. Liu, Jianhong, 1954–   III. Zhang,
    Lening, 1956–   IV. Messner, Steven F., 1951–   V. Contributions in criminology and
    penology ; no. 53.
    HV7118.5.C75   2001   00–069514
    364.951—dc21

British Library Cataloguing in Publication Data is available.

Library of Congress Catalog Card Number: 00–069514
ISBN: 0–313–31652–X
ISSN: 0732–4464

First published in 2001

Greenwood Press, 88 Post Road West, Westport, CT 06881
An imprint of Greenwood Publishing Group, Inc.
www.greenwood.com

Printed in the United States of America

The paper used in this book complies with the
Permanent Paper Standard issued by the National
Information Standards Organization (Z39.48–1984).

10 9 8 7 6 5 4 3 2 1

**Recent Titles in Contributions in
Criminology and Penology**

To our parents, our wives, and our children

Contents

Acknowledgments

This book is a collective effort to bring up-to-date research on Chinese crime and social control to a Western audience. The editors have had to do an unusual amount of editing, especially of the papers coming from authors in China. Chinese conventions of scholarship differ in certain respects from those in the West. In particular, conventions for referencing and footnoting are quite different. We have tried to make all chapters conform to standard, U.S. journal format. This has required repeated contacts with our colleagues in China for additional information. We are very grateful to them for honoring our somewhat chauvinistic requests, and we appreciate their patience.

The help of others should also be acknowledged. Professor Paul Friday reviewed the paper by Guoan Ma and offered important input for revisions. John Liu performed a great amount of secretarial work and research assistance. Our editor at Greenwood, Suzanne Staszak-Silva, offered much appreciated encouragement for the project. Finally, the editors' families deserve special thanks. Jianhong Liu is grateful to his parents, Jinshan Liu and Xianfang Yang; to his wife, Li Wang; and to his children John Liu and Vivian Liu. Lening Zhang expresses thanks to his parents; to his wife, Aiming; and to his daughter, Shangshang, for their invaluable support. Steven F. Messner similarly expresses his gratitude to his parents, Vye and Fred; to his wife, Jill; and to his daughter, Alison. Without the care and support of our families, the arduous task of completing this volume would have been an unbearable burden.

Introduction: Impact of Market Transition—Changing Crime and Social Control in China

Jianhong Liu, Lening Zhang, and Steven F. Messner

Interest in the comparative study of crime and justice has grown steadily in recent decades. The theme of the 1995 annual meeting of the American Society of Criminology was "Crime and Justice: National and International." The selection of this theme indicates a common awareness that criminology is an international enterprise. In her presidential address to the annual meeting, Freda Adler identified the benefits derived from comparative study. She observed that we can learn valuable lessons about social control from developments in other countries. As a practical matter, it is particularly important to learn "from each other's experiences in order that costly mistakes are not repeated and that useful practices are replicated" (Adler 1996, p. 4). Moreover, in academe, "globalization affords us the opportunity to do cross-cultural testing and development of criminological theory" (Adler 1996, p. 5).

Although some scholars are engaged in international efforts to initiate joint projects, "most of the contacts have been between Western industrialized countries" (Farrington 2000, p. 3). As many Westerners have observed, Chinese society represents a distinct and unique social and cultural system that differs significantly from Western societies. Since the late 1970s and early 1980s, China has opened its "door" and implemented economic reform. This economic reform has brought about immense changes in all aspects of Chinese society. Especially since 1992, the socioeconomic transition has accelerated dramatically. As the economic system has been transformed by the introduction of market dynamics, many other social institutions have also experienced profound changes, including legal institutions and other institutions responsible for social control. The modernization and economic development stimulated by market reforms have created unprecedented growth and a significant rise in the standard of living of the Chinese people. However, at the same time, levels of crime have risen sharply. Official statistics indicate that the total crime rate has tripled since the reform started (see chapters 1 and 9 in this volume). Crimes never seen before in China are spreading. China thus provides a fascinating opportunity to study crime and social control in a comparative context.

Various aspects of social change in China have become the subjects of research in the West. However, work on the impact of the recent social transformation on crime, social control, and the Chinese criminal justice system has been rather sparse for several reasons. First, the language barrier obviously limits the pool of scholars who can work with original materials. Second, political considerations have impeded access to information on crime and criminal justice. Third, many Western criminologists have an insufficient understanding of Chinese society and culture to be able to interpret fully the crime situation in China.

To overcome these limitations, we have organized a group of authors actively engaged in research on crime and social control in China. A few of the authors are U.S. natives who have developed scholarly expertise on China. However, many of the authors are originally from China, have lived and grown up in China, earned their doctorates in the United States, and now are professors at American colleges and universities. Further, our authors include a group of leading Chinese criminologists who are in a unique position to bring the current perspectives and contributions of Chinese criminology to the awareness of a Western audience.

The book is organized into four sections. Part I, "Social Transition and Crime in China," addresses patterns of crime in China under conditions of social change. As noted earlier, crime rates have risen steadily over recent decades. Facing these "crime waves," the government has responded with several "severe strikes," but the general trend has been persistent. Among the greatest changes in crime are the large increases in "economic crimes" and corruption, which are most often related by researchers to the economic transition. One of the most striking developments is the recurrence of illicit drug-related crimes. The drug problem was virtually eliminated in the early 1950s, but it is becoming a more and more severe problem today. These patterns of Chinese crime reflect features of changing Chinese society. The chapters in part I of the book are designed to describe these patterns and relate them to the special features of Chinese social change, cultural characteristics, and the concerns of the Chinese.

The first chapter in part I is "Modernization and Crime Trends in China's Reform Era," by Jianhong Liu and Steven F. Messner. They apply modernization theory to interpret trends in various kinds of crime in China over the period between 1978 and 1998. The chapter begins with a detailed description of patterns of crime in China, paying particular attention to the historical events that are likely to have affected both criminal offending and the recording of crime in the official statistics. They then perform time series analyses on Chinese crime data to determine whether the recent economic reforms have had similar or different effects on selected types of property and violent offenses.

Chapter 2, by Lening Zhang, is "White-Collar Crime: Bribery and Corruption in China." This chapter describes the reality of white-collar crime at both the individual and the organizational levels, especially among governmental officials and governments as organizations in China. Characteristics of bribery and corruption in China are analyzed in comparison to their counterparts in the West. Several sources of bribery and corruption are explored, including cultural, political, economic, social, and ideological sources. China's strategy to control bribery and corruption is also analyzed.

Chapter 3, "Narcotics Control in China: A Growing Challenge," analyzes the trend of growing drug trafficking and drug use in recent years. Based upon firsthand and secondary sources, this study systematically examines narcotics crimes and related problems in China. Peter Liu and Yingyi Situ first review the historical context and the current extent of narcotics crimes. Next, the causes of rapid increases in drug offenses are discussed, and the Chinese government's efforts against drug crimes are evaluated. Finally, these issues are placed in comparative perspective.

Part II of the book, "Chinese Perspectives and the Social Sources of Crime," addresses the question of the social correlates of changing patterns of crime. Facing the new challenges from rising crime waves, criminology as a new discipline has emerged and developed in China. Chinese scholars have been actively studying the sources of crime in the new era. This part first introduces perspectives and developments in Chinese criminology, and then analyzes whether various structural and cultural changes in China can be linked to increases in crime and delinquency.

Chinese social structure has experienced great change as the economy shifts from state socialism to a market economy. As the development of the private sector in the economy becomes more and more important, the changing nature of the economy has altered the social organization and welfare of the majority. Economic reforms create opportunities for many to get rich, especially in the growing private sector, while others, such as laid-off workers, are left out of the economic prosperity. Social inequality is developing on a scale never before seen. The emergence of a labor market created by economic transition, coupled with the leftover labor force created by rural reform, has led to unprecedented population migration from rural areas to cities. The structural change and new inequality are likely to promote anomie; according to classical sociological theory, crime and deviance are therefore expected to rise. Chapters in this section describe how these changes in social structure occurred, and explore how they are linked to rising levels of crime and delinquency.

The chapter "Criminology in China: Perspectives and Development," by the Chinese criminologists Lu Zhou and Mei Cong, introduces the audience to Chinese criminology. The chapter briefly describes the development of criminology, its theory, and its research since the 1920s, especially since the late 1970s. Although the chapter is relatively short, it offers an insider's view of criminology in China.

Chapter 5, "Population Migration and Crime in Beijing, China," addresses a new source of crime in urban areas: rural workers migrating into cities. Official data show that migrants are responsible for a large proportion of offenses. According to the statistics of some cities, more than half of the crimes are committed by the migrants from the rural areas. The population migration has played a prominent role in the rising crime waves during the social and economic transition in China. Guoan Ma's chapter offers rich data on this subject. It explores the relationship between population migration and crime by focusing on a large city, Beijing.

Chapter 6, "Inequality and Crime in China," by Liqun Cao and Yisheng Dai, analyzes the relationship between inequality and crime in the social transition. It argues that it is not economic growth per se that causes the acceleration in crime, nor is it simply the weakening of state control over migration. Instead, the widening inequality in income is largely responsible for soaring levels of crime.

Part III, "Social Control and Crime Prevention in a Changing Chinese Society," addresses the impact of social transition on the changes in the grassroots level of social control. China has long been a communitarian society, and it has traditionally relied on informal social control in grassroots-level social organizations. The traditional grassroots-based programs of "helping and educating" (bangjiao) and informal arbitration (tiaojie) have been very effective. The persistently low crime rates throughout most of the twentieth century can be reasonably attributed to the effectiveness of this control. Economic reform has greatly changed the workings of grassroots social organizations. The communitarian nature of the society has been profoundly altered. These changes have greatly affected the social control mechanism in China. The society and government have responded to the changes and developed new programs. A national program of comprehensive strategy for crime control has been developed and implemented. The chapters in part III explain the impact of changes in the nature of communitarianism on crime prevention strategies in recent China.

Chapter 7, "Chinese Social Control: From Shaming and Reintegration to Getting Rich Is Glorious," by Dean Rojek, analyzes the philosophical and cultural foundations of Chinese social control and the recent movement away from the communitarian tradition. It explains how far-reaching social changes have affected social control. The chapter further describes new measures of crime control that have been instituted in response to the social changes.

Chapter 8, "Community Integration and the Effectiveness of Social Control," by Hong Lu and Terance D. Miethe, examines the relationship between community integration and the effectiveness of social control in the city of Shanghai. It starts with a discussion of Western theory and research on community integration and social control. Issues of changing community integration and formal and informal responses to crimes in China are then discussed. After analyzing data on community integration and social control in two Shanghai neighborhoods, the chapter concludes with a discussion of the theoretical and policy implications of the findings.

The chapter by Shuliang Feng, vice president of the Chinese Society of Criminology, offers a Chinese perspective on crime control in China. "Crime and Crime Control in a Changing China" describes crime problems and discusses the strategies and measures adopted by the Chinese government. The general strategy for the control and prevention of crime is called the "comprehensive and systematic strategy." The basic principle of this strategy is the integration of punishment and prevention, with an emphasis on the latter. Prevention focuses on the grassroots levels of both the cities and countryside "to nip crime in the bud." The comprehensive strategy requires joint efforts of various social sectors under the unified leadership of the Chinese Communist Party and the government through political, economic, administrative, legal, cultural, and educational means. The ultimate goal of crime prevention is to guard social stability in order to ensure the development of economic reform. The chapter describes how these strategies developed through three stages in the past 20 years since the early 1980s.

Finally, part IV, "Social Transition and the Changing Criminal Justice System," addresses the changes in Chinese law and criminal justice. The Chinese justice system has been transformed fundamentally, sometimes unintentionally and sometimes as a result of systematic legal reform. The revised 1997 criminal law and criminal procedural law illustrate the influence of both social change and legal reform. The court procedure is much more formalized. In addition, the Chinese police have moved toward greater "professionalism." A juvenile justice system has been created, and children's rights have been codified in the law. Part IV explains these changes within the context of more general social transition.

Chapter 10, "Mixing Inquisitorial and Adversarial Models: Changes in Criminal Procedure in a Changing China," focuses on trials. China's criminal trial procedure in the past was characterized as a judge-dominated inquisitorial system. The 1996 criminal procedure law has improved the system to meet the needs of modernization. Based upon secondary data analysis and field study, this article uncovers some of the important adversarial elements that have been introduced into the Chinese criminal trial. First, the judges' responsibilities in court are now substantially reduced. Second, both procurator and defense counsel are designated as advocates, and therefore become much more active. Third, the rights of defendants and victims are extended. However, the legal reforms under the revised criminal procedure law have been limited. Important legal principles such as separation of powers and equality before the law have not been addressed well. As a result, the new criminal procedure is a mixture of the adversarial system and the inquisitorial system long associated with the socialist context.

Chapter 11, "New Directions of Chinese Policing in the Reform Era," by Yisheng Dai, describes the changes in police practices. Dai analyzes the changing role and function of the police since the start of the reform era. The chapter reviews the modifications in government household registration policy and the resulting challenges to policing. It illustrates the processes of professionalization of the police force and police legal reform, and it explains the newly developed policing strategies and security work.

Chapter 12, by Allan Jiao, analyzes the traditions and changes of police culture. The "Party Line," the "Mass Line," and the "Prevention Line" are examined as traditions of police culture in China. These traditions are rooted in China's cultural, political, and social systems. The social and economic transition in China is changing and modifying these traditions. Jiao speculates about the future impact of China's transition on those traditions of police culture.

Professor Guoling Zhao's chapter, "The Recent Development of Juvenile Justice in China," offers much needed information on the newly developed Chinese juvenile justice system. China opened its first juvenile court in 1984. Since then, the juvenile justice policies have developed into a full-fledged system. The chapter reviews the history of juvenile justice and juvenile protection in China. In 1991, China adopted the Law of the People's Republic of China on the Protection of Minors, and in 1999, the Law of the People's Republic of China on the Prevention of Juvenile Delinquency, the first of its kind in the world. This chapter describes the development and nature of these laws in detail. It illustrates the operation of the juvenile justice system within the distinctive context of China's social, cultural, and political systems.

The book is intended to serve as a valuable text for scholars and students in multiple academic disciplines, including sociology, criminology, law and legal studies, and political science. The book should also be of interest to nonacademics who are interested in Chinese society. As has been widely observed, the world is becoming an ever more closely connected, global system. We hope that the book will open a "window" for both scholars and the general public to learn about contemporary China, a nation with approximately one-fourth of the world's population.

REFERENCES

Adler, Freda. 1996. "Our American Society of Criminology, the World, and the State of the Art—the American Society of Criminology 1995 Presidential Address." *Criminology* 34: 1–9.

Farrington, David P. 2000. "Explaining and Preventing Crime: The Globalization of Knowledge—the American Society of Criminology 1999 Presidential Address." *Criminology* 38: 1–24.

Leng, Shao-Chuan, and Hung-Dah Chiu. 1985. *Criminal Justice in Post-Mao China*. Albany: State University of New York Press.

Ren, Xin. 1997. *Tradition of the Law and Law of the Tradition: Law, State, and Social Control in China*. Westport, CT: Greenwood Press.

Shaw, Victor. 1996. *Social Control in China: Study of Chinese Work Units*. Westport, CT: Praeger.

Troyer, Ronald J., John P. Clark, and Dean G. Rojek, eds. 1989. *Social Control in the People's Republic of China*. New York: Praeger.

PART I

Social Transition and Crime in China

CHAPTER 1

Modernization and Crime Trends in China's Reform Era

Jianhong Liu and Steven F. Messner

Economic reform in China, especially the dramatic transition to a market economy in the 1990's, brought about profound social change and unprecedented economic growth in the last two decades. From 1990 to 1998, China's real GDP increased an average of 11.9 percent annually. China's 1998 GDP was $964 billion, making China the seventh largest economy in the world. The industrial sector grew at an average rate of 18.8 percent during 1990–1997, and Chinese exports expanded by 16.3 percent annually during that time span. With $352 billion in exports in 1997, China was the world's third largest exporter, surpassing Japan and following only the United States and Germany.

During this period of modernization and economic development in China, official statistics and scholarly studies reported increased levels of crime. In 1978, the total crime rate was 55.91 per 100,000 population; in 1998, it reached 163.19 per 100,000 people (*China Law Yearbooks*). Some Chinese scholars propose that modernization inevitably causes crime to increase (Xiao, 1988). Studies have generally agreed on an observed association between modernization, social transition, and rising crime in China. They speculate on and suggest specific links and mechanisms accounting for this general association. These include increased inequality (see chapter 6 in this volume), changing cultural beliefs and norms (especially the introduction of Western values into China; see chapter 7 in this volume), disruption of traditional social control mechanisms (see chapter 9 in this volume), decreased social integration (see chapter 8 in this volume), massive migration of the rural population into urban areas (see chapter 5 in this volume), and an altered age structure of the population (Deng and Cordilia, 1999; Rojek, 1996; Curran, 1998).

In the West, a fairly extensive body of literature has emerged assessing the effects of modernization on crime. This research has been guided largely by "modernization theory," which draws heavily upon a Durkheimian heritage. The results of empirical analyses testing modernization theory have been mixed at best (see LaFree, 1999; LaFree and Kick, 1986; Neapolitan, 1997; and Neuman and Berger, 1988 for reviews of the literature). However, this research is limited in three important respects. First, the versions of modernization theory tested in quantitative analyses are somewhat oversimplified, especially with respect to the implications of the theory for violent versus property crimes. Second, the research is based, with few exceptions, on cross-sectional designs. Modernization theory refers intrinsically to processes of change, and thus longitudinal designs are best suited for assessing its claims. Third, Western criminologists have largely neglected China, and Chinese scholars have yet to apply formal statistical techniques to assess the consequences of economic reform for levels of crime.

In this chapter, we apply modernization theory to interpret trends in various kinds of crime in China over the period between 1978 and 1998. We begin with a detailed description of patterns of crime in China, paying particular attention to the historical events that are likely to have affected both criminal offending and the recording of crime in the official statistics. We then perform time series analyses on Chinese crime data to determine whether the recent economic reforms have had similar or different effects on selected types of property and violent offenses.

THEORETICAL BACKGROUND

As noted above, modernization theory has its origins in Durkheimian sociology. Durkheim studied French society during the industrial revolution. He observed that industrialization ushered in profound changes in France. In particular, the rapid pace of social change at the time undermined the norms associated with traditional society. He referred to this breakdown in the normative order as "anomie" and suggested that widespread anomie is likely to lead to increases in crime and deviance (Durkheim, 1933; 1950). Given his emphasis on the weakening of social norms in general, Durkheim's argument is generally understood to imply that rapid social transition and the concomitant anomie are likely to be associated with increased levels of all types of crime.

Various scholars have drawn upon Durkheim's insights in the study of crime, but the person usually credited with developing the most elaborate criminological variant of modernization theory is Louise Shelley (1981). Shelley's thesis posits that as nations modernize, social structures are fundamentally altered, and levels and patterns of criminal activity change. The precise nature of these changes depends on the stage of development and the offense under consideration. At early stages of urban and industrial growth, traditional social structures are undermined in the growing cities. The concomitant social disorganization, anomie, and weak control promote increases in property crimes. At the same time the newly arrived migrants from the countryside bring with them the traditions of violence associated with rural life, which leads to increases in violent crime. At later stages of development, patterns of crime change. Property crimes continue to rise, becoming the most prominent type of criminal activity. In contrast, the growth in criminal violence subsides as rural migrants become adjusted to urban life. The nature of violent crime is also changed. Increasingly, when criminal violence occurs, it does so in the context of the commission of property crimes. Shelley's thesis thus posits changes in levels of crime and the preponderance of different kinds of offenses at varying stages of the modernization process.

In the empirical literature, most researchers have interpreted the modernization thesis as implying positive effects of indicators of economic development on measures of crime in general. The results of this research have yielded findings largely contrary to this prediction (Neuman and Berger, 1988; Hartnagel, 1982; Krohn, 1976, 1978; Krohn and Wellford, 1977; McDonald, 1976; Wellford, 1974; Avison and Loring, 1986; Braithwaite and Braithwaite, 1980; Conklin and Simpson, 1985; Groves et al., 1985; Hansmann and Quigley, 1982; Messner, 1980, 1982, 1985; LaFree and Kick, 1986). Research findings are especially inconsistent with the notion that the process of economic development causes both violent and property crimes to increase. Instead, studies based on cross-national data have commonly reported that modernization and development are associated with increases in property crime (mostly measured by theft) and decreases in violent crime (mostly measured by homicide—for an opposing view, see Bennett, 1991; and Ortega et al., 1992). To account for this pattern, Kick and LaFree (1985) proposed an "opportunity" explanation to serve as an alternative to the conventional modernization thesis. They maintained that development is negatively related to homicide opportunities because it enhances urbanization, which decreases interpersonal ties and contacts among intimates and acquaintances, thereby reducing interpersonal violence. At the same time, development increases opportunities for theft by providing a vast supply of readily available commodities in environments generally characterized by ineffective surveillance (Kick and LaFree, 1985; LaFree and Kick, 1986).

In sum, the conventional wisdom is that the accumulated body of evidence on economic development and crime has not been particularly kind to the modernization thesis. However, the research testing this thesis is flawed in several respects. With regard to the analysis of violent crimes, researchers have generally ignored Shelley's arguments about the importance of stages of development. Violent crime is expected to increase at early stages of development, then stabilize (and possibly decrease) at later stages. The simple prediction of positive effects of modernization on all types of crime fails to accommodate the richness of the modernization thesis.

In addition, both Durkheim's and Shelley's arguments are intended to explain how deviance and crime are generated in a society where dramatic social transition leads to a breakdown of prior beliefs and the normal social order. The focus of these arguments is on processes involving a temporal sequence. Most studies ostensibly challenging the modernization thesis, however, are based on cross-sectional data for multinational samples. This is a critical limitation because cross-sectional and longitudinal relationships can vary markedly, depending on the nature of the underlying causal processes (Firebaugh, 1980). The modernization thesis is by its very nature most applicable to the analysis of the effects of changes in development on changes in crime within particular societies.

A test of the modernization thesis based on longitudinal analyses can be found in Bennett (1991). This study employed time series analysis for a sample of fifty-two nations from 1960 to 1984. The analysis tested the hypothesis that the rate of increase in crime is proportional to the rate of economic growth. The results indicate that both theft and homicide increase during the period of rapid growth. In contrast, the level of development does not affect the crime rate; only the rate of change has a significant effect. Though Bennett's use of time series data is a notable improvement over previous research, his analysis can be challenged on statistical grounds. Specifically, he used the AR model without testing the specification of the series. The AR model assumes that the time series are stationary with the error term following an autoregressive process. This is a strong assumption that is suspect. As a result, Bennett's model is likely to be based on an incorrect specification for the crime trend process.

Finally, it is important to emphasize that an adequate design for assessing the modernization thesis, especially its Durkheimian variant, would use data from a society that has experienced profound social transition over a short period of time. Durkheim (1933), unlike Marx, does not view the advanced capitalist societies as necessarily prone to self-destruction. Instead, new forms of solidarity could replace the older forms that had held together traditional societies. Social change becomes problematic for Durkheim when it is unusually rapid. Under such circumstances there is insufficient time for the existing social norms to become adjusted to the newly emerging social reality, leading to anomie and weak social control. China would seem to constitute an ideal case for applying this model of social change. Over the course of a generation, the economic foundations of the social order have changed fundamentally. To what extent has the social transition associated with economic reform led to increases in crime? Have any such increases been limited to the types of crimes most directly related to the nature of the reforms—property crimes—or have they affected crimes more generally, including violent crimes? We apply time series techniques using Chinese crime statistics to address these questions about the effects of modernization on crime in a non-Western society.

SOCIAL CHANGE AND CRIME TRENDS IN CHINA

As noted, the economic reform over the last two decades has dramatically changed Chinese society. These changes are so profound, complex, and far-reaching that the basic characteristics of China have been permanently altered (Deng and Cordilia, 1999; Anderson and Gil, 1998). One of the most remarkable consequences of social reform is the breakdown of traditional socialist cultural values. Before the reform era, China was a society where there was a remarkable degree of consensus on beliefs and norms among the citizens and the government. The value system emphasized egalitarianism, and the social structure was remarkably homogeneous (see chapter 7 in this volume). This social arrangement was partially due to the strong traditional cultural emphasis on the collective as opposed to individuals, and partially due to the Communists' reinforcement of the traditional collective social values and political education. The government effectively used all ideological means, including education and political and social organizations, at all levels to strengthen the socialist values and norms. The society shared basic values and a collective conscience to a remarkable degree (Deng and Cordilia, 1999). The core values emphasized the common good as the only goal for all members of society. Similarly, the interests of the community or the group were placed above the interests of the individual. Individualistic concerns with personal gain were despised (Ci, 1994; Deng and Cordilia, 1999). Politically, people were taught to believe in the socialist values and norms, and Mao Zedong's thought was recognized as the leading ideology. The socialist and Communist goal was held to be the future for the whole of mankind (Madsen, 1984). Most Chinese genuinely accepted these socialist values and felt that their government was working for the benefit of all. China was a society characterized by a communitarian social life infused with altruistic values and collective goals.

Although traditional orientations have by no means completely disappeared in China, economic reform has brought Western individualistic values. To facilitate the country's economic advances, the government started to promote cultural values that encouraged entrepreneurship and personal economic advancement. Previously the most often heard slogan was "to serve the people"; now a popular slogan endorsed by the government is "getting rich is glorious" (Schell, 1988; Deng and Cordilia, 1999; also see chapter 7 in this volume). The Chinese tradition of frugality, diligence, and self-sacrifice that was passed down for generations is now in conflict with the popular values of pursuing indulgence and self-interest. Consumerism and money worship have become much more prevalent. The new values encourage competition with others in the pursuit of wealth, rather than sharing prosperity with all.

The result of these changes is "anomie" in the classic Durkheimian sense. The government pursues conflicting policies and laws in the reform era. New policies and laws are blurry because of the ambiguity of right and wrong created by social transition as well as by the underdeveloped legal systems. Indeed, the laws are not adequate to deal with the complexities of transition to the market economy and modern social life.

The breakdown of the conventional cultural values and norms in China is strikingly similar to what Durkheim observed in nineteenth-century France during the industrialization era: society has experienced a normless state, and achieving wealth has become the supreme end of individuals. China is in fact developing far faster than nineteenth-century France and any other Western countries during their eras of industrialization. The social transition has created a relatively normless state in which the unconstrained pursuit of material indulgence and individual economic advancement has been embraced by large sections of the Chinese population.

According to Durkheim's thesis, the severe anomie experienced by Chinese society will cause all types of crime to increase, at least in the short run. Similarly, assuming that China is still in the early stages of development, Shelley's modernization thesis implies that both violent and property crimes will exhibit increasing trends during the era of reform. This hypothesis can be contrasted with LaFree and Kick's opportunity explanation, which predicts an increasing trend in property crimes and a decreasing trend in violent crimes (Lafree and Kick, 1986; Kick and Lafree, 1985). Below, we assess these competing hypotheses about the implications of economic reform in China for different types of crime.

MODELING TRENDS IN CRIME RATES

Previous work on crime trends in China has been rather preliminary. Various studies and news reports cite increases in crimes and deviance in China since the reforms began in 1978 (Rojek, 1996; Deng and Cordilia, 1999). Most of these reports are based on limited and incomplete official statistics. In addition, all of these reports are descriptive. At best they only describe the change in the number of crimes without testing for statistically reliable patterns. Even within this limited descriptive research on crime trends, there is little account of the historical context and the social and criminal justice events that directly influenced high and low crime counts. This reflects the limited familiarity of Western scholars with Chinese criminal justice.

Although descriptive studies are important, they cannot be used to distinguish the systematic component from random fluctuations of a time series. Crime rates change from year to year but contain stochastic components that cause the rates to fluctuate and that may affect the rates over more than a single year. Establishing a trend involves demonstrating a systematic year-to-year change in the data over a number of years. Time series modeling is the most suitable method for consistent and efficient estimation of trends in the face of stochastic components, autocorrelated residuals, and the retention of past stochastic shocks or innovations.

One well-known fact in the time series literature is that a series may visually seem to show a linear trend, even though there is in fact no trend. This occurs when a series appears to trend but is in fact a product of a "random walk," that is, the previous value plus a random shock generated the series. This fact makes it difficult to distinguish a series that contains a systematic trend component from one that does not. In this situation, descriptive methods will tend to conclude incorrectly that there is a trend when there is not. Time series modeling is especially useful for differentiating a "random walk" from a true trend.

When there is a trend in the data, time series methods are useful for detecting the way the data are generated. Time series analysis can test what model best reflects the nature of the trend. It is particularly important to determine if the trend is generated by a stationary process or by a random walk with a drift. These are very different processes with different characteristics.

In the following section, we will describe the change in the total crime rates in the historical context of the Chinese criminal justice system. We will then use formal time series methods to analyze the data on major Chinese crimes from 1978 to 1998 to answer questions about Chinese crime trends. Are there systematic trends of increases in Chinese crimes? Do violent crimes and property crimes exhibit similar or different trends? Answers to these questions will provide unique evidence from a non-Western society that is relevant to the modernization thesis on crime.

DATA AND ANALYSES

In the literature on Chinese crime and criminal justice, there has been no attempt to analyze the official statistics quantitatively, for at least two reasons. One is the difficulty in acquiring crime statistics. The data available to researchers have been very limited; often they are just total crime rates for limited years. Two, there is a lack of in-depth knowledge of the criminal justice system and of the political changes and policy implementations in China. This knowledge is indispensable for adequately understanding the official statistics and addressing their problems.

Acquiring data on Chinese crime and criminal justice is indeed a formidable task. Due to political and historical considerations, the Chinese government published little crime data until 1987, when the first *Chinese Law Yearbook* was published. The *Chinese Law Yearbook*, which is published in Chinese, includes a section on crime and criminal justice statistics. The Ministry of Public Security collects the crime data; the data are sent to the State Statistics Bureau; and the *Chinese Law Yearbook* selectively publishes some of these data.

Although these data provide important information on many aspects of Chinese crime and criminal justice, like any other official statistics, they are imperfect. A large literature has developed in criminology to deal with problems of official statistics (Shelley, 1981; Biderman and Lynch, 1991; O'Brien, 1985). Many of these concerns also apply to the Chinese statistics. Studies have found that Chinese official data suffer from underreporting (He and Marshall, 1997; Yu and Zhang, 1999) and underestimation (Dutton and Lee, 1993; Dai, 1995). Studies also indicate that the Chinese tend to report relatively few crimes (Zhu et al., 1995). It is not possible to circumvent these problems completely, but the official statistics can be regarded as a useful indication of crime patterns, given knowledge about the larger social context of China.

We first offer a descriptive analysis of the crime rates, focusing on the total crimes and their historical changes. Several studies have reported the increase in crimes and have cited official crime statistics as the major evidence in support of this claim. However, authors typically do not explain the details of the developmental history of the observed crime rates in the reform years.

Figure 1.1 shows the trend of the total crime rate from 1978 to 1998. Figure 1.2 shows the rates for common types of property crime—larceny, grand larceny, and bicycle theft. These offenses are presented separately from other offenses because they are relatively common and thus require a large scale in the graph. Figure 1.3 displays the trends for other major types of crime, including violent crime. All crime rates are measured by number of criminal cases filed by the police per 100,000 population. In China, not all reported crimes are filed by police for further investigation. Only cases that are assessed as having sufficient evidence to indicate that a crime has occurred, and that reach a minimum level of severity, are formally filed and recorded.

Figure 1.1 reveals a sharp increase in crime in China. The total crime rate tripled from 55.91 in 1978 to 163.19 per 100,000 in 1998. The chart also shows dramatic fluctuations over the period. The total crime rate started to increase as reform began in 1978, reached a first peak in 1981, then decreased over the next few years. The rate remained relatively low until 1988, when a sharp increase started. The total crime rate reached a second peak in 1991. A pronounced decrease followed after 1991. Levels were fairly steady from 1992 to 1995. The rate once again moved upward between 1997 and 1998.

To explain the observed trends in crime rates in depth, it must first be understood that the change in crime rates reflects at least four major components. The first is change in the true rate of offending. The second is the change in the definitions of crimes. The third is methodological change in the reporting and collecting of crime records by the police. The fourth is unique historical events that may disrupt an otherwise "normal" change in crime.

To interpret the patterns observed in the charts, we focus on the timing of the shifts in the curves. It turns out that the points of decrease correspond to several widely publicized "severe strikes" against crime as the government responded to the perceived crime problem at the time. The first of these strikes started in 1983. To place the "severe strike" action on a legal foundation, the Standing Committee of the National Congress passed revisions of the criminal law in September of that year and also passed two resolutions: "the resolution on severely punishing serious criminal offenders for crimes against public security" and "the resolution on the

Figure 1.1
Total Crime Rate, 1978–1998

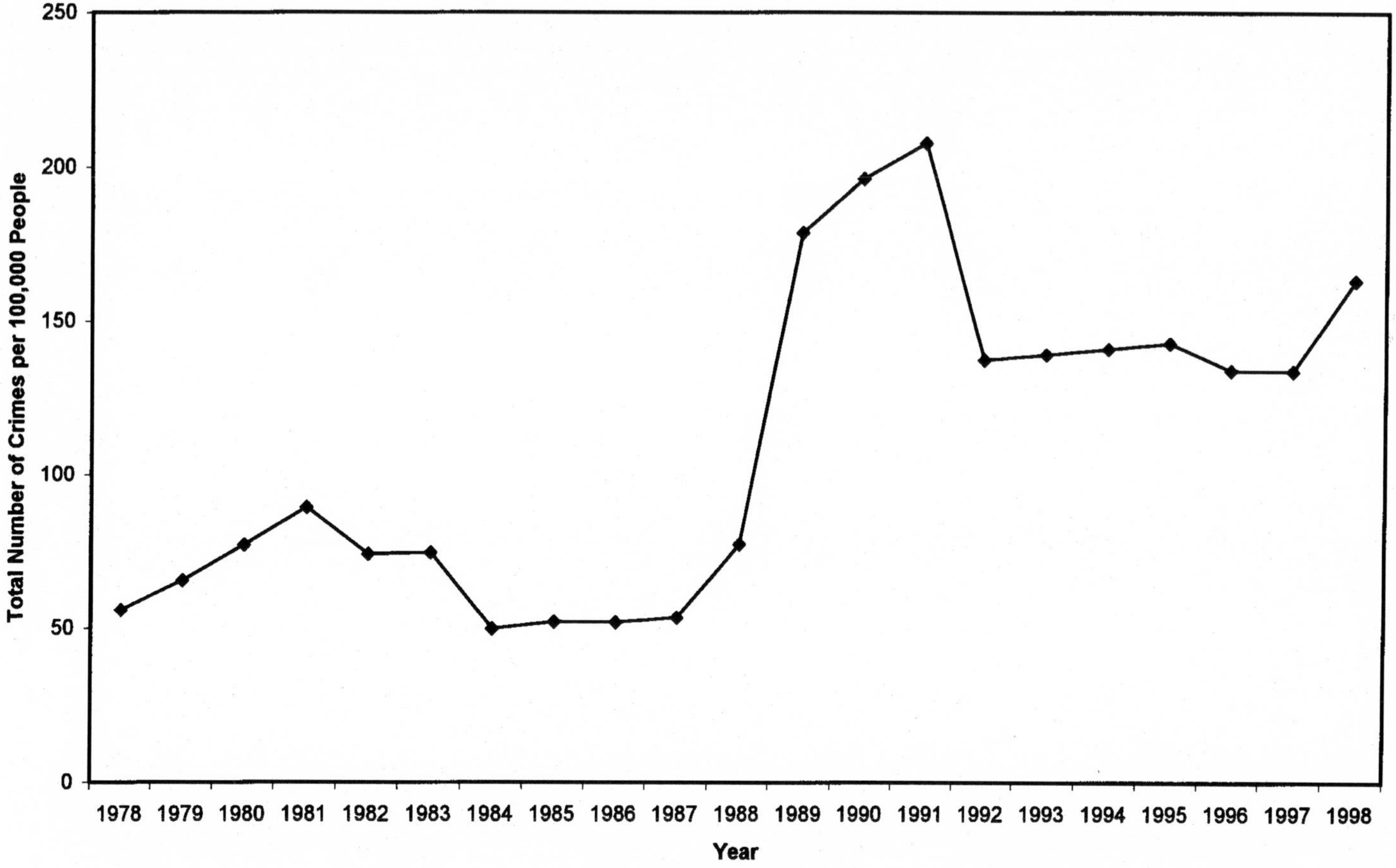

Figure 1.2
Larceny Crime Rates, 1978–1998

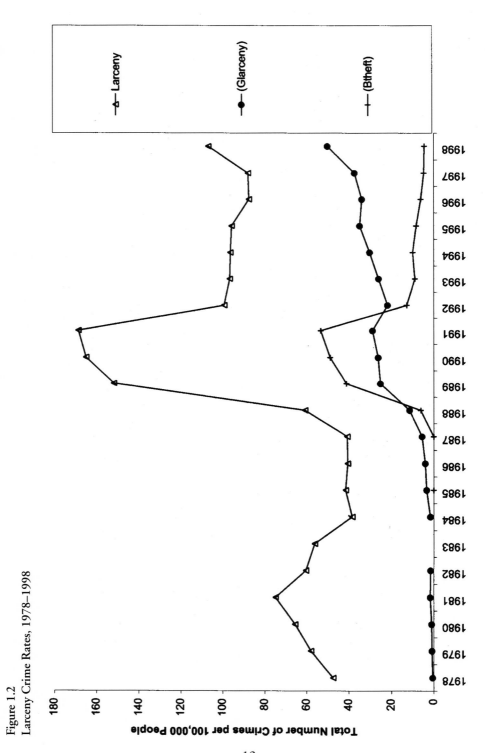

Figure 1.3
Major Crime Rates, Excluding Larcenies, 1978–1998

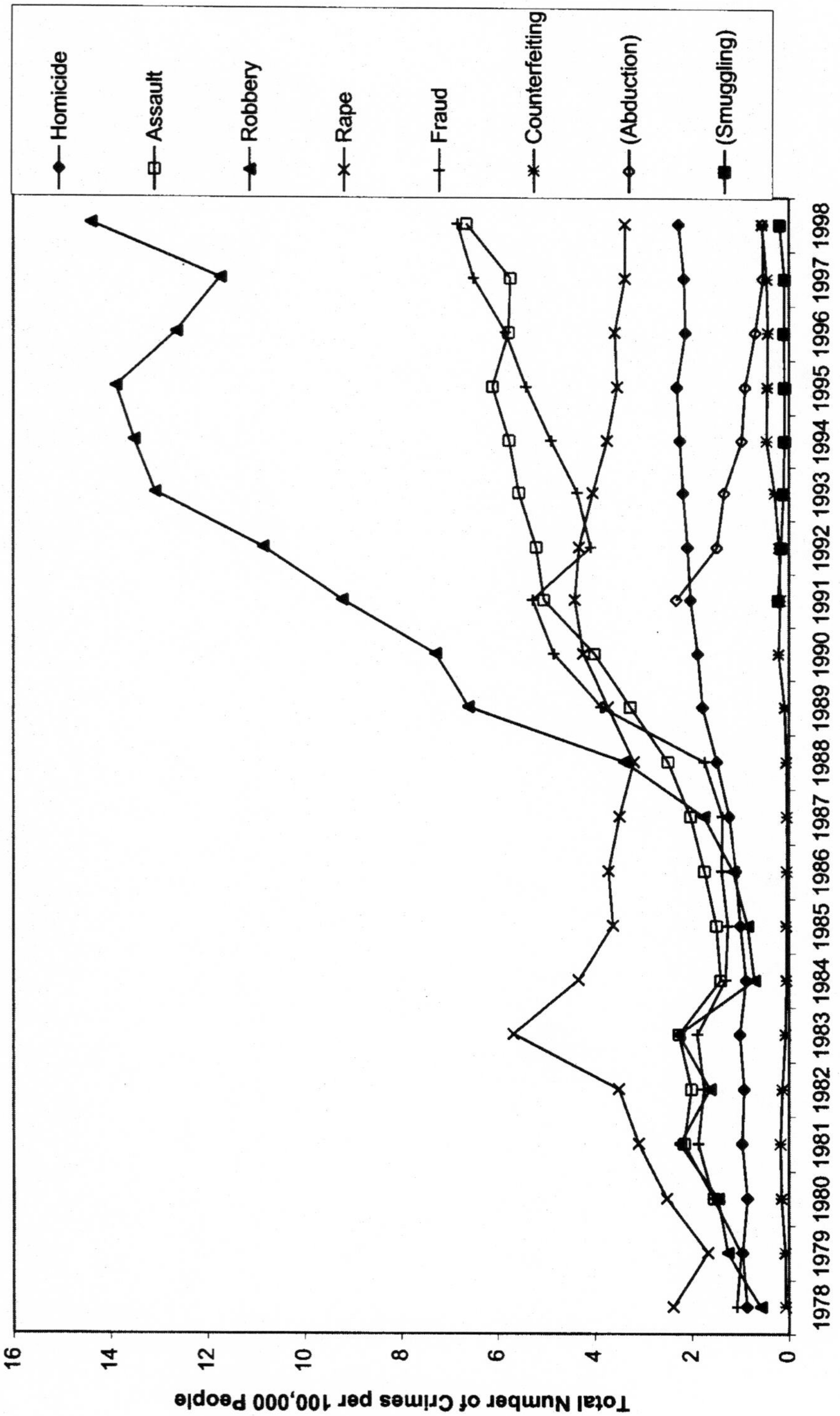

speedy procedure for punishing serious criminal offenders for crimes against public security." The first "severe strike" lasted from August 1983 to January 1987. During the three-and-a-half-year campaign, more than 1.77 million offenders were arrested and sentenced and more than 322,000 offenders were sent to reeducation through labor camp (referred to as *lao jiao* in Chinese). The campaign temporarily suppressed the crime wave, but the crime trend surged soon after the end of the campaign in January 1987. Crime rates soared to a historical high in 1991.

In response to the new wave of crime, the government carried out a second "severe strike" campaign in 1991. It is important to point out that part of the rise in crime rate from 1989 to 1991 is due to a correction of the statistical reporting practice by the local police. It is estimated that previously about one-third of the crimes were not reported from the local police units to the national police because local officials wanted to "look better" in their efforts to secure social order. A correction for this underreporting partially accounts for the higher number of recorded crimes in 1990 and 1991. A similar correction effort by the government occurred again in 1998. It is partially responsible for the increase in recorded crimes in 1998. Figure 1.1 shows that the total crime level dropped sharply in 1991, suggesting some effect of the "severe strike" campaign.

However, another factor that also accounts for the lower rate in 1992 and thereafter is the change of the definition of criminal theft, which was defined as stealing 25 Chinese yuan in rural areas, or 80 yuan in city areas. This was changed to stealing 300 yuan in rural areas and 600 in urban areas. Similar to other countries, theft constitutes 60–80 percent of the total crime in China. Accordingly, fluctuation in theft rates largely determines the change of the total crime rate. The definitional change surely had an appreciable influence on the crime statistics.

The total crime rate remained relatively stable with a slight increasing trend from 1992 to 1995. In April and November 1996, the government carried out two more "severe strike" campaigns. Following these campaigns, the total number of crimes was reduced from about 1.69 million to 1.60 million. In 1998, the total crime rate increased once again. Overall, these descriptive observations suggest that levels of crime in China have been generally increasing, but with interruptions and reversals during the "severe strike" campaigns.

As explained above, although descriptive studies provide valuable insights into the change in crime rates, they have severe limitations in investigating a trend. We next employ time series analysis to formally model any trends in Chinese crime rates. We first conduct the unit root test to investigate the correct specification of the crime series. Then, we estimate the trend component of the series to determine if there is a significant trend for each crime series.

To find out if a series has a nonrandom trend, we need to investigate the generating process of the series. One possibility is that the series is generated by a linear trend process:

$$y_t = \alpha + \beta_t + \rho y_{t-1} + \varepsilon_t$$

where $\varepsilon_t = \gamma \varepsilon_{t-1}$ or $\varepsilon_t = \upsilon_t + \theta \upsilon_{t-1}$ or other higher-order ARMA processes (Hamilton, 1994, p. 435). Alternatively, the series may be generated by a random walk process:

$$y_t = y_{t-1} + \varepsilon_t$$

The coefficient of the term y_{t-1} in the random walk process is 1. This is called a unit root process. Taking the first difference of the process, we have a first differenced series:

$$\Delta y = y_t - y_{t-1} = \varepsilon_t$$

If the first differenced series has no additional unit root, the process is said to be integrated of order 1, denoted I(1) (Johnston and DiNardo, 1997, p. 220). A process y_t without a unit root is referred to as integrated of order 0, or an I(0) process.

It is well known in the time series literature that a random walk process can appear to have a linear trend. If we mistakenly fit such a series with a linear trend, the misspecification will lead to incorrect conclusions about the trend. Conventional tests for trends are strongly biased toward finding a trend when none is present (Nelson and Kang, 1984). The model would nevertheless be meaningless, because the future value of the random walk cannot be predicted by previous values of the series.

When a random walk has a nonzero intercept α, it is called a random walk with a drift:

$$y_t = \alpha + y_{t-1} = \varepsilon_t$$

The intercept will produce a systematic trend in the sense of a drift in a particular direction. When α is positive, the trend is upward; when α is negative, the trend is downward.

In our data analysis, we carry out the unit root test to determine the correct model specification for each crime series. We use the Dickey-Fuller unit root test to determine if the process is a unit root process. The results of the test are reported in table 1.1. If there is a unit root, we will difference the series and test for the unit root in the first differenced series. If there is no additional unit root, we will then proceed to estimate the intercept α. The results of estimation of α are reported in table 1.2. We report the test of the null hypothesis that $\alpha = 0$. The sign of the α will indicate whether the trend (i.e., the drift) is upward or downward.

Data used in the analyses are from 1978 to 1998 for all crimes except assault, for which data are available only from 1980 to 1998. As mentioned above, the defini-

Table 1.1
Dickey-Fuller Test for Crime Rates[a]

	Estimated Value of ρ	Number of Lagged Differences
Homicide	0.98[b]	1
Assault	0.92[b]	2
Robbery	0.99[b]	1
Rape	0.59[c]	0
Counterfeiting	1.02[b]	1
Fraud	0.96[b]	1
Larceny	0.92[b]	1
Grand Larceny	1.05[b]	1

[a]The augmented Dickey-Fuller test is based on the test equation $y_t = \alpha + \rho y_{t-1} + \delta_1(y_{t-1} - y_{t-1}) + \delta_2(y_{t-2} + y_{t-3}) + u_t$, where equations contain zero, one, or two lagged difference terms, depending on the number needed to eliminate autocorrelation.
[b]Fails to reject the null hypothesis that $\rho = 1$ at the 0.10 level.
[c]Rejects the null hypothesis that $\rho = 1$ at the 0.05 level.

Table 1.2
Estimates of the Intercept for Crime Series[a]

	Estimated Value of α	Number of Lagged Differences
Homicide	0.07**	0
Assault	0.283**	0
Robbery	0.691**	0
Rape	0.093	1
Counterfeiting	0.024*	0
Fraud	0.288**	0
Larceny	2.968	1
Grand Larceny	2.472**	0

[a]The equations are based on the following specifications: $y_t - y_{t-1} = \alpha + \rho y_{t-1} + \delta_1(y_{t-1} - y_{t-1}) + u_t$, where equations contain zero, one, or two lagged difference terms, depending on the number needed to eliminate autocorrelation.
*$p < 0.10$.
**$p < 0.05$.

tion of larceny changed in 1992, which led to a lower larceny rate after 1992. We make an adjustment to the larceny rates after 1992 following the method used by Cantor and Land (1985) to make the pre- and post-1992 data more compatible. We calculate a multiplier for larceny rates after 1992 in the following way:

$$m = \frac{((1990\,rate + 1991\,rate)/2)}{((1992\,rate + 1993\,rate)/2)}.$$

We then use this multiplier, which is 1.7026, times the larceny rate after 1992 to adjust for the lower recorded rates due to the definitional change. Although this adjustment seems reasonable, caution must be exercised in the interpretation of the results for the total larceny category. Grand larcenies are thefts of more than 3,000 yuan. Grand larceny is subject to less fluctuation in recording, and it therefore provides a good indicator of changes for property crimes more generally.

Table 1.1 shows the result from unit root tests (Dickey-Fuller tests) of the time series for the different offenses. The first column reports the estimated ρ value and whether it is significantly different from 1. The second column reports the number of lagged differences added to the test equation necessary to eliminate autocorrelation. When lagged difference terms are added to the equation, the test is called the augmented Dickey-Fuller test. The results of the tests show that for all offenses other than rape, we cannot reject the null hypothesis that $\rho = 1$ at the 0.10 level of significance. This indicates that all the crime series except rape appear to have a unit root. This implies that fitting a linear time trend would be a misspecification of the process generating the data. Different numbers of lagged difference terms (reported in the second column) are used in the augmented Dickey-Fuller tests to eliminate autocorrelations. To address the concern of the low power of the Dickey-Fuller test—the series has only twenty-one cases—we estimated the coefficients of the y_{t-1} term ρ and report them in table 1.1. The results show that these coefficients are very close to 1 except for rape, confirming the existence of the unit roots.

To test for additional unit roots, we differenced each crime series, and tested them for unit root again for the differenced series. Results indicate that none of the series has additional unit roots. Thus all crime series are I(1).

Because there is no additional unit root in the first differenced series, we use the intercept α to test for a systematic mean increase or decrease for these series. A significant α will indicate that a systematic trend exists for the crime series. (A positive α indicates an upward trend, and a negative α indicates a downward trend of the crime series.)

Table 1.2 reports the results of the estimation of the intercept α. Because the degrees of freedom involved in the estimation of the drift parameter reported in this table are relatively modest, we use $\alpha = .10$ as a criterion for statistical significance in the case of counterfeiting. For twenty degrees of freedom, this requires t-values greater than 1.725 for a two-tailed test.

The results reveal that all crimes except rape and the total larceny category show statistically significant trends of increase. Note in particular the significantly positive effects of grand larceny and homicide. These are serious forms of property and violent crime, respectively, and they are less likely to be subject to definitional and reporting changes than are several other offenses. In addition, the intercepts for rape and larceny, though not statistically significant, are positive. Overall, then, the results are strongly suggestive of increasing trends of crime in general in China during recent decades of economic reform.

DISCUSSION

Our analyses demonstrate the utility of applying the modernization thesis to the explanation of recent developments in crime in China. Consistent with observations based on Western nations, noteworthy increases in crime have accompanied the development process in China. These increases cannot be explained away as normal, "random" fluctuations around a steady base rate of crime. Rather, the observed changes are suggestive of a statistically significant move upward in offending.

The increasing trends in Chinese crime rates evidently apply to both violent and property offenses. The similarity across offenses is contrary to variants of "opportunity" theory but is quite consistent with both Durkheimian anomie theory and Shelley's modernization thesis, assuming that China is in the early stages of the modernization process. It will be interesting to see in the years ahead whether patterns of crime continue to change in a manner similar to the changes observed in the West. Modernization theory implies that property crimes are likely to continue their increase, whereas the growth in violent crime will subside. This is an important topic for future research on crime in China.

In closing, we emphasize once again the distinctiveness of the Chinese context for studying modernization, economic development, and crime. Chinese society is based on an ancient civilization that has been characterized by extensive informal social control and a strong emphasis on internal social control as reflected in the personal quality of "virtue." In addition, Chinese society has for centuries been organized in a highly communitarian manner, and people have been oriented toward collective rather than individual goals. Nevertheless, the introduction of dramatic economic reforms over a relatively brief period of time apparently has undermined many of the traditional social protections against crime. The experience of China at the close of the twentieth century offers striking affirmation of Durkheim's insights from a century ago about the profound social destabilization that often accompanies rapid social change.

REFERENCES

Anderson, Allen F., and Vincent E. Gil. 1998. "China's Modernization and the Decline of Communitarianism: The Control of Sex Crimes and Implications for the Fate of Informal Social Control." *Journal of Contemporary Criminal Justice* 14: 248–261.

Avison, William R., and Pamela L. Loring. 1986. "Population Diversity and Cross-National Homicide: The Effects of Inequality and Heterogeneity." *Criminology* 24: 733–749.

Bennett, Richard R. 1991. "Development and Crime." *Sociological Quarterly* 32: 343–363.

Biderman, Albert D., and James P. Lynch. 1991. *Understanding Crime Incidence Statistics: Why the UCR Diverges from the NCS.* New York: Springer-Verlag.

Bonger, William A. 1916. *Criminality and Economic Conditions.* Boston: Little, Brown.

Braithwaite, John, and Valerie Braithwaite. 1980. "The Effect of Income Inequality and Social Democracy on Homicide: A Cross-National Comparison." *British Journal of Criminology* 20: 45–53.

Cantor, David, and Kenneth C. Land. 1985. "Unemployment and Crime Rates in the post–World War II United States: A Theoretical and Empirical Analysis." *American Sociological Review* 50: 317–322.

Ci Jiwei. 1994. *Dialectic of the Chinese Revolution: From Utopianism to Hedonism.* Stanford, CA: Stanford University Press.

Clinard, Marshall B., and Daniel J. Abbott. 1973. *Crime in Developing Countries.* New York: Wiley.

Conklin, George H., and Miles E. Simpson. 1985. "A Demographic Approach to the Cross-National Study of Homicide." *Comparative Social Research* 8: 171–186.

Curran, Daniel. 1998. "Economic Reform, the Floating Population, and Crime." *Journal of Contemporary Criminal Justice* 14: 262–280.

Dai Yisheng. 1995. "Expanding Economy and Growing Crime." *CJ International* 11, no. 2: 9–16.

Deng Xiaogang and Ann Cordilia. 1999. "To Get Rich is Glorious: Rising Expectations, Declining Control, and Escalating Crime in Contemporary China." *International Journal of Offender Therapy and Comparative Criminology* 423: 211–229.

Durkheim, Emile. 1933 (1893). *The Division of Labor in Society.* New York: Free Press.

Durkheim, Emile. 1950 (1897). *Suicide: A Study in Sociology.* New York: Free Press.

Dutton, Michael, and Tianfu Lee. 1993. "Missing the Target? Policing Strategies in the Period of Economic Reform." *Crime and Delinquency* 39, no. 3: 316–336.

Engels, Friedrich. 1958 (1887). *The Condition of the Working Class in England.* Oxford: Basil Blackwell.

Firebaugh, Glenn. 1980. "Cross-National versus Historical Regression Models: Conditions of Equivalence in Comparative Analysis." *Comparative Social Research* 3: 333–344.

Groves, W. Byron, Richard McCleary, and Graeme R. Newman. 1985. "Religion, Modernization and World Crime." *Comparative Social Research* 8: 59–78.

Hamilton, James D. 1994. *Time Series Analysis.* Princeton, NJ: Princeton University Press.

Hansmann, Henry B., and John M. Quigley. 1982. "Population Heterogeneity and the Sociogenesis of Homicide." *Social Forces* 61: 206–224.

Hartnagel, Timothy F. 1982. "Modernization, Female Social Roles and Female Crime: A Cross-National Investigation." *Sociological Quarterly* 23: 477–490.

He Ni and Ineke H. Marshall. 1997. "Social Production of Crime Data: A Critical Examination of Chinese Crime Statistics." *International Criminal Justice Review* 7: 46–63.

Johnston, Jack, and John DiNardo. 1997. *Econometric Methods*. New York: McGraw-Hill.

Kick, Edward L., and Gary D. Lafree. 1985. "Development and the Social Context of Murder and Theft." *Comparative Social Research* 8: 37–58.

Krohn, Marvin. 1976. "Inequality, Unemployment and Crime: A Cross-National Analysis." *Sociological Quarterly* 17: 303–313.

Krohn, Marvin. 1978. "A Durkheimian Analysis of International Crime Rates." *Social Forces* 57: 654–670.

Krohn, Marvin, and Charles F. Wellford. 1977. "A Static and Dynamic Analysis of Crime and the Primary Dimensions of Nations." *International Journal of Criminology and Penology* 5: 1–16.

Lafree, Gary, 1999. "A Summary and Review of Cross-National Comparative Studies of Homicide." In *Homicide: A Sourcebook of Social Research*, pp. 125–145. Edited by M. Dwayne Smith and Margaret A. Zahn. Thousand Oaks, CA: Sage.

Lafree, Gary D., and Edward L. Kick. 1986. "Cross-National Effects of Development, Distributional and Demographic Variables on Crime: A Review and Analysis." *International Annals of Criminology* 24: 213–236.

McDonald, Lynn. 1976. *The Sociology of Law and Order*. Boulder, CO: Westview.

Madsen, Richard. 1984. *Morality and Power in a Chinese Village*. Berkeley: University of California Press.

Messner, Steven F. 1980. "Income Inequality and Murder Rates: Some Cross-National Findings." *Comparative Social Research* 3: 185–198.

———. "Societal Development, Social Equality and Homicide: A Cross-National Test of the Durkheimian Model." *Social Forces* 61: 225–240.

———. 1985. "Sex Differences in Arrest Rates for Homicide: An Application of the General Theory of Structural Strain." *Comparative Social Research* 8: 187–201.

Neapolitan, Jerome. 1997. *Cross-National Crime: A Research Review and Sourcebook*. Westport, CT: Greenwood Press.

Nelson, Charles R., and Heejoon Kang. 1984. "Pitfalls in the Use of Time as an Explanatory Variable in Regression." *Journal of Business and Economic Statistics* 2: 73–82.

Neuman, W. Lawrence, and Robert J. Berger. 1988. "Competing Perspectives on Cross-National Crime: An Evaluation of Theory and Evidence." *Sociological Quarterly* 29: 281–313.

O'Brien, Robert M. 1985. *Crime and Victimization*. Beverly Hills, CA: Sage.

Ortega, Suzanne T., et al. 1992. "Modernization, Age Structure and Regional Context: A Cross-National Study of Crime." *Sociological Spectrum* 12: 257–277.

Park, Richard, Ernest Burgess, and Roderick McKenzie. 1967. *The City*. Chicago: University of Chicago Press.

Press of Law Yearbook of China. 1987–1998. *Law Yearbook of China*. Beijing: Press of Law Yearbook of China.

Quinney, Richard. 1965. "Suicide, Homicide and Economic Development." *Social Forces* 43: 401–406.

Rojek, Dean G. 1996. "Changing Directions of Chinese Social Control." In *Comparative Criminal Justice: Traditional and Nontraditional Systems of Law and Control*, pp.

234–249. Edited by Charles B. Fields and Richter H. Moore, Jr. Prospect Heights, IL: Waveland Press.

Schell, Orville. 1988. *Discos and Democracy*. New York: Pantheon.

Shelley, Louise I. 1981. Crime and Modernization: The Impact of Industrialization and Urbanization on Crime. Carbondale: Southern Illinois University Press.

Tarde, Gabriel. 1902. *La Criminalité comparée*. Paris: Flex Alcan.

Wellford, Charles F. 1974. "Crime and the Dimensions of Nations." *International Journal of Criminology and Penology* 2: 1–10.

Xiao, Jianming. 1988. "Economic Development and Crime Problem." *Juvenile Delinquency Studies* 5: 15. (In Chinese).

Yu, Olivia, and Lening Zhang. 1999. "The Under-recording of Crime by Police in China: A Case Study." *Policing: An International Journal of Police Strategies and Management* 22, no. 3: 252–263.

Zhu, Hongde, Lixian Wang, Jialun Lu, Jianan Guo, and Zhou Lu. 1995. "Result of the Crime (Victim) Survey in Beijing, China." In *Developmental and Policy Use of Criminal Justice Information: Proceedings of the Beijing Seminar, 12–16 September 1994*, pp. 185–217. Edited by Ugljesa Zvekic, Lixian Wang, and Richard Scherpenzeel. Rome: United Nations Interregional Crime and Justice Institute.

CHAPTER 2

White-Collar Crime: Bribery and Corruption in China

Lening Zhang

White-collar crime—bribery and corruption—has become a major public concern since China implemented economic reform and the "open door" policy in the
late 1970s and early 1980s. The present study describes the reality of bribery and
corruption at both individual and organizational levels, especially among governmental officials and governments as organizations in China. Further, the study explores the sources of bribery and corruption. Several sources are analyzed,
including cultural, political, economic, social, and ideological sources. Traditionally, people in power have been expected to use their positions to accumulate
assets for their family and relatives, no matter how this is done. Politically, the
Communist system lacks powerful mechanisms to prevent and control bribery
and corruption, and protection of the "face" of the system is generally believed to
be more important than punishment of any corrupted officers. Low income and
poor living conditions are other forces that push governmental officers to use illegitimate and illegal means to accumulate assets when getting rich becomes a basic
tenet of the nation during the course of economic transition. The "social anomie"
during the transition of China is creating many illicit opportunities to get rich, and
people who are losing their moral commitment to the Communist ideology and
self-control are likely to exploit these opportunities. Finally, the study reviews how
Chinese authorities deal with the problem of bribery and corruption through political, legal, and administrative measures.

STUDIES OF WHITE-COLLAR CRIME IN THE WEST

Edwin H. Sutherland formally introduced the concept of white-collar crime to criminology in his 1939 American Sociological Society presidential address (Coleman, 1991; Friedrichs, 1996; Poveda, 1994). He defined white-collar crime as "a crime committed by a person of respectability and high social status in the course of his [her] occupation" (Sutherland, 1983, p. 7). Although Sutherland's concept and definition raised a historical debate (Caldwell, 1958; Tappen, 1947), "criminologists have come to accept Sutherland's thesis that widespread criminality indeed exists among the rich and the powerful, even though they are seldom punished for their crimes" (Coleman, 1991, p. 220).

Building upon Sutherland's seminal concept, scholars commonly recognize three major characteristics of white-collar crime: respectability, trust, and risk calculation (Friedrichs, 1996). According to Sutherland's definition, white-collar criminals could be called "respectable criminals." Although "respectable" may have different meanings, here it implies the "good social standing" of these criminals. The good social standing is a powerful social force that may allow these criminals to take some advantages when they are processed by the criminal justice system. The claims of a "double standard" of justice in handling these "respectable" criminals are directly related to this characteristic (Poveda, 1994).

A second characteristic of white-collar crime is that it involves a "violation of delegated or implied trust" (Sutherland, 1947, p. 3). Some scholars argue that trust and its violation are key elements of white-collar crime (Friedrichs, 1996; Shapiro, 1990). These "trusted criminals" are especially difficult to prosecute because the violation of trust often occurs behind the closed doors of "suites." Offenders can often manipulate information and evidence to conceal their misconduct by using their high statuses and other available resources. As a result, people often ask: Is law enforcement more symbolic than real for white-collar crime?

Finally, risk calculation may be a basic element of any crime, but it is especially true for white-collar crime. Because of their high statuses, respectable or trusted criminals often perceive that "the chances of being caught and punished are quite remote compared with the benefits that accrue from committing crime" (Friedrichs, 1996, p. 14). A general formula of risk calculation for white-collar crime is that the risk strongly favors the offender because the probability of detection, prosecution, and sanctioning is typically very low. However, the formula is true only for the trusted criminal. For the public, the cost is far more than any street crime. The crime may cost the public enormous amounts of money, precious civil liberties, and even lives (Coleman, 1991). For instance, in the United States the average robbery netted about $628 and the average burglary about $953 in 1985. "The next year, a single respectable criminal, Ivan F. Boesky, agreed to pay $100 million in fines and penalties for his illegal stock market dealings—far more money than 150,000 average robberies would net" (Coleman, 1991, p. 219).

Although the typology and classification of white-collar crimes are diverse in different studies, bribery and corruption are typical forms of white-collar crime (Coleman, 1991; Friedrichs, 1996). Bribery can be classified in two types: commercial bribery and political bribery. It was estimated that the annual cost of both types of bribery was $3–15 billion in the United States (Coleman, 1985). The worst impact of bribery is the subversion of democratic government. Bribery and corruption can also be analyzed at two levels: individual and organizational. The individual level is concerned with occupational crimes committed by individuals or groups without organizational support and encouragement. The organizational level deals with crimes committed by "an organization as a whole or by individual members with the help, encouragement, and support of the organization" (Coleman, 1991, p. 221). The best-known example of such organizational crimes was New York Police Department corruption investigated by the Knapp Commission in the 1970s. In the United States, commercial bribery is believed to be a common practice in the business world, especially in the international business world, and has less serious consequences than political bribery and corruption. Many Westerners see bribery and corruption as a kind of Third World disease and less common in their own countries. This view reflects to some extent the reality of bribery and corruption in the developing countries.

The present study attempts to use the general conceptual and analytical framework of white-collar crime in the West to analyze bribery and corruption in a developing country, China. The analysis will be based upon information collected from Chinese documents, including newspapers, TV news, journal publications, and some unpublished official documents. These documents are limited, but they provide valuable information for exploring the problem of bribery and corruption in China.

BRIBERY AND CORRUPTION IN CHINA

Bribery and corruption are often government-related in China because the business world is not independent of political and governmental control. Although China has been transforming from a state-controlled economic system to a market-oriented economy since late 1979, the Communist Party and government still have a great deal of power in the business world. This power often becomes a means for some of the party's and government's officials to pursue personal or familial interests and benefits.

Bribery and corruption are not new in China. They have existed since the first official was created (Yang, 1997). China has dual cultural traditions regarding the official's image. The first one is that an official should be a "people's servant" with clean, ethical, and moral manners. The official should not gain any personal or family interest and benefit through his or her position. The Chinese have created many stylized figures with this official image to express their high expectation of government officials. A second tradition is entirely opposite: if an official does not accumulate assets and becomes rich by using his position, he is viewed as incompetent and stupid. Taking and holding an official position are believed to be an opportunity to collect and create assets. The role of these dual and opposite cultural traditions depends on social conditions, such as social constraints and opportunities. When social conditions are favorable, bribery and corruption are common among government officials.

When the Chinese Communists launched a revolution to gain national power, they did not have much in the way of social conditions and social statuses to be bribed and corrupted. Poverty and suffering were often part of their environment and life. When the Communists took over the state's power in 1949, bribery and corruption began emerging to a significant degree. Mao Zedong issued the death penalty to two high-ranking officials convicted of corruption in 1952. Each was a secretary of the party committee, in Shi Jiazhoung and in Tianjin city, respectively. They illegally used state funds (about 1,554,954 Chinese dollars), in addition to other illegal income, for personal expenses and pleasure-seeking (Huang and Liu, 1997, p. 83). Both of them had made significant contributions to the Communist revolution. On the one hand, the death penalty was an indicator of the surging of official corruption in the Communist government. On the other hand, the death penalty was symbolic. It was a signal that warned all officials. Although bribery and corruption were part of the Communist government since the founding of the People's Republic of China, they did not become a national disease until the economic reform and open door policy were implemented in the early 1980s.

The purpose of the economic reform and open door policy is to modernize China in both economy and technology. The transition to a socialist market economy inevitably has weakened traditional social constraints on people's behavior, such as worship of the Communist ideology, and has provided new behavioral motives, such as "getting rich is glorious." Getting rich is a social movement that involves all Chinese people, including government officials. In this economic and social context, bribery and corruption, which were already part of the Communist government, spread rapidly at various levels. In the 1980s, bribery and corruption were a major concern of the public. In 1982, a campaign against officials' criminal activities in the economic area was launched. During one year of the campaign (1982–1983), 192,000 officials' economic cases were recorded and investigated, and 24,000 officials confessed their economic crimes to criminal justice agencies and other official agencies (Li and Li, 1995). During 1983–1984, the Communist Party launched another campaign against corruption and power abuse among its members. About 33,896 individuals lost their party membership, and 184,971 had their membership suspended, for corruption and power abuse (Li and Li, 1995). A factor that initiated the 1989 Tiananmen Square movement was bribery and corruption among government officials.

After the Tiananmen Square movement, the Chinese government promised to severely control officials' corruption. The Chinese Communist Party designated "cracking down on corruption" as one of the major political tasks in the Fourth Congress of the Thirteenth Central Committee in 1989. Following the party's decision, China's Supreme Court and the Department of Prosecution jointly issued a legal circular stating that all officials who were involved in illegal economic activities must confess to criminal justice agencies or party branches within two and a half months. As a result of this legal circular, 25,544 corrupted officials confessed their illegal activities and 133,765 cases were reported by informants. Some officials in high posts, such as the vice chairman of the Xinjiang government and the vice commissioner of China's Department of Railroads, were investigated and sanctioned by the party and criminal courts (Li and Li, 1995). Deng Xiaoping emphasized the importance of controlling corruption again in 1992 when he visited Shengzhen, a special economic zone in China. He warned that corruption was a serious "disease" that infected the party and government. He also claimed that the war against bribery and corruption was directly related to the fate of China's modernization.

Despite various campaigns and movements, bribery and corruption continued to spread at various levels of government. It was estimated that during 1992–1996, more than 263,000 middle-range officials were disciplined by administrative measures. About 731,000 cases were investigated by criminal justice agencies or the party's special agencies. About 121,500 officials lost their party membership as a political sanction, and 37,500 received criminal penalties (Zheng, 1999). The official reports showed that China's departments of prosecution at various levels processed 76,000 cases of corruption and other power abuse and investigated 26,800 cases during 1997–1999. Among them, 646 officials were of middle or high rank (chief officials in county, provincial, and central governments) (Han, 2000). In 1999, the people's courts at various levels punished 15,748 officials. The economic cost of their offenses was about 15 billion Chinese dollars (Xiao, 2000).

CHARACTERISTICS OF BRIBERY AND CORRUPTION IN CHINA

As in Western studies, bribery and corruption in China can be analyzed at individual and organizational levels. At the individual level, an official is corrupted as an individual without organizational support and encouragement. The well-known case of Hu Changquing is a typical example of corrupted individuals. Hu was vice chairman of Jiangxi province. In December 1999, he was arrested for receiving a large amount of bribes during 1994–1998. The official report indicated that during this period Hu received bribery eighty-seven times, for a total of about 4 million Chinese dollars. He also had 2 million Chinese dollars for which he could produce no legitimate or legal sources. On March 8, 2000, he was executed (*People's Daily*, overseas ed., March 8, 2000).

Organizational bribery and corruption have an organizational context and supports. Corrupted individual members are part of the corrupted organization. A typical example of such crimes is the corrupted Customs Service office of Shamen city, which was investigated for smuggling (Wang, 2000). More than 100 officials were involved with the case, including the vice commissioner of China's police department, the vice commissioner of the police department of Fujian province, the vice secretary of the Communist Party's committee of Shamen City, and the chief officer of the Shamen City Customs Service office. The estimated value of smuggled goods was 80 billion Chinese dollars. The Communist Party's Supervision and Discipline Committee assigned more than 300 officers to investigate the case.

It is especially true in China that corrupted officials often perceive that the chances of being caught and punished are quite remote, compared with the benefits derived from their illegal activities. Such a perception has multiple sources. First, the relationship between officials and common people is traditionally analogized to a relationship between parents and children. How a "parental" official behaves depends on his morals, ethics, self-discipline, and self-control. Common people, as "children," have no power to supervise and monitor the official's behavior. This political culture leaves much room for an official to abuse his power and use his official status to further personal interests and obtain benefits. Lack of intensive and effective external control and supervision of official behavior often leads to a perception that the risk of being caught and punished would be much lower than the benefits derived from the corrupt behaviors.

Second, a political tradition is that the legal penalty for an official should be avoided as much as possible, because any penalty would influence the "face" of the government and damage official authority. When corruption is widespread, a corrupt official may be punished as an example to warn all officials. Such punishment is more symbolic than real. Who is punished usually depends on "luck" and personal relationships with other officials. This political tradition often makes officials feel that they enjoy certain privileges in the criminal justice system. As a result, risk calculation for white-collar crime generally favors the offender.

Finally, although bribery and corruption have not been institutionalized in China (Zhang, 2000), they have become a political subculture. Many people believe that bribery—large or small—is a common practice among government officials. This subculture significantly influences officials' risk calculation for offending. The chances of being caught and punished will be low if bribery is common among officials. An official may use the subculture as a defense and excuse for being bribed. To the public, punishment of a corrupted official simply implies that the official has "bad luck."

The social standing of an official in China often becomes a means for him to cover up his criminal activities and take advantage of the criminal justice system. Official social standing in China is not only respected and trusted, but it also represents social privilege. Because bribery and corruption are a subculture among officials, fear and distrust of government officials are fairly common in China.

Although street crimes such as robbery, larceny, and burglary are seriously threatening public safety and security in China (Curran, 1998; Rojek, 1995), people's political, administrative, and economic safety and security are also severely threatened by a large number of "trusted" and "respectable" criminals. People are losing their faith and trust in, and respect for, their government.

EXPLANATION OF BRIBERY AND CORRUPTION IN CHINA

There are diverse theories and perspectives in explaining white-collar crime, such as differential association theory (Sutherland, 1947), social control theory (Hirschi, 1969), rational choice theory (Cornish and Clarke, 1986), self-control theory (Gottfredson and Hirschi, 1990), and integrated theories (Braithwaite, 1989; Coleman, 1987). Although these theories are different in conception and construction, they all, to a lesser or greater degree, concern three basic elements in explaining white-collar crime: social constraints, opportunities, and motivations. For example, for differential association theory, association with deviant companions provides a deviant environment in which an individual gains motivations and learns skills necessary for committing crime. Social control theory argues that strong social bonds to conventional institutions are likely to be related to low crime rates. Social bonds can be viewed as social constraints. Calculation of costs and rewards in committing crime, proposed by rational choice theory, is directly related to the availability of social constraints and attractiveness of crime opportunities. For Gottfredson and Hirschi's theory, low self-control provides a direct motivation to commit crime when such opportunities are available and attractive. Coleman's integrated theory directly explains white-collar crime by opportunities and motivations.

When explaining white-collar crime, social constraints and opportunities are primarily concerned with structural analysis of the distribution of power and the related legal system in modern capitalist societies. Social constraints and opportunities probably provide no more than half the answer to white-collar crime. Motivations should also be taken into account for the explanation (Coleman, 1991). Motivations are analyzed primarily at the individual level, and the analysis offers explanations of why some people pursue certain opportunities, and others do not, when the opportunities are available and attractive. These three conceptual elements are useful for providing an explanation of white-collar crime in China.

Since the late 1970s, economic reform and the open door policy have greatly changed the political and ideological climate for governmental officials in China. In the past, political and ideological worship of communism and collectivism imposed significant social constraints on officials' deviant behaviors, although such worship suppressed individual freedom. Now that China is transforming into a market economy, the capitalist tenets of individual interests and gains are replacing the Communist and collectivist tradition. Getting rich is becoming glorious (see chapter 7 in this volume). On the one hand, this transformation lifts the old social constraints, such as brainwashing and self-education, on officials' behavior. When getting rich becomes a basic tenet of the nation, why should officials be poor? On the other hand, the development of regulations and rules for people's economic behavior lags far behind the pace of economic transition. The Communist Party lacks an effective mechanism for preventing and controlling corruption during economic transition. For officials with low incomes and poor living conditions, a direct and handy source of getting rich is the power they hold, if no effective and clearly defined regulations and rules for the exercise of power are enforced. As a result, what we observe is power-money exchange.

The economic transition has created "social anomie" in the sense that many old social constraints are lifted and new ones have not been established. Consequently, the social anomie is creating many illicit opportunities for individuals, and for officials in particular, because of the power they hold. The motivation for officials who pursue these available and attractive opportunities is simple: getting rich. This motivation seems to be legitimate, given that the nation encourages everyone to get rich. The interesting phenomenon is that the nation is lifting old social constraints, the economic transition is producing opportunities, and the motivation (getting rich) is strongly socialized for committing corruption. What is blamed is the society, not the individuals who are corrupted.

Caution is called for when an uncorrupted official is evaluated, given the weak social constraints, attractive opportunities, and common motivations. The evaluation may be twofold. First, some officials are not corrupted because of their individual characteristics, such as stronger moral commitment or stronger risk estimate of crime commission. In China, these officials are often used as role models for educating other officials and urging them to be models. The second one is derived from the labeling perspective (Becker, 1963; Lemert, 1951; Schur, 1971). Who and what are defined as criminal is largely determined by extralegal factors rather than the act itself. In China, common sense dictates that the official who is charged with bribery and corruption had bad "luck." This means that the act or acts the official committed are not critical for criminal labeling. Some officials who are bribed and corrupted may escape criminal charges. They seem to be clean and respectable. Who is officially defined as criminal largely depends on his or her power, interpersonal relations with other officials, and skills in rationalizing and neutralizing his or her illicit acts. The issue is that some officials who are not charged with bribery and corruption may be in the "dark figure" of crime.

In sum, the proposed model for explaining bribery and corruption in the course of China's transition involves three primary variables—social constraints, opportunities, and motivations. The theoretical framework containing these three variables is the interaction of social constraints and opportunities (see figure 2.1). Weak social constraints are directly related to high opportunities, and high opportunities impose difficulties on the role of social constraints. Both social constraints and opportunities affect motivations to engage in bribery and corruption. This

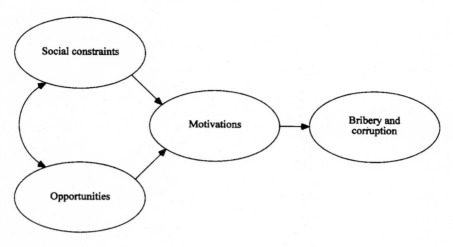

Figure 2.1
Model for Explaining Bribery and Corruption in China

model should be applied and tested in China as it undergoes the transformation to a market-oriented economic system.

CHINA'S STRATEGY AGAINST BRIBERY AND CORRUPTION

The strategy against bribery and corruption is carried out at three basic levels. Because most officials are members of the Communist Party, control at the first level takes place in the Communist Party. A special agency of the party that is directly responsible for investigation and punishment of party officials is the Central Committee of Supervision and Discipline, which was reestablished in 1979. The committee is in charge of investigating officials' criminal behaviors, imposing discipline and punishment on deviant officials, and turning officials over to the criminal justice system if they are considered to deserve further legal investigation and sanction. The committee has branches at local governmental levels to monitor officials' behaviors.

Control at the second level is carried out by the criminal justice agencies. The government agency that takes charge is the Prosecution Department of China. The department takes action after an official (a party member) is disciplined and punished by the party and is referred to the criminal justice system. The action is generally guided and instructed by the Central Committee, although laws stipulate how to define, investigate, and punish criminals. The Prosecution Department also has corresponding local departments and agencies.

At the first level of control, the Communist Party has launched campaigns and drives against bribery and corruption since 1982 (Li and Li, 1995). These campaigns generally serve two objectives: (1) pushing the party's officials to do self-inspection and self-critiques regarding deviant behaviors, including bribery and corruption, and urging those who have been bribed and corrupted to self-report to the party's committees or to criminal justice agencies; (2) conducting nationwide inspection and investigation of party officials regarding bribery and corruption by the Central Committee of Supervision and Discipline. If the party sees fit, some officials are disciplined and punished as examples during each campaign. For example, at the party's instruction, China's Supreme Court and China's Prosecution Department jointly issued the circular "Bribed, Corrupted, and Other Criminals Must Report Their Criminal Activities to Criminal Justice Agencies Within a Defined Period" in 1989. The circular announced that any bribed, corrupted, and other criminals must report their criminal activities between August 15 and October 30, 1989. Those who reported were promised lenient treatment; those who did not, were threatened with severe criminal sanction. These campaigns were often carried out along with the party's regulations and rules. Sometimes these regulations and rules were issued in specific legal forms. The combination of political and legal power and authority created a climate that can pressure some officials to report their criminal activities. However, who is punished publicly often depends on political considerations rather than legal standards. As a result, people usually perceive the punishment of any officials as symbolic rather than real.

The second level of control is directly involved with the criminal justice system. Justice is not independent of the party's leadership. Any legal action is often related to political instructions and decisions issued by the party. Since China began transforming to a market-oriented society, the Communist Party has become aware of the utility of using legal power in addition to political control to regulate people's behaviors. To fight against bribery and corruption among officials, the party has utilized several legal approaches. One is to promulgate laws through the National Congress. For example, the Criminal Law promulgated in 1979 stipulates that state officials and other personnel who use their positions to receive bribes should be sentenced to less than five years in prison. All bribes should be confiscated (China's Criminal Law, art. 185). In 1982, the National Congress amended the article in response to the increasing seriousness of bribery and corruption. The amendment stipulates that if a case involves serious criminal activities, the bribed official or other state employee may be sentenced to life in prison or to death.

Another approach is for the Supreme Court and Prosecution Department to issue special regulations and rules. In 1999, the Prosecution Department issued uniform criteria for investigating and prosecuting corrupted governmental officials who abuse power. These criteria are stipulated and detailed in a forty-one-page document. For example, the criteria state that a government official who receives a bribe of 5,000 Chinese dollars or more should be prosecuted. A governmental official who has an asset above 300,000 Chinese dollars and cannot provide legitimate sources for that asset should be prosecuted (*People's Daily*, overseas ed. September 16, 1999).

In the West, people often observe the failure of law enforcement in regard to white-collar crime. The reasons for such failure "can be summarized in a single word: power" held by those criminals (Coleman, 1991, p. 237). This is also true in China. Although laws and legal regulations are promulgated, an official's power derived from his or her position often allows him or her to evade criminal prosecution and sanction even though common people know about and witness his or her criminal behavior. When the vice commissioner of Jiangxi province was sentenced to death for bribery and corruption, a common popular response was "He should have been sanctioned much earlier." Another important factor affecting law enforcement in China is protecting the "face" of the party and the government. Legal sanctioning of any officials, especially high-ranking ones, is perceived as a shame and a threat to the party's and government's authority. Instead of turning a criminal official over to the criminal justice system, a common practice is pursuing an "internal resolution." Such internal resolution often leads to questions about a double standard for white-collar crimes and damages people's confidence in the criminal justice system.

China has begun to adopt administrative measures against bribery and corruption, which is the third level of control. For example, in 1998, the central government began to reduce its size by cutting 50 percent of its officials. The reduction was accompanied by the intention to significantly increase officials' wages. It was believed that such action might reduce the rates of bribery and corruption among officials. Also, since 1998, army forces and governmental departments have been prohibited from running businesses for profit, in order to reduce the opportunities of power-money exchange. These administrative measures are proactive, indicating China's efforts to increase social constraints and reduce opportunities for bribery and corruption.

DISCUSSION AND CONCLUSION

The present study is an attempt to describe and explain a complex phenomenon—bribery and corruption—in China based on limited information and data. The description and explanation are preliminary. As many people have observed, bribery and corruption are common in Asian countries. They are social diseases rooted in Asian cultural, political, social, and economic systems. China is not an exception, especially given the social and economic transition. When Chinese Communists worshiped the "socialist poor," the social constraints were relatively strong, opportunities were relatively low, and motivations were relatively weak for bribery and corruption. However, as China has been transforming to a market economy with the tenet of "getting rich is glorious," official power is becoming a major means for "poor" officials to achieve the goal of getting rich as the old measures of political control lose their power. The flourishing bribery and corruption among officials are a reflection of this "social anomie." The traditional political culture of "making rich from the position" also plays a role in the growth of bribery and corruption.

Although bribery and corruption have not been institutionalized, as in some other Asian countries, these criminal activities are fairly common among officials (Zhang, 2000). People's resentments about growing bribery and corruption are threatening the legitimacy of the Chinese government. The Chinese leadership has been aware of this problem, as shown in Deng Xiaoping's words about the need for "sanctioning corruption and restoring people's faith and trust" (Li and Li, 1995). China's political, legal, and administrative controls and measures can be viewed as a reaction to the problem. However, a large gap has been observed between the awareness of, and actual control of, bribery and corruption. This continues to be a great challenge to the leadership in China.

REFERENCES

Becker, Howard S. 1963. *Outsiders: Studies in the Sociology of Deviance*. London: Free Press of Glencoe.

Braithwaite, John. 1989. "Criminological Theory and Organizational Crime." *Justice Quarterly* 6: 333–358.

Caldwell, Robert G. 1958. "A Reexamination of the Concept of White-Collar Crime." *Federal Probation* 22: 30–36.

Coleman, James W. 1985. The Criminal Elite: The Sociology of White-Collar Crime. New York: St. Martin's Press.

———. 1987. "Toward an Integrated Theory of White-Collar Crime." *American Journal of Sociology* 93: 406–439.

———. 1991. "Respectable Crime." In *Criminology*, pp. 219–244. Edited by Joseph F. Sheley. Belmont, CA: Wadsworth.

Cornish, Derek, and Ronald Clarke. 1986. *The Reasoning Criminal: Rational Choice Perspectives on Offending*. New York: Springer-Verlag.

Curran, Daniel J. 1998. "Economic Reform, the Floating Population, and Crime: The Transformation of Social Control in China." *Journal of Contemporary Criminal Justice* 14: 262–280.

Friedrichs, David O. 1996. *White-Collar Crime in Contemporary Society*. Belmont, CA: Wadsworth.

Gottfredson, Michael R., and Travis Hirschi. 1990. *A General Theory of Crime*. Stanford, CA: Stanford University Press.

Han Rubin. 2000. "The Annual Report of China's Prosecution Department to the Third Conference of the Ninth National Congress of China." *People's Daily*, overseas ed., March 11.

Hirschi, Travis. 1969. *Causes of Delinquency*. Berkeley: University of California Press.

Huang Xirong and Songbin Liu. 1997. *The History of the Chinese Communist Party in Controlling Corruption*. Beijing: Fangzheng Publications.

Lemert, Edwin M. 1951. *Social Pathology: A Systematic Approach to the Theory of Sociopathic Behavior*. New York: McGraw-Hill.

Li Xieqin and Xiehui Li. 1995. *The Course of Controlling Corruption in the People's Republic of China*. Beijing: Chuengqiu Publications.

People's Daily. 1999. "China Issues Uniform Criteria for Prosecuting Occupational Crime." overseas ed., September 17.

———. 2000. "Former Vice Commissioner of Jiangxi Province, Hu Changqing, Executed . . . ." overseas ed., March 8.

Poveda, Tony G. 1994. *Rethinking White-Collar Crime*. Westport, CT: Praeger.

Rojek, Dean G. 1996. "Changing Directions of Chinese Social Control." In *Comparative Criminal Justice: Traditional and Nontraditional Systems of Law and Control*, pp. 234–249. Edited by Charles B. Fields and Richter H. Moore, Jr. Prospect Heights, IL: Waveland Press.

Schur, Edwin M. 1971. *Labeling Deviant Behavior: Its Sociological Implications*. New York: Harper & Row.

Shapiro, Susan P. 1990. "Collaring the Crime, Not the Criminal: Reconsidering the Concept of White-Collar Crime." *American Sociological Review* 55: 346–365.

Sutherland, Edwin H. 1947. *Criminology*. 4th ed. Philadelphia: Lippincott.

———. 1983. *White-Collar Crime: The Uncut Version*. New Haven, CT: Yale University Press.

Tappen, Paul W. 1977. "Who Is the Criminal?" in *White-Collar Crime: Offenses in Business, Politics, and the Professions*, pp. 272–282. Edited by Gilbert Geis and Robert Meier. New York: Free Press.

Wang Jian. 2000. "The Source of Serious Cases of Corruption in China." *Ming* magazine (March): 84–86.

Xiao Young. 2000. "The Annual Report of China's Supreme Court to the Third Conference of the Ninth National Congress of China." *People's Daily*, overseas ed., March 11.

Yang Enhan. 1997. "Reexamining Corruption." *Law Studies* (Beijing) 19: 139–141.

Zhang Wuchang. 2000. "Do Not Look Down upon Chinese." *Washington Chinese News*, April 29.

Zheng Shuping. 1999. "Legally Disciplining Cadres Is More Important Than Legally Ruling the Country." *Mainland China Studies* (Taipei, Taiwan). 42: 1–2.

CHAPTER 3

Narcotics Control in China: A Growing Challenge

Peter Liu and Yingyi Situ

China has had a disastrous history with narcotics. The use of opium has been associated with the fall of a great nation. The widespread use of, and addiction to, the drug in the nineteenth century led to the shameful labeling of the Chinese people as the "sick men of East Asia," and the nation fell into semicolonial status after it lost two Opium Wars to the Western powers.

The outlawing of the narcotics trade and of the use of narcotics were among the Communists' first acts after the establishment of the People's Republic of China in 1949. Since the 1950s, China has enjoyed the reputation of being drug free. However, after its once tightly closed door opened to the outside world in the 1980s, illicit drugs entered with other commercial goods, and drug crimes have been increasing, becoming one of the most serious social problems in the 1990s. According to Bai Jingfu, deputy director of the National Antidrug Commission, in 1998 there were 596,000 registered drug users in the nation (the government requires all drug users to register with the police); 2,033 counties (cities) reported drug crimes. The police seized 7.3 tons of heroin, up 34.3 percent from 1997; 1.6 tons of "ice" (methamphetamine), up 20.5 percent; and 5.1 tons of marijuana, up 137 percent. Some 270,000 people have been sentenced for drug offenses (*Legal Daily*, 1999b). The Chinese government has launched a people's war on illicit drugs.

This paper was undertaken to study drug crimes, their causes, and their control in the People's Republic of China. It attempts to answer the following research questions:

1. What are the history and the present status of drug crimes in China?

2. What are the causes of drug crimes today?

3. What effort is the government making to deal with drug crimes?

4. In what ways are China's and the United States' wars on drugs similar and in what ways are they different?

The study was based upon the information obtained in China during 1996 and 1999. Following an ethnosociological tradition, we combined interviews and field observations as our main data collection methods. During the summers of 1996 and 1999, we traveled to China and conducted a series of unstructured interviews with government officials, police officers, staff members of drug treatment centers, drug addicts, scholarly researchers, high school students and their teachers, and residents in the cities of Guangzhou and Beijing. We also visited drug rehabilitation clinics, neighborhoods, high schools, and a drug education exhibition in order to make direct observations. These field studies gave us deep insights into the natures of drug crimes, public opinion, government efforts, and the weaknesses and limitations of the control systems. In order to develop a more comprehensive view of the drug problem in today's China, we also used government documents, the official Xinhua News Agency, and several major government newspapers. This literature provided us with systematic statistics on drug problems at national and regional levels.

Although there is a lack of independent sources with which to verify the objectivity of the official statistics, we feel confident in using these data, based on the following considerations. First, they are the only systematic drug statistics available for researchers who are studying the drug problem in China. Second, the purpose of this study is not to find out the exact degree of the drug problem in China. Instead, we are concerned only with the general situation and trends. The available official statistics are sufficient for these goals. Third, our interviews and field observations were able to verify the governmental data to a certain degree.

DRUG PROBLEMS IN TODAY'S CHINA: NATURE AND IMPACTS

In the past, China experienced a painful drug problem. In the seventeenth century, opium, which was considered an effective weapon for opening the doors of imperial China to Western products, was first transported into China from India by the British. By the nineteenth century, foreign powers sold 4,000 tons of opium to China each year, valued at 1,000 tons of silver (Deng and Deng, 1993). The Chinese imperial authority tried to ban opium in several ways, from burning all of the found drugs to engaging in wars against Great Britain and other Western powers. However, agricultural China was no longer able to resist the invasion of the industrialized Westerners. As a result of the losses in the two Opium Wars (1839–1842, 1856–1860), Chinese authorities were forced to open the nation's door to narcotics, mainly opium.

The extensive use of opium among the Chinese people resulted in many profound negative social consequences, one of which was the rapid worsening of people's health. China became known as the "sick man of eastern Asia" in the late nineteenth and early twentieth centuries, while the nation retained the status of a semicolony of foreign powers. This stigma severely hurt the Chinese people's self-esteem and became a force that inspired their patriotism. When the Chinese Communists took power in 1949, the desire to remove this shameful stain motivated the new government to launch a massive antidrug movement.

According to the official statistics, there were over 300,000 drug producers and dealers, and over 20 million users, in 1949 (Huang, 1995). By 1953 about 220,000 drug cases had been tried, and over 80,000 drug offenders sentenced. Among them, over 800 were sentenced to death and executed. Hundreds of drug production sites were shut down, and millions of drug addicts were rehabilitated. It has been claimed that after three years of effort, the drug problem was thoroughly eliminated. After that, China enjoyed a reputation as "the nation free from drugs" (Ma and Bao, 1993).

However, since the early 1980s, China has once again encountered the problem of illegal drugs. Opium, heroin, morphine, methamphetamine (ice), *Cannabis sativa* (marijuana), cocaine, and controlled medical narcotics which can cause addiction quickly became common almost everywhere in the nation. Consequently, drug crimes, such as smuggling, selling, transporting, and producing illegal drugs; illegal possession of drugs; shielding drug offender(s); harboring, transferring, and concealing drugs or earnings from dealing drugs for drug offenders; disguising the illegal nature of drug earnings; dealing the materials that can be used to produce illegal drugs; illegally planting opium poppies; and luring others to use drugs are increasing in frequency and shocking the society. For example, in Guangdong province, the number of drug crimes (drug use not included) solved by the police in 1998 alone was more than four times that in the years between 1981 and 1990 (see table 3.1).

According to Jia Chunwang, director of the National Antinarcotics Commission and minister of public security, China has changed from being a transit coun-

Table 3.1
Drugs Seized in Guangdong, 1981–1998

	Cases Solved	Opium (kilo)	Heroin (kilo)	Others (kilo)	Dealers Arrested
1981–1990	850	1,377.3	299.9	N.A.	2,142
1994	3,045	11.3	306.0	1,509.7	4,064
1998	3,700	N.A.	669.5	6,050.4	4,600

Source: The Anti-Narcotics Commission of Guangdong Province.

try for narcotics to a transit and consumption country. In 1998, about 596,000 drug users were registered with the police, and drug crimes were found in 2,033 counties, cities, and districts, accounting for 71 percent of the nation's jurisdiction (*Legal Daily*, 1999a). According to Bai Jingfu, deputy director of the National Antinarcotics Commission and deputy minister of public security, in 1998 the Chinese police solved over 180,000 drug cases; confiscated over 7,300 kilos of heroin, 1,600 kilos of methamphetamine, and 5,100 kilos of marijuana; and arrested about 34,000 drug offenders. Courts convicted about 27,000 drug criminals (*Legal Daily*, 1999b).

The drug problem not only has become one of the main concerns of the Chinese criminal justice system, but also has drawn the attention of the entire society. Our field observations showed that drug education had been carried out in all the high schools we visited, public antidrug exhibitions were on view in both cities, that is, Guangzhou and Beijing antinarcotics slogans appeared on many main streets and in public transportation stations, drug treatment clinics were everywhere, and antinarcotics flyers were distributed in many hotels and restaurants. A director of a neighborhood residents' committee told us:

Dealing with the drug problem has become one of the main duties of my committee. We need to go out to check those highly susceptible places, such as small hotels, street corners, and the apartments occupied by temporary residents. We also try to educate the residents to be aware of drug problems and to help parents to deal with their drug-involved kids. I have been working on this committee for almost twenty years, [and] this is the first time that we have been seriously disturbed by drug-related problems. (interview note #4, 1996)

Based upon our interviews and secondary source analyses, several characteristics of the present drug activities have been identified. First, drug traffickers have become more professional, and drug organizations, from local groups to international ones, have been formed. Many drug organizations consist of citizens from various nations. The most common are Burmese, who sell drugs in the Sino-Burma border areas; other foreigners, such as Koreans, who buy and smuggle drugs out of China; Hong Kong residents, who buy and transport drugs in the Mainland-Hong Kong border areas; and Chinese who buy, sell, or transport drugs inside the country. In 1988, 5,177 drug offenders who resided outside of China were captured (Zhao and Yu, 1998, p. 33). Many groups were found to be highly organized and disciplined, equipped with firearms and high-tech communications (Liu, 1995; Zhao and Yu, 1998, p. 34). The number of drug organizations has increased rapidly. For example, prior to 1990, they were rarely heard of in Beijing, the capital city, but by the end of 1997, 312 drug groups were arrested and 1,261 members processed (interview note #18, 1999).

Second, major cases involving greater amounts and a higher quality of narcotics are increasing. In 1998, cases involving over 10 kilos of heroin had increased by 25.2 percent from 1997 (*Legal Daily*, 1999b). In one case, on October 24, 1998, the police seized 309.9 kilos of heroin in Yunnan province (Xinhua News Agency, 1999). On June 9, 1998, the Shenzhen police seized 16 kilos at the border of Hong Kong (Xinhua News Agency, 1998c). In another case, 11 kilos of heroin were seized in Beijing in 1996 (interview note #17, 1999).

In the past, heroin was the major drug found in China. Nowadays, cocaine, methamphetamine (ice), ecstasy, and other types of drugs are also seen frequently. In May 1997, Beijing police cracked a narcotics organization; arrested seven drug dealers, including three Korean citizens; and seized 9 kilos of methamphetamine (interview note #17, 1999).

Third, drug-selling networks have become more extensive and decentralized. In the past, drug trafficking and drug selling involved only a few people, the networks being highly organized and secretive. Nowadays, many ordinary drug users have joined the networks, making them more extensive and aggressive. The reason that ordinary users joined the networks is simple: they need money to support their expensive drug habit. According to our interviews with Beijing drug enforcement officers, an average user needs to consume 0.5 gram of heroin a day, and the street price for heroin was about 600 yuan per gram in Beijing in 1998. That means a heroin addict's monthly expenses for heroin could be as much as 9,000 yuan, whereas an average worker's monthly income is only about 1,000 yuan (interview note #16, 1999). Therefore, many users introduce this "high class" consumption goods to other people and develop their own small-scale markets. They do not intend to get rich by selling drugs, making only enough money to support their own habits. They sell small amounts of heroin to one individual at a time, usually less than a few grams. These drug dealers are great in number, more flexible in action, and more difficult to detect and prosecute because law enforcement cannot easily determine whether they are drug sellers or users if they find only 1 or 2 grams in their possession. These petty drug dealers are responsible for the fast growth of the narcotics market.

Fourth, drug crimes have joined with other felonies, such as sale of firearms, robbery, and burglary. Many drug addicts become regular criminals. Statistics of Guangzhou city, Guangdong province, show that among the 150 local residents charged with criminal acts in Yuexiu district during the first three months of 1995, 60.1 percent were drug users (Luo Yuqiu, 1995). The crimes committed by drug addicts included all types of illegal acts which can yield money to purchase drugs. The common crimes are selling drugs, theft, robbery, burglary, fraud, and prostitution. Statistics indicate that among the robbers arrested on the highway from Guangzhou to Conghua, 80 percent were drug users (Zhong and Huang, 1995).

Finally, young people account for a large proportion of drug addicts. Nationwide, 85 percent of drug users are under the age of thirty-five (Xinhua News Agency, 1998e). In Guangdong province, 80 percent of drug users are under the age of twenty-five. One of the cities of Guangdong province examined all of the candidates for military recruits in early 1995, and 20 percent of them tested positive for drugs (*Guangzhou Legal System Daily*, 1995b). A national sample for a drug study in 1990 found that more than 85 percent of 14,000 drug users were younger than thirty-five years old (Ma and Bao, 1993).

This increase in drug problems has created serious threats to the Chinese people. One threat is to public health. In Shajing township, Guangdong province, almost 90 percent of drug users have some type of disease: 30 percent of them have sexually transmitted diseases and 50 percent carry hepatitis (Zheng Yanxiong, 1995, p. 64). Nationwide, there were 1,132 drug users who had been infected with AIDS, accounting for 70 percent of all AIDS patients (Tao, 1995).

Another threat is unemployment among drug users. According to the statistics of Yuexiu district, Guangzhou city, 71.5 percent of the 611 found drug users were unemployed (Luo, 1995). Many employers lay off the employees who are found using drugs. When unemployment is considered in combination with the high cost of drug use, the problem becomes more threatening. A survey conducted in 1995 among 300 drug users in Guangdong province indicated that 21 percent of them spent 1,500–2,000 yuan a month to buy drugs (the national average monthly wage was less than 500 yuan in 1995), 30 percent spent 2,000–3,000 yuan, and 40 percent spent 3,000–6,000 yuan (Zheng Yanxiong, 1995). Even people who used to be well-off, including business owners, often fell into bankruptcy when they could no longer cover the gap between income and expenses. Many drug users sold everything they had to support the habit, and many more were in great debt.

The last threat is to the social order. Because drug addicts tend to turn into regular criminals, public safety in China has become a serious concern as the number of drug abusers and dealers has increased. Our study found four classes of crime associated with drug use. First is the crime that necessarily accompanies the distribution and sale of illegal drugs, such as the violation of laws against the importation, distribution, sale, and possession of illegal drugs; the corruption of the criminal justice system and of legitimate businesses; and the violent crime that is associated with drug trafficking. The second class includes the violent, nonviolent property-intrusive, and "white collar" money-raising crime committed by persons who need funds to buy illegal drugs. For instance, one of our interviewees told us that he started using drugs after being persuaded to do so by his associates, soon got divorced because his wife did not want to spend her life with a drug addict, was fired by his boss when he found out about his involvement with drugs, and finally ended up in jail three times because he committed burglaries. The third class is crime committed under the influence of drugs: violation of motor vehicle statutes and regulations, and interpersonal violence. The fourth class of drug-related crime is income, sales, and excise tax evasion. Although there are no systematic and empirical data to support our classifications here, each of these types of crime has been identified in our interview and field observations.

According to the above analysis of drug problems in China, it is clear that drug abuse and dealing have once again attacked Chinese society after a drug-free period of thirty years. Although the degree and prevalence of drug problems among the Chinese may be not comparable to those in the United States, the nature and impacts of the problems are very similar. Obviously, drug problems in today's China are not simply a repeat of its history. Instead, they are characterized by many new features found only in the twentieth century.

CAUSES OF DRUG PROBLEMS IN CHINA

There are many factors that contribute to the causation of drug problems in a contemporary society. Criminological theories to explain drug abuse and crime have been well developed in the United States. At the individual level, drug problems can be explained by physiological, psychological, psychoanalytic, and learning perspectives. At the societal and group level, the available theories include anomie, differential association, delinquent subculture and symbolic interactionism. At the economic level, the availability of drugs is the most frequently cited factor associated with drug problems. However, we argue that no single theory is able to explain the causes of drug crimes in China and that a full understanding of the problem requires a more sophisticated strategy. According to Frank and Lynch (1992), a "good" theory of crime should address the key issues of motivation, opportunity, and social control. This integrative approach is adopted here to explain the growing drug problem in modern China.

Motivation

It has been generally agreed that making a profit is the leading motivation for drug trafficking. This is also appropriate for explaining drug dealing in China. It is reported that the value of 1 kilo of heroin in Yunnan province, which borders Burma, is around $1,000. In Guangdong, which borders Hong Kong, 1 kilo of heroin is worth $40,000. And in the United States, the same amount of heroin is worth $100,000 (Ma and Bao, 1993). The large profit leads many people to risk imprisonment (and even their lives) to commit drug crimes. But why did the motivation of making money not lead the Chinese to engage in drug trade before the 1980s? Our field study explored the dynamic behind this change. From 1949 to the end of the 1970s, when China was under Mao Zedong's leadership, the priority of the state was class struggle, and the improvement of the Chinese living standard was not part of the agenda. "The poorer, the more honor" was implanted into Chinese minds and became an acceptable social value. The movement of economic reform, which began in the early 1980s, brought about a total reversal of Mao's ideology. The slogan "It is glorious to get rich" was posted in every place where we conducted our field observations. People are encouraged to create innovative ways to make quick money and to become rich overnight. High-tech products and Western luxury goods which poured into China's markets shocked the Chinese, who had lived in poverty for so long, and further stimulated their desire for money. As a result, finding a way to be rich has become the most urgent goal for many Chinese. Drug dealing provides a shortcut to reach such a goal. The findings from our interviews with drug dealers support this source of motivation.

Opportunity

Drug crime is not the only way to make money. Only when such motivation combines with opportunity does illegal drug activity become more likely. The opportunity here refers to the availability of drug sources from abroad. According to the police, drugs found in China are mainly transported from the Golden Triangle, which is the world's largest opium-growing region. The Golden Triangle lies in the mountains and jungles of northeast Burma, northern Thailand, and northwest Laos. The area is as large as 193,000 square kilometers, with a small population and a large quantity of opium poppy plants. The "Golden Triangle" produces 2,030 tons of opium annually (Gelbard, 1995), enough to produce more than 200 tons of heroin. Traditionally, opium and heroin produced in the Golden Triangle were transported south to Bangkok and Yangon, and exported to international markets. Since the 1980s, the Thai and Burmese governments have launched a series of attacks on this traditional passage. The drug organizations therefore opened a new way north to China's Yunnan province, a jungle area that borders Burma. Originally, Hong Kong was the target of most of the drugs; Yunnan, Guangdong, and other areas were only a corridor to Hong Kong. However, with the rapid increase of people who seek to make huge profits by dealing illegal substances, China has finally become a large market for the drugs. In recent years, illegal drugs imported from the Golden Triangle to China amount to approximately 200 tons annually (Ma and Bao, 1993). The availability of drugs makes widespread drug abuse and obtaining a large amount of money from the drug trade possible.

Social Control

Drug abuse and trafficking may occur when crime-prone individuals (who are willing to make money by illegitimate means) have the opportunity to obtain sufficient amounts of drugs. The quality of social control affects the likelihood of this outcome. According to the social control theory, when there is a lack of external control (legal system and social organs, such as family, school, and church) and internal control (moral and social values, self-concept, self-control, etc.) in a given society, an increase in the crime rate can be expected (Akers, 1994). From the perspective of external control, several facts are relevant here. First, in the early 1980s, when China had just opened its door to the outside world under its policy of economic reform, loose customs inspection made it easy for foreigners to bring illegal drugs to the areas designated for border trade. Second, the government was not aware of the seriousness of the drug problem until the 1980s. No new drug legislation had been promulgated, and no drug programs had been carried out to educate citizens, since the early 1950s. Third, law enforcement was severely restricted by the goverment's intent to maintain China's reputation as a drug-free nation. As a result, the fight against drug use and the drug trade was conducted underground, without public knowledge and participation and without designated resources. The legal system was prepared to deal with only the most serious drug crimes, and left the majority of cases unsolved.

From the internal control point of view, a unified social norm on drugs was not established because public opinion had not considered drug problems for thirty years. In the Sino-Burmese border areas, where the use of opium has been popular historically, drug dealing was generally acceptable. A number of drug abusers that we interviewed in the treatment centers told us that they didn't know using drugs is illegal and can cause addiction. Our findings show that having grown up in a social environment where there were no social norms about drugs, the young generation will probably fail to develop self-control against the lure of drugs and, therefore, is very vulnerable to their use.

Due to these factors, the drug problem has become an inevitable development in Chinese society since the early 1980s. In Yunnan, tens of thousands of people became drug dealers. During the years from 1982 to 1989, 33,294 drug dealers were arrested in this province. Many of them were millionaires (Ma and Bao, 1993). Those people not only did not feel shame for what they had done (shame is a strong internal control factor in the Chinese society), but they told others about their experience of how to get rich quickly. The weakness of external and internal control encouraged drug crimes.

To explain the rising drug problems in modern China, we must integrate the three factors—motivation, opportunity and social control—in our considerations. However, it is important to realize that though the motivation for making easy money and the opportunity to get drugs easily are very commonly cited factors of drug trafficking of many other countries, the weakness of external and internal social control is unique to the Chinese society. As we have seen, China is a country with a long tradition of strict external and internal social control. Its effective social control mechanism has been regarded as the most important element contributing to the low crime rate in the period from 1949 to 1979 (Troyer et al., 1989). However, the modernization process resulting from the economic reform has had two critical consequences. On the one hand, the value system of the Chinese has been modified. In the past, working hard, sacrificing oneself, and making a contribution to society were encouraged and praised. Now, getting rich in order to have the best life and higher social status has become the priority. On the other hand, the social control mechanisms that used to be effective in regulating people's behaviors as well as their minds have been shaken. For example, the emergence of private business breaks the traditional lifetime employment in state enterprises. Consequently, the bars on population movement from rural to urban areas and the switch from one job to another have been lifted. These changes to a great extent have paralyzed the once-effective social control of neighborhoods and work units. Thus, as people's desire for more money has been promoted and some formal and informal supervision of their activities has disappeared, drug problems have inevitably appeared.

The increasing drug crime problem in China strongly supports both anomie theory and social disorganization theory, which have been generally tested on other types of crimes and have been proven valid by many empirical studies conducted in the United States. However, with regard to the causes of drug crimes in China and the United States, several differences have been identified. The current drug problem in China emerged along with its modernization process since the 1980s, whereas drug abuse reached its largest youthful audience in American history in the 1960s and was probably associated with a distrust of authority and of government policies, caused by the widespread anti-Vietnam War sentiment (Lyman and Potter, 1991).

GOVERNMENT EFFORTS TO CONTROL DRUG PROBLEMS

The Chinese government's long-term antinarcotics goal is to eradicate illicit drugs, and its short-term goal is to prohibit planting, selling, and use of illicit drugs (Xinhua News Agency, 1998b) in order to control both the supplies of and the demand for illicit drugs.

Although opium poppy cultivation is not a devastating problem in China, it has become a serious concern. Opium poppy plants have been found in remote areas of southwest, northwest, southeast, and northeast provinces. In 1997, Fujian province alone destroyed 2 million opium poppy plants (Xinhua News Agency, 1998a).

In order to curb border drug trafficking, China has signed multilateral and bilateral drug control agreements with Myanmar (Burma), Thailand, Laos, Cambodia, Vietnam, Russia, Pakistan, India, the U.N. Development Program, and the U.N. Drug Control Program (*Beijing Review*, 1998). Ministry officials have stated that China will take part in more active international cooperation on drug control and will honor its commitments and obligations within international conventions regarding drugs.

Realizing that the main drug crime is trafficking, the Chinese government began to severely punish offenders during the 1990s. On December 28, 1990, the Standing Committee of the National People's Congress passed an antinarcotics law titled "The Decisions on Prohibition of Narcotics" (SCNPC, 1990). It was incorporated into the 1997 Criminal Code. The law stipulates that anyone who is classified in one of the following categories is subject to fifteen years' imprisonment, or life sentence, or death, along with confiscation of personal property:

1. Smuggling, or selling, or transporting, or producing 1,000 grams or more of opium, or 50 grams or more of heroin, or a large amount of other types of drugs

2. Being a core member of an organization that smuggles, or sells, or transports, or produces drugs

3. Using an armed shield during the operation of smuggling, or selling, or transporting, or producing drugs

4. Using force to resist police search, detention, or arrest

5. Being involved in organized international drug dealing.

The law also stipulates that anyone who is convicted of smuggling, selling, transporting, or producing 200 to 999 grams of opium, or 10 to 49 grams of heroin, or a fairly large amount of other types of drugs is subject to seven or more years' imprisonment, plus a fine. Anyone who is convicted of the above-mentioned crime but for less than 200 grams of opium, or 10 grams of heroin, or a small amount of other types of drugs is subject to less than seven years' imprisonment.

In implementing drug laws, the courts believe that severe, swift, and public punishment will deter the potential drug criminals. Severity is the core of deterrence. Courts at all levels have used the maximum penalty stipulated by the Decisions to punish drug offenders. For example, during the period between 1991 and 1994, 64 percent of convicted drug offenders were sentenced to more than five year's imprisonment, to life in prison, or to death (Liu, 1995; Ma, 1995). This percentage is much higher than for other types of common crimes. The National Supreme Court has granted provincial higher courts the power to review death penalty cases. That means the higher courts at the provincial level become the last resort in cases of drug crimes. Although systematic data about the death penalty are not available due to their being a "state secret," the executions are often reported in media. For example, on June 25, 1994, and June 23, 1995, thirty-six and forty-four drug criminals, respectively, were executed in Guangdong province (Luo Binyi, 1995). On June 23, 1995, Guangxi province executed thirty-four drug offenders (*Legal Daily*, June 23, 1995). In Jiangmen city, Guangdong province, three core members of a seven-person group that sold 785.1 grams of heroin in 1993 were executed on July 6, 1995 (Lei and He, 1995). On June 19, 1997, fourteen drug offenders were sentenced to death and executed immediately after the sentence in Shi Jing Shan district, Beijing city (*Legal Daily*, June 26, 1999). The effectiveness of deterrence is believed to depend on swift resolution. From 1991 to 1994, courts at all levels decided over 90 percent of drug cases within forty-five days (Liu, 1995).

Next, publicity is regarded as an important aspect of deterrence. Before the execution of drug criminals, the court holds a mass rally, publicly denouncing and parading the convicted. Television, radio broadcasts, and newspapers report these denouncements and executions. June 26 was set as Antinarcotics Day by the National People's Congress. According to the Announcement of Guangdong Province Government on Antinarcotics (Guangdong Government, 1995), those who had committed any type of drug crime, such as smuggling, selling, transporting, or producing drugs, or illegally possessing drugs, or shielding drug offenders, must turn themselves in to the police before June 26, 1995, in order to receive lenient treatment. If they reported other people's crimes, their punishment could be significantly reduced or eliminated altogether. This announcement was broadly proclaimed in Guangdong. Citizen's reports could bring awards of from 100 yuan to 30,000 yuan.

During the severe strikes against drug offenses, the incidence of drug dealing and drug abuse in China usually decreased. Open and semi-open drug activities were greatly eliminated. However, with offenses turning underground, further antinarcotics actions become more difficult. The government is considering a regular antinarcotics process which coordinates drug use prevention, drug control, public education, and drug treatment. For example, the Beijing police have signed narcotics-free responsibility contracts with neighborhood committees, which in turn contract with each street and household for the same responsibilities (*Legal Daily*, June 26, 1999). With this contract system, it is hoped, the fight against drugs can be carried out from the top of the central government to the neighborhood committees. A war involving the masses of Chinese is deemed likely to succeed.

Finally, treatment of drug users has increased. This approach to dealing with drug addiction is very different from what we found in the United States. The primary characteristic of drug treatment in China is its mandatory nature. On January 12, 1995, the State Council of the People's Republic of China enacted the Regulations on Forcible Termination of Drug Use (State Council, 1995). This made it mandatory for all drug users to receive treatment to terminate their drug use. By June 1999, there were 596,000 registered drug users. It is reported that the real number of drug users may be five to ten times this figure (interview note #17, 1999). There were 690 Centers for Forcible Termination of Drug Use, which can house 77,000 people; they had treated over 180,000 by the end of 1997 (Xinhua News Agency, July 30, 1998e).

The second characteristic is the direct involvement of police in the treatments given in the Centers for Forcible Termination of Drug use. They receive budgets from local governments to run the centers and are responsible for identifying drug users, making decisions on the treatment plans, and supervising administrative as well as disciplinary matters. Thus, the Centers for Forcible Termination of Drug Use are actually state agencies, and very different from the drug termination houses recently opened by many medical institutions. The drug users treated in these state centers are usually law violators with police records, and are handled as criminal offenders if they use drugs again after the treatment (Tao, 1995). Drug termination houses accept voluntary patients and run their treatment programs like businesses. Records in these centers are kept confidential. Therefore, although it is much more expensive to receive treatment in these institutes, many patients would rather go there because they are afraid of having a police record, and they are treated as clients who bring money to the business (interview note #18, 1999).

   The third characteristic is that the treatments in China include not only medical and psychological care and legal education (as given in some treatment programs in the United States), but also labor. It is believed that hard labor can wash out people's evil thoughts and change their habits. Therefore, though labor is not a required treatment for first-time drug users, it is mandatory for those who have failed to stay drug-free after the first treatment. The program of education through labor used in the drug treatment duplicates the program that has been implemented in the Chinese correctional system for decades.

   Treatment has been utilized as the main measure by the Chinese local governments to fight drug use. As a result, the number of people who receive treatment is growing rapidly everywhere in the country. For instance, the number of the patients in Guangdong Province in 1994 was eight times greater than that in 1991 (see table 3.2).

   The results of these programs are questionable. Besides problems like lack of enough beds for drug users and high costs of the treatment, ineffectiveness of the treatment caused by the poor quality of medical and psychiatric programs is the main concern. According to our interviews, 95 percent of the drug users treated in the forcible Centers used drugs again within six months after the treatment (interview note #21, 1999).

   Thus, our examination of the Chinese government's efforts against drug crime indicate that official control of the drug problem mainly relies on severe punishment and special strikes to crack down on illicit drug activities during a given period of time. These strategies are a reflection of the Chinese tradition in controlling unlawful behaviors rather than a special reaction to the current drug problems. Their implementation requires social environment (obedience and uniformity) and political conditions (centralization and the government's ability to mobilize its people on a large scale). Both social environment and political conditions are unique to China. Thus, even if the strategies of severe punishment and special strikes are effective and powerful in fighting drug crime in China, their applicability to other countries is very limited. In other words, it is very unlikely, if not im-

Table 3.2
Drug Users Receiving Treatment in Guangdong Province, 1991–1994

Year	Forcible Treatment	Voluntary Treatment	Treatment in Institutes of Education Through Labor
1991	over 5,000	over 1,000	1,202
1992	over 8,000	over 3,000	1,951
1993	over 16,000	over 6,000	2,609
1994	over 30,000	over 15,000	3,107

Source: Anti-Narcotics Commission of Guangdong Province.

possible, for a democratic country like the United States to carry out the same policies in its war on drugs.

DISCUSSION AND CONCLUSION

China, once a drug-free nation, has witnessed a serious growth in drug problems since the 1980s. In order to fight back, the Chinese government has made great efforts to cut off drug supplies, punish drug law violators, give treatments to addicts, and educate/threaten the general public. However, these are only the beginning of the battle. By the time of our second trip to China, the approach of a people's war on drugs has been developed systematically. Under this proposal, the leadership in antinarcotics activity at all government levels must be improved; the drug law enforcement must be strengthened; new institutions of drug education and prevention must be created; and the responsibility for a drug-free environment must be assigned to neighborhoods, schools, workplaces, villages, and other small social units. The Chinese government believes that only when the entire society is mobilized in this "people's war" against narcotics, can the disaster be controlled to the minimum level (interview note #18, 1999).

Ironically, while a people's war on drugs is being zealously launched in China, the war on drugs in the United States has been declared a failure. The measurement of such failure can be found in two aspects. One is the incidence of drug crime: a significant increase in drug use among Americans, more availability of drugs in the streets, and lower drug prices. The other aspect is related to law enforcement: more corruption among police officers, more violation of individuals' rights, more racial conflicts among Americans, and greater social costs paid to detect, sentence, and incarcerate drug offenders. Therefore, instead of continuing the drug war, the legalization of drugs has been increasingly advocated by Americans including politicians, criminal justice practitioners, and researchers. The contradictory realities found in both China and the United States raise serious questions for those who are interested in comparing drug policies across nations: Can China be successful in its people's war on drugs, while the United States is losing its drug war?

To answer this question, we have to consider two other questions. First, are the antidrug policies similar in important respects in both countries? The answer is yes. Our examination of the Chinese drug approach shows no substantial difference between the Chinese policy and the American strategies. Both countries have implemented a national drug-control policy that seeks eradication of drug-producing crops at home and abroad, interdiction of drug smuggling, prosecution of drug traffickers, and penalization of drug users. If these policies have caused America's war on drugs to come "crashing down in the cold light of reality" (Miranda, 1998), it is very likely that the same policies would lead the Chinese war on drugs to a dead end.

Second, is there any difference between the two countries' wars on drugs? Our response is yes. Four differences can be addressed here. The primary difference is found in the political systems. China is a nation with an extremely centralized government under the leadership of the Communist Party. This gives the central government the ability to undertake a people's war on drugs by mobilizing every social force, concentrating its economic and political resources, and engaging its military power. This cannot happen in the United States, a country with a very decentralized federal system and two-party politics.

The next difference exists in the severity of punishment. Although under America's mandatory drug sentencing laws, millions of drug dealers and abusers have been apprehended, processed, convicted, and incarcerated by the nation's criminal justice system, the sentences given to American drug offenders are much less severe than those given by Chinese judges. In particular, the death penalty has been extensively imposed on drug criminals in China. Apparently, such extremely severe sentences, accompanied by swift execution, can produce strong deterrence of drug violations.

The third difference is the scope and time frame of drug problems. On the one hand, drug abuse is much more prevalent among Americans than among the Chinese people. On the other hand, America's war on drugs has been undertaken for more than two decades, whereas the Chinese war on drugs is just beginning. Thus, if the American government is losing its war on drugs partially because the drug problems have become too serious to be dealt with, it may be possible for the Chinese government, with its unique power, to control drug problems and keep them at a minimum level.

The last difference concerns the popularity of the war on drugs. In the United States, the call for legalization of drugs has tended to be more popular recently. If gaining the support of the people is the first prerequisite for victory in modern warfare, as claimed by the American opponents (Miranda, 1998), then the Chinese government has such support from the masses. The Chinese can never forget their history as the "sick men of Eastern Asia," which was caused by drug abuse. "Zero tolerance for drugs" is socially accepted, and decriminalization of drugs has no voice in China. The popularity of the war on drugs provides the Chinese government with a basic condition to win.

It is a difficult task to predict the final result of China's war on drugs. But it is certain that the Chinese government will continue the war regardless of its costs and consequences. Drug legalization is not an alternative for the Chinese, so fighting drugs is their only choice.

REFERENCES

Akers, Ronald L. 1994. *Criminological Theories: Introduction and Evaluation*. Los Angeles: Roxbury.
Beijing Review. 1998. "China Strengthens Drug Control." 41, no. 28 (July 13): 6.

Deng Youtian and Deng Gang. 1993. *Lun dupin fanzui* (On Drug Crimes). In *Chengzhi dupin fanzui lilun yu shijian* (Theories and Practices in Punishing Drug Crimes). Edited by High Court of Yunnan Province. Beijing: Press of the Chinese Political and Legal University.

Frank, N., and M. Lynch. 1992. *Corporate Crime, Corporate Violence: A Primer.* Albany, NY: Harrow & Heston.

Gelbard, Robert. 1995. "Assessment of U.S. Counter Narcotics Efforts in Asia." Statement Before the Subcommittee on Foreign Operations of the Senate Appropriations Committee. Washington, DC, July 24.

Guangdong Government. 1995. *Guangdongsheng zhengfu guanyu jindu de tongzhi* (Announcement of Guangdong Provincial Government on Anti-illegal Drugs). Document no. 25.

Guangzhou Legal System Daily. 1994. "Guangxi panchu yipi zhongda dupin anfan" (A Batch of Drug Dealers Executed in Guangxi). June 25.

———. 1995b. "Guojia jindu weiyuanhui quanti huiyi tichu yao zhonghe zhili dupin wenti" (The Plenary Session of the National Antinarcotics Commission Proposes Comprehensive Treatment for Drug Problems). June 23.

———. 1999a. "Dupin manyan zhongguo qicheng xianshi" (Narcotics Extended to 70 Percent of China's Counties and Cities). June 11.

———. 1999b. "Jindu douzheng renzhong daoyuan" (Antinarcotics Battles Will be Difficult and Long). June 26.

Huang Hongwu. 1995. *Duhuo taotian* (Monstrous Drug Disaster). In *Duhuo* (Drug Disaster). Edited by Antinarcotics Commission of Guangdong Province. Guangzhou: Guangdong People's Press.

Lei Ming and He Jongzhao. 1995. "Shale fandu de, bile dajie de" (Drug Dealers Executed, Robbers Shot). *Yangcheng Evening News,* July 8.

Li Anding and Zhang Jinsheng. 1995. "Gaige kaifang gei zhongguoren dailai shihui" (Reform and Opening to the Outside World Bring Benefits to the Chinese). *People's Daily,* overseas ed., October 2.

Liu Jiachen. 1995. "Shiyi zhongdian, yancheng budai" (Imposing Heavy Sentences to Severely Punish Drug Offenders). *Guangzhou Legal System Daily,* June 26.

Luo Bingyi. 1995. "Fengleidong—Guangzhou sao huang du du xingdong jishi" (Fast Moves—Sweeping Out Porno, Gambling, and Drugs in Guangzhou). *Guangzhou Legal System Daily,* January 30.

Luo Yuqiu. 1995. "Yinjunzi lunwei xingshifan, congsu jindu yicheng ranmei zhiji" (Drug Addicts Becoming Criminals, Prohibition of Drugs Being Emergent). *Guangdong Legal System Daily,* April 1.

Lyman, Michael, and Gary Potter. 1991. *Drugs in Society: Causes, Concepts and Control.* Cincinnati, OH: Anderson.

Ma Jianwen. 1995. "Tantan feifa chiyou dupin zui" (Talking About the Crime of Illegal Possession of Drugs). *Guangdong Legal System Daily,* February 24.

Ma Kechang and Bao Suixian. 1993. "Zhongguo dupin fanzui de xianzhuang yuanyi yu duice" (Present Drug Crimes in China: Causes and Countermeasures). In *Chengzhi dupin fanzui lilun yu shijian* (Theories and Practices in Punishing Drug Crimes). Edited by High Court of Yunnan Province. Beijing: Press of the Chinese Political and Legal University.

Miranda, Joseph. 1998. "War or Pseudo-War?" *Social Justice* 25, no. 2 (Summer): 65.

Standing Committee of National People's Congress (*SCNPC*). 1990. "Guanyu jindu de jueding" (The Decisions on Anti-illegal Drugs). In *Daji dupin fanzui shiyong* (Practice in Striking Drug Crimes). Edited by Wang Yongcheng. Beijing: People's Court Press, 1992.

State Council of the People's Republic of China. 1995. "Qiangzhi jiedu banfa" (The Regulations on Forcible Treatment of Drug Users). In *Guangdong Legal System Daily*, January 19.

Tao Siju (Commissioner of the National Anti-Narcotics Commission). 1995. "Guojia Jindu Weiyuanhui Zhuren Tao Siju Tan Jindu Wenti" (On Issues of Antinarcotics). *Legal Daily*, June 23.

Troyer, Ronald, John Clark, and Dean Rojek, eds. 1989. *Social Control in the People's Republic of China*. New York: Praeger.

Xinhua News Agency. 1998a. "Fujian jindu douzheng zaizhou kaige" (Another Victory in Battling Narcotics in Fujian). February 25.

———. 1998b. "Zhongguo jiangwei quanqiuxing jindu zuo gongxian" (China Will Contribute to the Global Antinarcotics Effort). June 8.

———. 1998c. "Shenzhen jingfang pohuo teda fandu an" (Shenzhen Police Crack Big-Time Drug Sale). June 26.

———. 1998d. "Yunnan chengli jindu ju" (Antinarcotics Bureau Created in Yunnan). July 11.

———. 1998e. "166 wan renci canguan quanguo jindu zhanlan" (1.66 Million Persons Visit the National Antinarcotics Exhibition). July 30.

———. 1999. "Quanguo gongan bianfang budui quenian jiaohuo dupin 7000 duo gongjin" (Over 7,000 Kilos of Drugs Seized in 1998). January 17.

Zhao Binzhi and Yu Zhigang. 1998. *Dupin fanzui* (Narcotics Crimes). Beijing: Press of the People's Public Security University.

Zheng Yanxiong. 1995. "Mogui de cishang" (Rewards of Demons). In *Duhuo* (Drug Disaster). Edited by Antidrug Commission of Guangdong Province. Guangzhou: Guangdong People's Press.

Zhong Jianping and Huang Ying. 1995. "Qingshaonian xidu de jingshi" (The Warning of Juvenile Drug Use). *Guangdong Legal System Daily*. June 6.

PART II

Chinese Perspectives and the Social Sources of Crime

CHAPTER 4

Criminology in China: Perspectives and Development

Lu Zhou and Mei Cong

Criminology as an independent discipline has a history of more than 100 years in the West. However, criminological research in China has developed significantly only in the period following the initiation of the social and economic transition (1978–1998). This chapter describes the development of criminology in China by discussing its theories, methods, and research.

A BRIEF HISTORY OF CRIMINOLOGICAL RESEARCH IN CHINA

In China, criminology has gone through an uneven development since the 1920s. Before the founding of the People's Republic of China in 1949, Chinese scholars began criminological research in the late 1920s, when the Revolution of 1911 led by Dr. Sun Yat-sen had achieved success. During the late 1920s to 1930s, teaching and research on criminology were relatively active in China. Western and Japanese publications in criminology were translated and imported into the Chinese academic community. With this intellectual stimulation Chinese scholars began to conduct research on crime in China. A typical example of such research was Yan Jingyao's work. Yan received education in sociology at Yanjing University. Seeing the serious crime problems at that time, Yan decided to devote his academic efforts to criminological research. Primarily, he did field research. During the summer of 1927, he went to No. 1 Metropolitan Prison in Beijing as a voluntary "prisoner" to collect crime information. Through fieldwork, he learned the criminals' histories, family backgrounds, social statuses and how they became criminals. He also observed an abusive and dehumanizing aspect of the prison administration. According to the investigation on the prison and the prisoners, he wrote quite a few papers, such as "Social Analysis of Beijing's Crime" and "Problems of Chinese Prisons." In 1934, he gathered his observations and ideas into his doctoral dissertation, "*Social Change and Crime in China*" (in English), which was published by Columbia University Press. The book has become a significant work in the field of Chinese criminology. However, despite those efforts, criminology did not develop well at that time due to the civil war in China and the Japanese invasion.

Although criminological research continued after the Chinese Communist Party took power in 1949, it was greatly influenced by political struggle. At that time, the general task for the state was to establish its power and control, and to start economic construction. Systematic crime research was rare and could be found only in other fields, such as law enforcement and criminal rehabilitation. During 1958–1978, criminological research totally died due to the spread of political struggle in the Communist Party, as shown in the campaign against the "Right Wing" of Communist ideology and the "Cultural Revolution."

Since late 1979 criminological research has been revitalized in response to the surge in crime during the social and economic transition in China. In August 1979, the Communist Party central committee endorsed a report on the problem of juvenile delinquency. This endorsement stimulated and promoted nationwide research on crime, especially on juvenile delinquency. In March 1980, the Institute of Adolescent Study was founded in the Chinese Academy of Social Sciences. The institute includes a branch of crime research, the first academic body engaging specifically in the study of juvenile delinquency. The branch sponsored the first academic crime journal, *Studies of Juvenile Delinquency*.

Later, similar research bodies were established in universities and academies of social sciences. Courses in criminology began to be offered in universities and colleges. In June 1982, the Chinese Society of Juvenile Delinquency Study was founded by scholars and experts who were interested in research on juvenile delinquency. In 1992, the Chinese Society of Criminology was established as an academic community. Following these national establishments, similar local academic communities were founded in major cities. Although criminology is considered part of both law and sociology in China, most professionals in criminology formerly engaged in teaching and researching law. This academic phenomenon reflects the lack of professionals in sociology. Sociology as an independent discipline has experienced a development similar to that of criminology.

Professional criminology journals in China include *Studies of Juvenile Delinquency*, *Juvenile Delinquency*, *Studies of Public Security and Safety*, and *Crime and Rehabilitation*. By the early 1990s, over 200 books and more than 2,000 articles and reports were published in criminology. Professional conferences are held by the Chinese Society of Juvenile Delinquency Study and the Chinese Society of Criminology each year.

THEORIES OF CHINESE CRIMINOLOGY

Given the recent development of criminology in China, theories of crime and delinquency are relatively preliminary.

Perspectives on Criminology

Chinese scholars have two major views on criminology. The first one focuses on the causes and prevention of crime. The scholars holding this view advocate classifying criminology into two categories—research on the causes of crime and research on the prevention of crime. They argue that the causes of crime are the central content of criminological research (Zhou, 1991). The second view emphasizes the study of criminal cases through classification and characterization. It is a first step to study rates, classes, times, regions, and composition of crime. It is argued that the empirical facts of crime are the starting point to explore the causes of crime. Without the study of empirical facts of crime, criminology is only a form of social philosophy (Kang, 1998; Zhou, 1995).

Typology of Crime

Chinese criminologists usually classify criminal acts according to different standards. First, the criminals can be classified into three age categories—juvenile delinquent, adult offenders in middle age, and offenders of the aged. The category of juvenile delinquent includes juvenile offenders (ages fourteen–eighteen) and youthful offenders (ages eighteen–twenty-five). For the adult offenders in middle age, the age range is generally from twenty-five to fifty. Offenders aged above fifty are usually called offenders of the aged.

Second, according to occupations, crime can be classified into worker's crime, peasant's crime, and white-collar crime. White-collar crime includes "corporate crime" and "occupational crime." "Corporate crime" refers to organizational acts that violate laws, such as institutional smuggling and institutionally producing or selling fake or inferior products. "Occupational crime" refers to an act whereby the individual illegally uses his or her position for personal benefit.

Third, according to the nature of the crime organization, crime can be classified into gang crime and Mafia-style crime. Gang crime is committed by more than three criminals who join together and have a certain organizational form. A crime gang is loosely organized, with no clearly defined structure. Over the past decade, gang crime has become more professional and organized, and is likely to be Mafia-style crime.

Causes of Crime

Studies generally focus on three analytical levels to explore the causes of crime in China: the structural level, such as change of social structure and economic development (see chapter 1 in this volume); the cultural level, such as deviant subculture; and the psychological/biological level, such as motivation and the interaction between internal and external factors. These levels are applied to the analysis of the rising crime rate in China since the economic reform (Xiao and Pi, 1992).

Strategies of Crime Prevention and Correction

China has proposed the comprehensive management of public order, a national strategy that fights the rising crime rate. In February 1991, the Communist Party central committee and the State Council jointly issued the Decision on Strengthening Comprehensive Management of Public Order. In March of the same year, the Standing Committee of the Seventh National People's Congress passed the Decision on Strengthening Comprehensive Management of Public Order (Yang and Zhou, 1994; also see chapter 9 in this volume).

The major content of China's comprehensive management of public order includes the following: under the united leadership of the Communist Party and government at various levels, relying totally on the public and using multiple means, such as political, economic, administrative, legal, cultural, and educational means, all social units and organizations should make coordinated efforts to control the public order, by cracking down on and preventing crime, to ensure the stability of society and create a social environment for socialist modernization.

The requirements of comprehensive management of public order include (1) branches of the Communist Party and government at various levels place the comprehensive management as an important agenda item; (2) all departments and units work together to implement the policy of management responsibility; (3) branches of the Communist Party and government at various levels implement measures at the grassroots level of urban and rural areas, conduct mass prevention, and improve the awareness of the masses about laws and regulations, in order to mobilize the public to be involved in crime prevention.

The tasks of comprehensive management of public order include cracking down on crime, prevention, education, administration, construction, and correction. "Cracking down" refers to penalizing criminal activities that harm the society. "Prevention" is to prevent crime before it occurs. "Education" refers to strengthening the ideological, political and legal education for citizens, especially for adolescents. "Administration" refers to strengthening administrative work in every social aspect to reduce crime opportunities. "Construction" refers to establishing and developing organizations and systems at grassroots levels. "Correction" is reforming and rehabilitating criminals in order to prevent them from committing crimes again. The key to comprehensive management of public order is that all party, government, and military departments, mass organizations, enterprises, and institutions clearly define their responsibility in preventing crime and maintaining the public order.

RESEARCH METHODS OF CHINESE CRIMINOLOGY

Generally, Chinese scholars advocate the integration of theory and empirical research. Because criminological research in China is in a preliminary stage, it lacks standardized research methods. Philosophical thinking and speculation on crime are fairly common. However, Chinese scholars commonly view research methods as having two parts—methodology and applied methods/techniques. Methodology is concerned with philosophical and logical issues, such as how to study crime and delinquency, and what type of analytical logic (induction or deduction) to be used. The applied methods/techniques include crime surveys, crime statistics, and content analysis. Basically, these methods and techniques are imported and learned from crime research in Western countries. Traditionally, the Chinese are likely to do philosophical thinking and speculation about social phenomena. The application of research methods and techniques imported from the West is fairly limited. The importation is also limited and incomplete (Kang, 1996).

CRIME RESEARCH IN CHINA

Crime research has diverse and multiple areas in China. The present study will briefly discuss several areas, including studies of juvenile delinquency, drug-related crime, and violent crime, as examples. Studies have characterized juvenile delinquency as (1) gang crime; (2) violent and brutal offending; (3) offending as well as being victimized; and (4) high recidivism (Wu and Wang, 2000).

The causes of juvenile delinquency are first attributed to external factors such as the impact of the Cultural Revolution, the change of the social structure, and social conflict in ideology, morality, and norms. The causes are also attributed to psychological factors, such as personal values, morals, and cognition; and biological factors, such as congenital defects, hereditary diseases, anomalies of the endocrine and/or nervous system. Finally, the causes of juvenile delinquency are examined with reference to the interaction between external and internal factors. The external factors are conditions, and the internal factors are the direct causes. The external factors play a role through internal factors (Cao, 1993; Yin, 1997).

Drug crime is another research focus of criminology in China. Historically, China suffered great harm from opium. Before the founding of the People's Republic in 1949, about 1 million hectares were devoted to growing opium poppies. Among the population of more than 400 million, over 300,000 engaged in manufacturing and trafficking in drugs, and 20 million people were drug addicts. After the founding of the People's Republic, the government developed a nationwide drug-suppression movement. In February 1950, the State Council issued the General Order on Prohibiting Drugs. As a result of the severe control, 20 million drug addicts gave up opium smoking successfully, and more than 800 drug recidivists were sentenced to death. China was well known as a country without narcotics. However, since China has implemented economic reform and the open door policy, drugs and drug-related crime have spread increasingly in China and have become a social problem. Studies show that drug-related crimes include smuggling and trafficking in drugs, growing and producing illicit drugs, possessing illicit drugs, distributing illicit drugs and inducing drug use, and concealing illicit drugs (Guo and Che, 1995; Ling, 1999; also see chapter 3 in this volume).

Violent crime is also a major research target. Some studies classify violent crime into several types: violence against state governments; violence against citizens' legal rights; violence against public security and safety; violence against collective or personal property; violence in marriage and family; violence against social administration and management.

The cause of violent crime is analyzed in terms of biological instinct, the relationship between the rate of total crimes and the rate of violent crime, inequality, personal disputes and conflicts, and antisocial tendencies.

DISCUSSION AND CONCLUSION

This study has briefly discussed the development of criminology, theories of crime, research methods, and crime research in China. As noted, although Chinese criminology has developed significantly since the late 1970s, it is still in a preliminary stage due to China's unique historical, political, and academic background. Its theories, methods, and research are fairly underdeveloped in comparison with their counterparts in the West, and in the United States in particular. However, the revitalization of criminology is mainly a reaction to the rising crime rates during the social and economic transition. Although the rising crime rates and related problems are unexpected, they provide rich opportunities for the Chinese to develop the criminological enterprise. As Chinese scholars are becoming aware of the relationship between crime research and policy-making for controlling crime, the social need will greatly promote crime research in China.

The globalization of criminology, as recognized by many scholars, may also be a force to promote the development of crime research in China. Chinese scholars participating in the process of the globalization would learn from other countries and would also offer lessons to other countries. We believe that Chinese criminology will fully develop in these domestic and international climates in the years ahead.

REFERENCES

Cao Zidan. 1993. *Survey of Research on the Causes of China's Crime*. Beijing: Press of the Chinese People's Public Security University.

Guo Xiang and Che Weijian. 1995. *Cross-Border Crime and the Countermeasures*. Beijing: Chinese Social Sciences Press.

Kang Shuhua 1996. *General Criminology*. 2nd ed. Beijing: Beijing University Press.

———. 1998. *Criminology*. Beijing: Press of the Masses.

Ling Qing. 1999. "Enhance the Education of Drug-Expression to Adolescents." *Studies of Juvenile Delinquency* 5–6: 4.

Wu Qiangjun and Wang Minyuan. 2000. "Review of Research on Criminology in 1999." *Juristic Research* 1: 112.

Xiao Jianming and Pi Yijun. 1992. *Introduction to Criminology*. Beijing, China: Police Officers Education Press.

Yang Ruohe and Zhou Lu. 1994. *A New Theory of Comprehensive Management of Public Order*. Chong Qing, China: Chong Qing Press.

Yin Jiabao. 1997. *Survey of Criminological Research in New China (1949–1995)*. Beijing: China Democracy and Legal System Press.

Zhou Lu. 1995. *Empirical Criminology*. Tianjin: Press of Tianjin Academy of Social Sciences.

Zhou Mi. 1991. *Theoretical Criminology*. Beijing: Press of the Masses.

CHAPTER 5

Population Migration and Crime in Beijing, China

Guoan Ma

Since the early 1980s, reduced migration control by the state and increasing economic liberalization have led to the movement of millions of peasants to the cities in China, creating various types of new "urban areas" and "underground areas" (Davis et al., 1995). The "floating population" accounted for 11.1–27.5 percent of the total urban population in eight of China's largest cities in 1990 (Wang and Hu, 1996, p. 42).[1] The movement has fundamentally changed the social, spatial, and economic landscapes of Chinese cities and has made the urban scene much more diverse, lively, and dynamic—but less safe and orderly—than in the Maoist era. Official data show that migrants are responsible for a large proportion of offenses. According to the statistics of some cities, more than half of the criminal cases are committed by the migrants from the countryside, and the migrants account for 70 to 80 percent of theft cases (Yu, 1993, p. 79). The population migration has had a great impact on the rising crime rates during the course of social and economic transition in China. This study explores the relationship between population migration and crime by focusing on a large city, Beijing.

RURAL-URBAN MIGRATION IN BEIJING

"Migration" in this context refers to internal "migration" in China, and migrants or "transient people" refers to unregistered residents in the cities.[2] It is estimated that the migration involves 80 million people annually. Many of the migrants face transitional problems and are confronted with a different value system and lifestyle when they reach the cities. One of the problems is crime.

The formation and growth of migrant enclaves in post-Mao urban China have been affected by two factors. The first is institutional reforms and economic restructuring at the national level since 1978 that have made rural-urban migration possible. The second factor is related to the policies and attitudes of the Chinese government toward migration.

Rural reform since the late 1970s greatly improved farm efficiency, which quickly rendered a large number of farm laborers redundant and gave rise to millions of surplus agricultural workers (*nongye shengyu laodongli*). A survey of China's surplus farm labor conducted by scholars at the Chinese Academy of Sciences reveals that as early as 1984, 95 million peasants were in the category of surplus labor (Li, 1996, p. 12). In 1986, there were between 114 and 152 million surplus farmworkers, and by 1990 the number had swelled to 170 million (see Taylor, 1988, p. 737; Cai, 1995, p. 181). In 1994, the number exceeded 200 million, and by 2000 it was expected to reach 300 million (Li, 1996, p. 12). Though millions of surplus farm laborers have been absorbed by the rural industries that have blossomed since the abandonment of the commune system in the early 1980s, millions more have sought their fortunes in cities and towns.

In 1984, the State Council issued a directive that permitted peasants to move to and settle in towns (Chen and Yu, 1993). This new policy officially loosened the rigorous restriction of population mobility to urban areas which had been in place since the Chinese household registration system (*hukou*) was implemented in 1958 (Guowuyuan, 1984).[3] With the tacit consent of the state, millions of peasants have moved not only to towns but also to cities. An unprecedented era of massive migration (*da qianyi*) thus began, and since then the migrating waves of peasant workers (*mingongchao*) have been increasing rapidly.

The size of China's floating population has been estimated by various sources to be 70 to 100 million. The national census reported some 20 million floaters in 1982, about 64 million in 1990, and approximately 80 million in 1995. Most of these floaters came from rural areas.[4]

In Beijing as well as other cities, the only data available for the floating population were official residential registrations at the local public security offices before 1984. The number of migrants who did not register was likely to be relatively small, because urban communities during the prereform period were much more tightly controlled than they are today (Wang and Hu, 1996, p. 41). Few outsiders could stay in the city without legitimate reasons, and few strangers could wander around in an urban neighborhood without being questioned by neighborhood watchers (typically old women, wearing a red armband, stationed at strategic points on the street) or by public security officers. Since 1984, however, the term "floating population" has been widely used to include both the registered "temporary migrants" and the unregistered.

As the nation's capital, Beijing has attracted large numbers of floating and temporary populations. Before the late 1970s and early 1980s, the size of the floating population was relatively small in Beijing. For example, during the decade

1960–1970, Beijing's temporary population never exceeded 130,000. Most of them were visitors or persons seeking medical care. Some of them were hired by urban enterprises on contract. Little is known about the number of migrants during the latter part of the Cultural Revolution (1970–1976) due to the turmoil at the time. By 1978, Beijing's temporary population had reached nearly 220,000. During the 1980s, the floating and temporary populations increased rapidly. From 1988 to 1994, Beijing's floating population more than doubled. The proportion of floating population that has not registered as temporary residents has been growing, and in 1994 it exceeded 50 percent.[5]

The reasons for the great increase of peasant mobility to Beijing changed drastically over the years. During the 1950s and the 1960s, visiting relatives and friends was a major reason for going to Beijing, followed by official business and medical care. But since the early 1980s, dynamic structural change in the economy has created numerous urban jobs for the peasants. Many of the jobs are low-paying, dirty, or tedious ones which are avoided by the local residents even when unemployed, but some are offered by state-owned work units with a short-term contract. Such work units are willing to hire peasants, because they do not have to provide regular staff housing or such benefits as retirement pension and health care for family dependents. At the same time, the state's decision to allow the nonstate sectors of the economy to grow has made numerous jobs in the tertiary sector available to rural peasants. It is under these changing economic conditions that a large number of peasants have moved to Beijing.

CRIME AMONG THE FLOATING POPULATION IN BEIJING

Among the criminal suspects captured by Beijing police stations, the percentage of floating people increased year by year. Official reports show that 18.5 percent of all the criminal suspects were floating people in 1986, 22.5 percent in 1990, 37.6 percent in 1992, 43 percent in 1993, and 50 percent in 1994 (Jiao, 1994). In some areas where floating people are quite concentrated, the percentage is up to 80 or even to 90 percent. In the "belt" areas of the city (*chengxiangjiehebu*), the percentage is as high as 70 percent. The Public Transportation Division of the Beijing Public Security Bureau caught more than 10,000 pickpockets on city buses, 3,400 per year between 1995 and 1997 (Du, 1998). Most of them were floating people from rural areas. Furthermore, serious and violent offenses which are significantly related to gambling, prostitution, and illicit drugs are increasing quickly in the enclaves of the floating people.

The official reports of offenses committed by the floating people in 1990 to 1995 by the No. 1 Intermediate People's Court of Beijing show the following characteristics. First, offenses committed by the floating people were increasing. Of all criminal cases tried by the Court, 12.5 percent were committed by the floating people in 1990, 13.6 percent in 1991, 22.6 percent in 1992, 20.6 percent in 1993,

25.9 percent in 1994, and 34.1 percent in 1995. Second, the severity of official punishment was rising in response to the increase of seriousness of offenses committed by the floating people. The data show that 42.4 percent of all the criminals among the floating people were sentenced to life imprisonment in 1990, 41.4 percent in 1991, 44.6 percent in 1992, 50.3 percent in 1993, and 63.7 percent in 1994. Third, the types of crime committed by the floating people were concentrated on property offenses, especially robbery and theft. Property offenses accounted for about 40 percent of all crimes committed by the floating people during 1990–1995. In addition to property crime, other crime types included murder, homicide, and aggravated assault. Finally, joint crimes or gang crimes were common among the floating population. They accounted for 23 percent of the crimes committed by the floating people. These crimes usually had a family basis and local ties.

Serious offenses among Beijing's floating population are rising. According to a 1994 survey of floating people offenders by the Inquisition Division of the Beijing Public Security Bureau, there were ninety-eight serious criminal cases in 1993, which accounted for 28 percent of all criminal cases dealt by the Inquisition Division of the Beijing Public Security. In 1994, the number of cases increased to 128, accounting for 32 percent of all criminal cases. These serious offenses included larceny, murder, homicide, aggravated assault, robbery, fraud, and drug trafficking.

THEORETICAL PERSPECTIVES ON THE RELATIONSHIP BETWEEN POPULATION MIGRATION AND CRIME

The emergence of population migration in China is the consequence of a variety of factors. The immediate factor was the state's decision to relax migration control in the early 1980s. In addition, a large development gap between urban and rural areas may also be viewed as a major factor.

The theory that can explain the relationship between population migration and crime in China is relative deprivation theory (Ma, 1999; also see chapter 6 in this volume). A large income gap between urban and rural areas would lead to strong perceptions of relative deprivation among rural populations. These strong perceptions may become motives pushing rural people to use illegal means to get rich. This theory could explain why many migrants are involved in property crime.

In the West, most countries adopt the Gini coefficient to measure income inequality. The Gini coefficient ranges from 0, a condition of perfect equality of income, to 1, a condition of maximum inequality. Observed values of the Gini coefficient range between 0 and 1. The smaller the Gini coefficient, the more equal the income; the larger the Gini coefficient, the more unequal the income. According to international experience, if the Gini coefficient is less than 0.2, the society is quite equal in income distribution. If the Gini coefficient is between 0.2 and 0.3, the income distribution is relatively equal. If the Gini coefficient is between 0.3

and 0.4, the society is moderately unequal. But if the Gini coefficient is larger than 0.4, the society is quite unequal. Now, let's look at the Gini coefficient in China (see table 5.1).

The table shows that the distance between the rich and the poor has been enlarged in both cities and countryside. The Gini coefficient of city and countryside is up to 0.434 in 1994, which means that inequality between city and countryside is quite large in China. A large degree of inequality is likely to produce perceptions of relative deprivation for the rural population when they reach the cities. Crime may be an outlet for those rural migrants to relieve their relative deprivation.

Another explanation is that after the floating people migrate from the "poor" countryside to the "rich" city, they lose traditional support from their family and any home-province or home-county associations comparable to earlier *huiguan* (provincial or county guild hall) and *tongxianghui* (an association of fellow provincials or townsmen). This is especially true for migrants who are guided by nothing more than the expectation of finding urban employment and "flow blindly" into the cities. Normlessness and lack of social support in cities constitute additional causes of crime committed by migrants.

SUMMARY AND CONCLUSIONS

In this chapter, the author explains the relationship between population migration and crime by taking Beijing as an example. The reduction of migration control by the government and the economic reform that started in 1978 in the countryside made it possible for people living in the countryside to migrate into the cities. When they migrated to the cities, they faced a totally different value system and lifestyle. When they reached the cities, they found they were relatively deprived. The loss of traditional family support, combined with an inability to

Table 5.1
Gini Coefficients in China Urban and Rural Areas, 1978–1994

City Residents		Rural Residents		City and Rural Residents	
1978	0.16	1978	0.21	1979	0.31
1986	0.19	1982	0.22	1988	0.382
1987	0.20	1983	0.25	1994	0.434
1988	0.23	1984	0.27		
1990	0.23	1985	0.30		
1991	0.24	1986	0.31		
1992	0.25	1988	0.34		
1994	0.37	1994	0.41		

Source: Xinhua Digest 2 (1996), 16–19.

improve their poor status, increased the likelihood that the migrants would commit crimes. In a sense, the increasing crime of the migrants is a cost associated with the transformation from a planned economy to a free economy. Now, the Chinese government, especially in the large cities like Beijing, strictly controls the migrating population both in the floating-out places (the countryside) and the floating-in places (the cities).

As part of this control effort, local city governments have divided the types of jobs into Labor A, B, and C. The migrants can be employed only in Labor C, which is usually dirty, difficult, and dangerous (the so-called 3–D jobs). Companies and enterprises that illegally employ migrants are fined heavily. In the long run, rural migration to cities constitutes a real challenge to the Chinese government. Urbanization is a major dimension of China's modernization, but coping with the consequences of urbanization, such as crime, will be a difficult and important task for the Chinese in the years ahead.

NOTES

1. In this chapter, "urban population" refers to the registered local resident population (*huji renkou* or *changzhu renkou*) plus the floaters who have registered as "temporary population" (*zhanzhu renkou*)."

2. In this chapter "migration" and "migrants" are used as generic terms without implying that they are officially approved. The difference between "migration" and "population movement" will be clarified below.

3. *Hukou* regulations were passed in 1958, but their systematic enforcement actually began in 1960.

4. There was a slowdown between 1989 and 1991 that corresponded to the national belt-tightening, which curtailed urban construction.

5. On prereform urban society, see Whyte and Parish (1984), esp. chapters 8 and 9.

REFERENCES

Cai Fang. 1995. "Zhongguo liudong renkou: Xingcheng yuanyin yu yingdui zhi ce" (China's floating population: Factors of formation and coping strategies). In *Zhongguo Renkou Liudong Shitai Yu Guanli* (The Situation and Management of Chinese Population Movement). Edited by Dangsheng Ji and Qin Shao. Beijing: Zhongguo Renkou Chubanshe.

Chen Jiyuan and Yu Dechang, eds. 1993. *Zhongguo nongye laodongli zhuanyi* (The Transformation of China's Agricultural Labor). Beijing: Renmin Chubanshe.

Davis, Deborah S., Richard Kraus, Barry Naughton, and Elizabeth J. Perry, eds. 1995. *Urban Spaces in Contemporary China: The Potential for Autonomy and Community in Post-Mao China*. New York: Cambridge University Press.

Du Jun. 1998. "Dangqian paqie de franzui xindongxiang" (The New Trends of Pickpocket Crime at Present). *Beijing Youth Daily*, October 2, p. 7.

Guowuyuan. 1984. "Guowuyuan guanyu nongmin jinru jizhen luohu wenti de tongzhi" (Circular of the State Council Concerning the Question of Peasants Entering Market Towns for Settlement). *Guowuyuan gongbao* (Gazette of the State Council) 26: 919–920.

Jiao Qingle. 1994. "Yingjie tiaozhan—Wailai renkou zhi'an guanli wenti tantao" (Welcome the Challenge—Research on the Control of the Migration Population). *Legal Daily*, July 21, p. 1.

Li Qiang. 1996. "Woguo shehui ge jiecheng souru chajiu fengxi" (Analysis of the Income Distance of the Different Classes in Chinese Society). *Xinhua Digest* 2: 16–19.

Li Rongshi. 1996. "Dangqian woguo liudong renkou de renshi he sikao" (Some Considerations on the Floating Population in Contemporary China). *Renkou Yanjiu* (Population Research) 20, no. 1: 12–17.

Ma Guoan. 1999. "Relative Deprivation Theory—An Explanation for the Crimes Committed by the Migrants." *Faxue yanjiu* (Legal Research Journal) 6: 123–134.

Taylor, Jeffrey R. 1988. "Rural Employment Trends and the Legacy of Surplus Labor, 1978–86." *China Quarterly* 116: 737–739.

Wang Jianmin and Qu Hu. 1996. *Zhongguo liudong renkou* (China's Floating Population). Shanghai: Shanghai University of Finance and Economics Press.

Whyte, Martin King, and William L. Parish. 1984. *Urban Life in Contemporary China*. Chicago: University of Chicago Press.

Yu Lei. 1993. *Crime Research in Today's China*. Beijing: Chinese People's Public Security University Press.

Zuo Lanchun. 1996. *Beijing de liudong renkou* (Beijing's Floating Population). Beijing: Zhongguo Renkou Chubanshe.

CHAPTER 6

Inequality and Crime in China

Liqun Cao and Yisheng Dai

China has enjoyed a sustained and unbroken annual economic growth rate of nearly 10 percent since 1979. At the same time, the crime rate has increased at an unprecedented pace. The government has periodically attempted to reduce the crime rate through "crackdown drives" and "comprehensive management of public order" programs (Dutton and Lee, 1993; Jiang and Dai, 1990; Rojek, 1996; Situ and Liu, 1996). However, neither of these efforts seems to have achieved the expected results. For example, the government launched the first barrage of crime crackdowns in 1983, facing what it considered an unacceptable level of criminal activity: 74 cases per 100,000 residents in 1982. By 1994, the figure was 140 per 100,000 residents, almost double the previous "unacceptable" level. As for the newly implemented "comprehensive management of public order" program, it seems to target only certain populations, and the results would not permit a long-term solution (Curran, 1996; Dutton and Lee, 1993; Friday, 1998).

The present study attempts to analyze the causes of crime in China by focusing on the relationship between inequality and crime. It applies the structural explanation of Western criminological theories to the Chinese situation. It is argued that one of the important causes of the current crime upsurge in China is the widened income distribution in general and socioeconomic inequalities between urban and rural people in particular. Urban crimes are closely related to the large exodus of peasants to cities. Inaccessibility of urban-centered economic fruits causes many new migrants to turn to crime.

WESTERN THEORIES OF INEQUALITY AND CRIME

Many criminological theories are concerned with the relationship between inequality and crime. For example, Marx (1867) and Engels (1845) derived their thesis of "poverty causes crime" from their observations of the English working class in the nineteenth century. They argued that capitalist economic growth was built on the sacrifice and exploitation of proletarians. An ever-growing mass of dispossessed and exploited workers scrabbling for a living was forced into crime in order to survive. Mainly built on Durkheim's modernization perspective (1893), but also partially inspired by stratification analysis of Marx and Engels, the American sociologist Robert Merton proposed his anomie theory in 1938. He argues that when there is incongruity between the cultural goal and the structural means to reach that goal, anomie results. American society encourages people to be materially successful, but opportunities for achieving success are not available to all. Racial minorities and people in poverty-stricken neighborhoods do not have equal access to success. As a result, crime is produced by the values of the society itself—encouraging high material aspirations as a sign of individual success without adequately providing approved means for all to reach these goals.

The relationship between inequality and crime has been considered in many other theories, such as subcultural theories, opportunity theories, social disorganization theory (Braithwaite, 1979; Cao and Maume, 1993; Patterson, 1991). Blau and Blau (1982) go beyond the question of whether poverty or income inequality has an independent effect on crime rates and focus on contingencies in the relationship between inequality and crime in the United States. They argue that where ascribed inequality is present, the rate of violent behavior will be high. Specifically, they suggest that "ascriptive socioeconomic inequality undermines the social integration of a community by creating multiple parallel social differences which widen the separation between social classes, and it creates a situation characterized by much social disorganization and prevalent latent animosities" (p. 119). They pinpoint the ethnic inequality in resources in America and the widespread resentment, frustration, hopelessness, and alienation—a state of anomie—among these people. Relying on the data for statistical metropolitan areas in the United States, Blau and Blau empirically verify their thesis. They conclude that the cost of inequality is a high rate of theft and violence.

China offers an interesting setting to study the relationship between inequality and crime. China has gone through ambitious economic reform. It has brought about great economic progress, but also some unintended consequences, such as rising crime rates and increased inequality. Guided by the Western theories of inequality and crime, the present study addresses the relationship between inequality and crime in changing China.

CRIME TREND IN CHINA

Figure 6.1 shows the total crime rates in China from 1950 to 1993. In reading Chinese official data, several points need to be kept in mind. First, the numbers cannot be compared directly with official statistics of the United States, which include attempted crimes, such as robbery, rape, and burglary. In China, only the completed acts count. Second, many violations of the law are handled informally by neighborhood committees. Incidents such as domestic violence and neighbor conflicts are more likely to end up in mediation than in the police files or the courts. Third, Chinese are known for their avoidance of legal procedures and for their tendency to settle their disputes privately, even without the involvement of neighborhood committees (David and Brierley, 1978; Dutton, 1992; Fairbank, 1987).

Fourth, the police have more discretionary power to deal with many violations without putting the incidents on record. The Security Administration Punishment Act of 1986 enumerates offenses that are to be handled administratively (i.e., outside of the criminal courts) (Bracey, 1996). The act gives the police the power to impose warnings, fines of up to 200 yuan, or fifteen days of detention, and these offenses are not included in official crime statistics. Fifth, there have been two major changes in the definition of grave theft (Rojek, 1996; Dai 1997). The first occurred in 1984 and the second in 1991. Many cases have been dropped from official statistics for being minor offenses. Last but not least, fudging the data according to the leadership's will is more widespread in China than in the United States (Dutton and Lee, 1993; Yu and Zhang, 1999). The official data suffer from underrecording by authorities rather than underreporting by victims (Yu and Zhang, 1999). However, these official figures are the only sources of crime data in China, and they provide a reasonable overview of the crime trend.

Figure 6.1 indicates that crime rates were two-digit figures per 100,000 in 1988. They reached three digits in 1989, and they have never come down. There is little sign of the effects of severe crackdowns on crime between 1983 and 1994. The crime rates from 1984 to 1988 appear to be lower, but this should not be attributed solely to the highly publicized 1983 crackdown on crime (He, 1992). It should be attributed, at least partially, to a change in the definition of larceny in 1984, when the value for recorded larceny rose from 40 yuan or more in cities and 20 yuan or more in rural areas to 80 yuan or more in cities and 40 yuan or more in rural areas (Rojek, 1996). Another change in the definition of larceny in 1991 (Dai, 1997) resulted in another sharp crime drop from 1992 to 1994.

Many scholars are puzzled by the claim that a crime crackdown would instantly result in a lower official rate of crime when more people turn themselves in for their previously unclaimed crimes, when the clearance rate is high, and when the police assign more manpower to dealing with crimes. In the United States, President George Bush announced the war on drugs in 1989, and crime rates increased in the following years.

Figure 6.1
Crime per 100,000 Residents in China

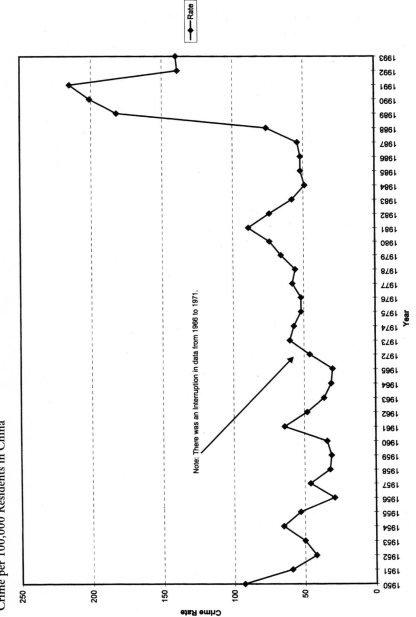

Source: Deng Xiaogang and Ann Cordilia, "To Get Rich Is Glorious: Rising Expectations, Declining Control, and Escalating Crime in Contemporary China," *International Journal of Offender Therapy and Comparative Criminology* 43, 2 (1999): 211–229.

There is yet another worrisome trend that is not visible in figure 6.1: the rapid rise in the proportion of crime committed by young offenders (Curran and Cook, 1993; Dai, 1997; Friday, 1998; He, 1992). Young offenders' proportion to the total crime rate increased from 18.7 percent in 1988 to 33 percent in 1994 (Dai, 1997).

With crime surging upward in the 1980s and 1990s, the image of cities and coastal regions has changed dramatically. To prevent burglary, residents install iron bars over their windows and balconies, and replace their wooden doors with steel doors. Such jail-like apartments constitute more than 90 percent of all residences in Guangzhou (Situ and Liu, 1996), which is quite typical.

INEQUALITY AS A CAUSE OF RISING CRIME IN CHINA

The social changes that have occurred during the fifty years of the People's Republic of China are perhaps more dramatic than in any other half-century in China's long history. Mao Zedong's triumph in 1949 united China, ending a long civil war and predatory treatment by foreign powers. Through periodic political movements and a frozen population movement, the first generation of leadership under Mao succeeded in creating a society free of crime (Fairbank, 1987) and without lawyers (Li, 1978). It also created a society in which everyone was equally poor despite the noticeable progress in heavy industry. To revitalize the stagnant planned economy, the second generation of leadership under Deng Xiaoping launched market-oriented economic reform in 1979 with a single overriding concern: the four modernizations drive. Without being fully prepared for its consequences or knowing exactly where this drive would lead China, the government simply adopted the approach of "crossing the river by feeling for the stone." The progress of China's modernization is undeniable, and so are its consequences: greater income inequality and rising crime, including corruption, drug abuse, prostitution, underground societies, superstitions and cults—the troubles of the pre-1949 society that Mao ended through ruthless suppression are flourishing anew.

Official propaganda organs still blame the residual aftermath of the Great Proletarian Cultural Revolution as a primary source of crime, and the "spiritual pollution" caused by the "open-door" policy to the West as the secondary source of crime (Dutton, 1992; He, 1992; Troyer, 1989). However, Jieli Li (1996) argues that the Cultural Revolution reinforced rather than weakened social control in China. By all accounts, crime rates were not particularly high (see figure 6.1) during the Cultural Revolution (1966–1976). The crime rates during this period did not exceed 60 per 100,000. In 1954 and 1961, the rates had peaked at 65 and 64 per 100,000 respectively. Both of these figures are higher than the average crime rate during the Cultural Revolution. Comparative research indicates that Western ideology or capitalist economies do not inevitably lead to high crime rates. Developed industrialized societies, such as Japan and Germany, are considered to be nations not obsessed with crime (Adler, 1983).

We argue that it is the rapidly widened income inequality that may be the real culprit. The linkage between economic growth and rising crime is complex. Economic growth per se is not a direct cause of crime. To break up economic stagnation, the second generation of leadership under Deng Xiaoping started their reform with two slogans: "Regardless of its color as black or white, a good cat is the one that can catch the mouse" and "To get rich is glorious." Over the following years, China's revitalized economy widened its stratification, first rapidly in the rural areas and then in the urban regions. Thus, economic development caused widened stratification, and in turn, the widened stratification caused crime to increase.

Table 6.1 shows the income distribution of different population groups in China and in the United States in 1994. The top 20 percent of Chinese households received more than 50 percent of the total national income of that year. In comparison, the top 20 percent of U.S. households had about 44 percent of the total national income. There is almost a 6 percent difference between the two figures. Using another measure of inequality, China does not fare well either. A common measure of income inequality is the Gini coefficient, which is frequently used by economists to summarize the degree of inequality in income distribution. It varies from a minimum of 0 to a maximum of 1. The greater the Gini coefficient, the greater the inequality of income distribution. Typically, this coefficient for the industrialized societies varies from a low of .25 to a high of .40 (Nagle, 1998). In 1994, a national study conducted by the People's University showed that China's Gini ratio was 0.45; another researcher's calculation pushed this figure to 0.59, higher than that of the United States (Dai, 1997).

Table 6.2 presents Gini coefficients from the *World Bank Report* (1994). The urban data and rural data are calculated separately. As late as 1986, the Gini coefficients in Chinese cities and rural areas were as low as .19 and .30, respectively. However, in 1994, both figures reached .37 and .41, respectively. In addition, table 6.2 shows that, paralleling this widened inequality, crime rates rose in both cities

Table 6.1
Income Distributions of Different Population Groups, China and United States, 1994

Groups	Percentage of Total National Income	
	China	U.S.A.
Top 20 percent households	50.2	44.3
Bottom 20 percent households	4.7	4.6

Source: Adapted from *DongFang* (Orient Journal) (May 1995).

Table 6.2
Gini Ratio in China and Crime Rate

Year	Gini Coefficient	Total Crime/100,000
	In Cities	
1986	0.19	11.2
1990	0.23	44.6
1994	0.37	34.0
	In Rural Areas	
1986	0.30	3.7
1990	0.34	5.4
1994	0.41	7.9

Source: Gini coefficients adapted from *World Bank Report*; crime rates, from Ministry of Public Security of China data.

and rural areas during the selected years. The Chinese economic reform started in the rural areas, abandoning all people's communes by 1986. That is why the inequality in rural areas was higher than in the urban areas in 1986. However, with the deepening measures of economic reform, urban residents also felt the pinch. In 1994, the inequality level in urban areas was close to that of the rural areas.

The data from the World Bank do not contradict the data from Dai's citation (1997) because in China, the sharpest contrast has been between the richest people living in the coastal areas and/or big cities and the poorest people living in the remote mountainous areas. In big cities and some areas of the coastal provinces, per capita annual income has approached 1000 dollars. In the remote areas, this figure remains a little more than 50 dollars. It is known that about 70 million people, accounting for 6 percent of China's population, are still living under the official poverty line (per capita annual income below 40 dollars). Most of them dwell in the mountainous areas or barren areas of southwest and northwest China.

Before the economic reform of 1979, some inequality existed. Generally speaking, the relatively rich people and the relatively poor people were not living in the same region, same city, or same neighborhood because migration into cities and between cities was controlled effectively through household registration (*hu-kou*) and labor-personnel dossiers (*dang-an*) (Li, 1996; Troyer, 1989). Since 1979, however, the breakup of the communes and the commercialization of agriculture have revealed an enormous reservoir of redundant labor. The rapid development in cities demands more cheap labor, and opportunities in the newly established special economic zones attract skilled workers and experienced management. As a result, two forces of migration have been formed: one from the inland cities to special economic zones in coastal areas, and the other from small towns or rural areas to big cities. These two forces joined to dismantle the system of control, but they did so differently: the first, through bribery and corruption; the second, through simply turning a deaf ear to policy makers. In short, the new market economy has created new opportunities and incentives, and it has eroded the system of control based on *hukou* and *dang-an*.

The economic reform brought booms to the Chinese society with familiar social consequences. While average living standards continued to rise, the fruits of economic progress were distributed in an increasingly inequitable fashion. In big cities and coastal areas, China's nouveaux riches—an assortment of engineers, managers of transnational corporations, private entrepreneurs, small industrialists, and profiteering bureaucrats—flaunt their wealth at expensive nightclubs and restaurants, drive imported automobiles, and often complain that there is not enough to do with their money. In contrast, migrants from the rural areas live in shantytowns or on the streets. The more fortunate among them work as low-paid contract laborers on around-the-clock construction sites or, in the case of young women, labor in sweatshops under oppressive conditions that harken back to the early decades of the century. Some are employed as servants, nannies, and house cleaners in the homes of urban professionals. But most are day laborers—"one-day mules," as they are called—who gather on street corners early in the morning to compete for jobs. The distance between the newly rich and the impoverished migrant laborers makes for as wide a social gap as is likely to be found in any society in the world, developed or developing.

It is estimated that since 1980, more than 100 million peasants have been allowed to leave their villages, and a "floating" or "transient" population has been roaming in the cities, looking for better opportunities (Curran, 1996; Situ and Liu, 1996). This means the haves and the have-nots are living side by side. Controlling the "floating" or "transient" population becomes a serious challenge in big cities. Currently, about 60 percent of criminals arrested in cities are from the floating population (Dai, 1997; see also chapter 5 in this volume).

The main cause of current massive migration is not "a blind influx" (*mang liu*). Instead, it is rooted in the disparities of income distribution caused by historical factors but widened by the current economic policy that favors coastal areas and big city development. Forests of glassy skyscrapers, modern expressways, elegant shopping malls, and upscale apartment buildings attest to the new wealth. Farmers in remote, barren regions are barely kept from starvation by government handouts. Schools lacking government support charge fees too steep for many villagers; girls often go unschooled. Even the most miserably paid of the new industrial workers earn more than they would have if they had remained on the land. Even the most miserably paid of workers in special economic zones earn more than they would have if they had remained in inland cities. People in China do not willingly leave their homes to work in strange places. They do so, for the most part, only out of necessity, a necessity now ensured by the market. The recent lackluster policies favorable for investment in poor areas, in order to reduce the gap between rich and poor regions are late and not yet enough to keep people from migrating to coastal areas and rich regions, or to keep people from migrating from rural areas or small towns to big cities.

The rural population in contemporary Chinese society qualifies as an ascriptive group (Blau, 1977). Peasants and farmers are born into their statuses. Their ascribed status denies them many political rights and economic opportunities that urban residents enjoy. According to Blau and Blau (1982), such inborn inequalities exist if membership in ascriptive groups is strongly related to socioeconomic position. Pronounced rural-urban inequality in resources implies that there are great riches within view but not within reach of many people destined to live in poverty. As a result, there is much resentment, frustration, hopelessness, and alienation—the state of anomie. Coser (1968) argues that interests that cannot find realistic expression to achieve desired goals frequently find expression as diffuse aggression: people being more driven by hostile impulses than governed by rational pursuit of their interests. It is such diffuse hostility that ascriptive inequalities engender and that criminal violence manifests.

It must be emphasized that the floating population provides cities with much-needed cheap labor to sustain their boom and to take jobs that city dwellers are unwilling to take. Their manpower has shouldered the construction boom since about 1980. It is only a small percentage among the floating population who are causing problems, but the majority of rural people seem to bear the brunt of the crime crackdowns. Furthermore, there is no implication in this analysis that there should be a return to the "good old days" when everyone was equally poor; nobody had much freedom in terms of job, migration, choice of lifestyle, and even the color of clothing. Moreover, everyone feared being singled out for prosecution in the political movement. Under Deng Xiaoping, Chinese were the freest they had ever been to choose their own lifestyles and line of work.

DISCUSSION AND CONCLUSION

The origins and the nature of China's economic system are unique, but its social consequences are surprisingly typical. If Deng Xiaoping did not foresee where modernization would lead China, the new leadership under Jiang Zeming should appreciate the consequences better. Deng's bold reform brought prosperity to the nation, but the mounting inequality caused an upsurge in crime. In the new millennium, the third generation of leadership under Jiang still has a choice on its road to modernization with Chinese characteristics (i.e., modernization with fewer crimes). As a late starter, China has the advantage: it can avoid the errors other nations had made before it.

Modernization is a complex and sometimes difficult process (Durkheim, 1893; Friday, 1998; Heiland and Shelley, 1991; also see chapter 1 in this volume). Economic development produces significant social changes, including migration for economic improvement, the spatial separation of extended family, increased urban density and cultural diversity, and a breakdown in the traditional means of social control. These social changes also come with changing values and the failure of some groups to attain the new educational and technical standards demanded by industrialization. The equilibrium of traditional society is disrupted. From this perspective, contemporary China is not an exception. In fact, some scholars argue that an increase in crime is inevitable during the process of change (He, 1992). However, there are also examples that suggest crime is not necessarily a consequence of economic change and development (Adler, 1983; Austin, 1987). Rather, crime is the result of the type of development; that is, when development leads eventually to a more inequitable distribution of benefits, crime will increase. In other words, crime is generated by the uneven expansion of economic change and the subsequent restructuring of social classes. Messner (1989), for example, concludes from his study of fifty-two nations that the structuring of economic inequality on the basis of ascribed characteristics is a particularly important source of lethal violence in contemporary societies.

In the United States, crime is considered a cost of inequality (Blau and Blau, 1982). The stratification system results in permanent and distinguishable neighborhoods in big cities, and this arrangement insulates most middle and upper classes from vicious street crime. The majority of street crimes occur in lower-income or poverty-stricken neighborhoods. These neighborhoods have become a fixture in U.S. cities. Japan and Singapore, both as Asian societies that share some of their values and culture with China and as late starters in modernization, offer an alternative road of economic growth without radically increasing their stratification (and, as a result, without much increase in crime). Other major industrial nations, such as the Scandinavian nations, also developed without widening their stratification systems and are able to maintain a low crime rate. There are lessons to be learned: economic growth and crime are not necessarily correlated when inequality is controlled for.

Thus, we call for continued economic reform, abandoning policies that favor coastal and big city development so that people in the vast inland and small towns can also benefit from the reform and do not have to dislocate themselves. Furthermore, China should not deprive the rich and divide their wealth for the sake of equality, as Mao did in the 1950s. The Chinese government should continue to rely on the real market mechanism, not the "man-made" market mechanism, to solve the problem of inequality by including more people, from both urban and rural areas, in the ranks of the wealthy (i.e., enlargement of the middle class and shrinkage of the lower class). It is particularly crucial to reform the current legal system, making it a rule of law, not a rule by law (Unger, 1976). Only in this way can China complete its transformation from a planned economy to a market economy, as well as its transformation from state ownership to multiple ownership, including the private sector and foreign capital.

China can also learn from Durkheim's view that crime is a barometer of broader social conditions. Though certainly disturbing in the individual case, as a phenomenon crime is like pain, an unpleasant experience but normal and necessary to indicate a condition needing attention. Crime and criminals are separable. Criminals, in particular those from rural areas, cannot be simply regarded as "social dregs" (*shehui zazi*); they are victims of rapid social change and of existing inequality who are worthy of help. Accepting the philosophy of "to get rich is glorious," rural people find themselves without access to legal opportunities to achieve economic success, compared with urban residents and people with political connections. Their ascriptive status, characterized by rural origins, determines their position in the Chinese social structure. Witnessing the affluent urban life and faced with blocked opportunity, migrants are more likely to seek innovative means to achieve economic success, as structural theories predict. From this perspective, draconian measures will not be able to curb their criminal activities. Only through increased job opportunities and other measures that will enable them to enjoy economic prosperity will their criminal activities be effectively reduced. In other words, the government has to address the root cause of crime—inequality—by spreading the fruits of economic progress to more people, not by regurgitating the old practices of the past.

Crime is not simply an issue of quality of life, but an indicator of deeper tension within a society. If China continues the current development process without paying enough attention to the widened inequality, it is possible that some areas of big cities will form slumlike neighborhoods and the crime rate will surely increase. This paper discusses only the causes of more obvious crimes, such as property crimes and violent crimes. Another type of crime, corruption, is more latent, but potentially more threatening to the Chinese government. A detailed discussion of its causes is beyond the scope of this paper. (See Chapter 2 in this volume.) However, we believe that addressing corruption also calls for the continued reform of the current system. Whereas street crime forces people to live in a jail-like environment, corruption weakens the legitimacy of the state, limits the capacity of those in power to govern, and restricts attempts to create a more extensive rule of law in China. Both types of crimes threaten not only the social order but also the reform itself. If they are not addressed properly, the consequences are highly unpredictable. This is particularly true for China, which used to be a crime-free society (Fairbank, 1987) where the ruling party claimed its legitimacy to rule on the basis of rectitude.

Apparently China, emerging from the vestiges of the Maoist era and burying the instruments of the Orwellian state and command economy during the Deng era, remains in the throes of unfinished and incomplete reform. More than fifty years after Mao Zedong stood atop the crimson Gate of Heavenly Peace and proclaimed the People's Republic, China remains a nation caught between extremes: poverty and wealth, change and continuity, order and chaos. On the cusp of a new millennium, China needs to resolve one important issue: whether to operate under the rule of law or the rule by law.

NOTE

We want to thank Professor Melissa Motschall for her helpful comments on this chapter.

REFERENCES

Adler, Freda. 1983. *Nations Not Obsessed with Crime*. Littleton, CO: Fred B. Rothman.

Austin, W. Timothy. 1987. "Crime and Custom in an Orderly Society." *Criminology* 25: 279–294.

Blau, Peter M. 1977. *Inequality and Heterogeneity*. New York: Free Press.

Blau, Judith R., and Peter M. Blau. 1982. "The Cost of Inequality: Metropolitan Structure and Violent Crime." *American Sociological Review* 47: 114–129.

Bracey, Dorothy H. 1996. "Civil Liberties and the Mass Line: Police and Administrative Punishment in the People's Republic of China." In *Comparative Criminal Justice*, pp. 225–233. Edited by C. B. Fields and R. H. Moore, Jr. Prospect Heights, IL: Waveland Press.

Braithwaite, John. 1979. *Inequality, Crime, and Public Policy*. London: Routledge and Kegan Paul.

Cao Liqun and David J. Maume, Jr. 1993. "Urbanization, Inequality, Lifestyle, and Robbery: A Comprehensive Model." *Sociological Focus* 26, no. 1: 11–26.

Coser, Lewis A. 1968. "Conflict: Social Aspects." In *International Encyclopedia of the Social Sciences*. Edited by David L. Sills. Vol. 3, pp. 232–236. New York: Macmillan.

Curran, Daniel J. 1996. "The New People's Justice: Adjusting the Justice System to Complement Economic Change." In *Comparative Criminal Justice*, pp. 48–60. Edited by C. B. Fields and R. H. Moore, Jr. Prospect Heights, IL: Waveland Press.

Curran, Daniel J., and Sandra Cook. 1993. "Growing Fears, Rising Crime: Juveniles and China's Justice System." *Crime and Delinquency* 39: 296–315.

Dai Yisheng. 1997. "Crime Wave and Relative Deprivation in China: Are the 'Wolves' Really Coming?" Paper presented at the 1997 annual meeting of the American Society of Criminology.

David, Rene, and John E. C. Brierley. 1978. *Major Legal Systems in the World Today*. New York: Free Press.

Durkheim, Emile. 1947 (1893). *The Division of Labor in Society*. New York: Free Press.

Dutton, Michael R. 1992. *Policing and Punishment in China*. Cambridge: Cambridge University Press.

Dutton, Michael R., and Tianfu Lee. 1993. "Missing the Target? Police Strategies in the Period of Economic Reform." *Crime and Delinquency* 39, no. 3: 316–336.

Engels, Friedrich. 1968 (1845). *The Condition of the Working Class in England*. Stanford, CA: Stanford University Press.

Fairbank, John King. 1987. *The Great Chinese Revolution: 1800–1985*. New York: Harper & Row.

Friday, Paul. 1998. "Crime and Crime Prevention in China: A Challenge to the Development-Crime Nexus." *Contemporary Criminal Justice* 14: 296–314.

He Bingsong. 1991. "Crime and Control in China." In *Crime and Control in Comparative Perspectives*, pp. 241–257. Edited by H. Heiland, L. I. Shelley, and H. Katoh. New York: Walter de Gruyter.

Heiland, Hans-Gunther, and Louise Shelley. 1991. "Civilization, Modernization and the Development of Crime and Control." In *Crime and Control in Comparative Perspectives*, pp. 1–19. Edited by H. Heiland, L. I. Shelley, and H. Katoh. New York: Walter de Gruyter.

Jiang Bo and Yisheng Dai. 1990. "Mobilize All Possible Social Forces to Strengthen Public Security—A Must for Crime Prevention." *Police Studies* 13, no. 1: 1–9.

Li, Jieli. 1996. "The Structural Strains of China's Socio-legal System: A Transition to Formal Legalism?" *International Journal of the Sociology of Law* 24: 41–59.

Li, Victor H. 1978. *Law Without Lawyers: A Comparative View of Law in China and the United States.* Boulder, CO: Westview Press.

Marx, Karl. 1967 (1867). *Capital.* New York: International Publishers.

Merton, Robert K. 1938. "Social Structure and Anomie." *American Sociological Review* 3: 672–682.

Messner, Steven F. 1989. "Economic Discrimination and Societal Homicide Rates: Further Evidence on the Cost of Inequality." *American Sociological Review* 54: 597–611.

Nagle, John D. 1998. *Introduction to Comparative Politics.* Chicago: Nelson-Hall.

Patterson, E. Britt. 1991. "Poverty, Income Inequality, and Community Crime Rates." *Criminology* 29: 755–766.

Rojek, Dean G. 1996. "Changing Directions of Chinese Social Control." In *Comparative Criminal Justice*, pp. 234–249. Edited by C. B. Fields and R. H. Moore, Jr. Prospect Heights, IL: Waveland Press.

Situ, Yingyi and Liu Weizheng. 1996. "Transient Population, Crime, and Solution: The Chinese Experience." *International Journal of Offender Therapy and Comparative Criminology* 40: 293–299.

Troyer, Ronald J. 1989. "Chinese Thinking About Crime and Social Control." In *Social Control in the People's Republic of China*, pp. 45–56. Edited by R. J. Troyer, J.P. Clark, and D. G. Rojek. New York: Praeger.

Unger, Roberto Mangabeira. 1976. *Law in Modern Society: Toward a Criticism of Social Theory.* Glencoe, IL: Free Press.

World Bank Report. 1994. Washington, DC: World Bank.

Yu, Olivia, and Lening Zhang. 1999. "The Under-Recording of Crime by Police in China: A Case Study." *Policing: An International Journal of Police and Strategies Management* 22, no. 3: 252–263.

PART III

Social Control and Crime Prevention in a Changing Chinese Society

CHAPTER 7

Chinese Social Control: From Shaming and Reintegration to "Getting Rich Is Glorious"

Dean G. Rojek

China has existed as a stable and organized society for some 7,000 years. During this time it made notable advances in printing, science, literature, art, and architecture, but advances in formal law and formal social control were not prominent. China never had a need for formal law because of informal social control mechanisms that started from the ground up (Whyte and Parish, 1984). The bedrock of Chinese society is the family, which evolved into the clan system. With the advent of urbanization, the clan system facilitated the creation of strong neighborhood organizations that became something of an extended family. To complement the neighborhood organization with its street committees, neighborhood mediation teams and residency registration requirement, there emerged the *danwei* (production unit). The *danwei* became the economic leg of Chinese society that included employment issues, nurseries, health clinics, pensions, and letters of credit. Butterfield (1982) comments that many Chinese would identify themselves by naming their work unit. Thus, China became the paragon of a tight, cohesive, exceedingly well-organized society. The logical outcome of this organizational efficiency was a society that had little crime and no need for formal law, courts, or law enforcement machinery.

CONFUCIANISM AND TAOISM

To complement these grassroots organizational systems, China adopted two philosophical perspectives that added to its social control effectiveness. The sage and philosopher Confucius (551–479 B.C.) became the essence of Chinese thinking. Confucius was born at a time of civil discord and strife, during which he sought to restore order and harmony. The English philosopher Thomas Hobbes (1588–1679) also was born at a time of social chaos and disunity. But it is interesting to compare how Confucius and Hobbes responded to the need for social order and unity. Hobbes, in his treatise titled *Leviathan,* argued that the natural state of man was to be at war with one another, and the only way to bring about social harmony was by imposing it through a superior power, the absolute sovereign. Hobbes's famous dictum was that the life of man was "solitary, poor, nasty, brutish, and short" (*Leviathan*). Hobbes's influence in Western civilization is quite pervasive, and the need for the power of a sovereign to impose order is taken for granted.

Chinese society followed a different path. Rather than imposing order from without, Confucius sought to create a sense of order from within. For Confucius, man is inner-directed, searching for *jen* (humanity). Human nature is perfectible, and man can be led to virtue and righteousness. Chinese society has little need for formal, external law when the dictates of Confucianism are followed. Western civilization adopted something akin to "the fallen nature of man," the concept of original sin that sees man as weak and crime-prone. The Freudian notion of the id, with its emphasis on self-centeredness and selfishness pervades Western thought. Confucius, on the other hand, saw inherent goodness in mankind, and filial piety and loyalty became the hallmark of Confucian ideology. Though Confucian thought is more of what Bellah (1970) might consider a "civic religion," it does permeate all of Chinese society and emphasizes the goodness of mankind. In the *Analects*, Confucius says, "The superior man is concerned with virtue; the inferior man is concerned with law" (Brooks and Brooks, 1998, p. 15). Another Confucian saying in the *Analects* reads "The superior man understands what is right; the inferior man understands what is profitable" (Brooks and Brooks, 1998, p. 36). What emerges from Confucian thought is a substructure for Chinese society that stresses the cultivation of self, the striving for virtue and righteousness, and the suppression of natural desires for the betterment of Chinese society. With Confucian thought as the bedrock of Chinese social organization, it is no wonder that crime and deviance were virtually nonexistent.

A second philosophical tradition emerged in China about the fourth century B.C. that became known as Taoism. Whereas Confucianism urged individuals to conform to the standards of an ideal social system, Taoism (the way) maintained that the individual should ignore the dictates of society and seek only to conform to the underlying pattern of the universe. To be in accord with Tao, one should "do nothing" (*wuwei),* that is, nothing strained, artificial, or unnatural. In its broadest sense, Taoism is to be accepting and yielding, which complements and yet opposes the duty-conscious and purposeful nature of Confucianism. Orthodox Confucianism limited its field of interest to the creation of a moral and political system, whereas Taoism represented a more personal and metaphysical perspective. The "superior virtue" of Taoism is a latent power that never lays claim to its achievements. "The man of superior virtue never acts, and yet there is nothing he leaves undone." It is action in accordance with nature such that "perfect activity leaves no mark." The sage who practices *wuwei* lives out of his original nature before it was tampered with by knowledge and morality. "He returns to the state of the un-carved block, uncut, unpainted" (Lagerwey, 1987, p. 115). For the Taoist, society carves the wood into specific shapes and robs it of its original existence: "Once the uncarved block is carved, it forms utensils (instruments of society) but the great craftsman (ruler) does not carve (rule)" (Lagerwey, 1987, p. 260). Thus, Taoism teaches that wisdom is to conform to the rhythm of the universe. The alternation of *yin* and *yang* (complementary energies) becomes two sides of the same coin. Armed with Taoism, with its emphasis on harmony, nature, and sense of oneness, and Confucianism, with its concern with social obligations, self-perfection, and virtuous activity, Chinese society emerged as the paragon of order, harmony, and inner direction.

SHAMING AND REINTEGRATION

China and several other Oriental societies have long been the epitomes of soci-eties that were tightly interconnected, having low crime rates and an ability to rein-corporate deviants back into society. Braithwaite (1989), in a seminal book titled *Crime, Shame and Reintegration*, argues that Western society has adopted a model of crime control based on deterrence that stresses shaming offenders by emphasiz-ing punishment. "The public visibility of the pillory and the chain-gang were re-placed by penal practices to warehouse offenders away from public view" (Braithwaite, 1989, p. 59). Offenders were subject to shaming by being placed in public view in such a way that stigmatization and ostracism were seen as the ac-cepted way to deal with offenders. Braithwaite argues that this became a means of permanently marking the criminal offender as deviant; as a result, the offender never gained full acceptance back into the community. "Punishment erects barri-ers between the offender and punisher" (Braithwaite, 1989, p. 73) and becomes what the labeling school referred to as a degradation ceremony. The offender is iso-lated from the rest of society, is stigmatized and isolated in a prison, and upon com-pletion of his or her prison term, must carry the "scarlet letter" of being an offender or an "ex-con." For Braithwaite, this approach alienates the offender from society, and the ex-offender can never be fully accepted back into the community.

What Braithwaite describes in his book is precisely the approach that is taken in China. He argues that crime is best controlled in those societies where there is a pervasive sense of familism and communitarianism (Zhang, 1995). That is, the more people are interconnected in social relationships, the greater the potential for more effective social control. In other words, the ostracism and stigmatization of offenders becomes a virtual guarantee that they will not be accepted back into soci-ety, and the only option may be a continued life of crime. On the other hand, shaming that is reintegrative, whereby the offender is accepted back into the community, is the essence of Braithwaite's argument. The objective is not to allow offenders to lose their "stake" in conformity by effectively cutting them off from full participation in conventional society (Vagg, 1998).

The theory of shaming and reintegration works the best in societies where there is a high level of interdependency between family members, and between workers and employers. There must be a high level of communitarianism whereby the interests of the community or the group are placed above the interests of the individual. Further, there must be a willingness of the community to accept a collective responsibility for the actions committed by the individual and a willingness to accept the offender back into the community. Braithwaite and Mugford (1994) argue that those societies with low crime rates have the ability to shame and reintegrate deviants back into society. Conversely, societies with high crime rates, such as the United States, shame and then stigmatize offenders. This leads to a continuous cycle of reoffending. The seminal thoughts of Garfinkel (1956) on the sociopsychological processes involved in degradation ceremonies, such as court appearances and punishment, that transform the deviant into an outsider are central to Braithwaite's thesis of shaming and reintegration.

The key to this approach is that the shame experienced by the deviant must be transformed into a process of reintegration. Braithwaite places an enormous burden on the victims of crime, who must confront their offender, convey their abhorrence of being victimized, but then allow the offender to come back to the community. Thus, he calls for empowering the victim, giving respect and support to the offender while condemning his or her act, and sensitizing the community to participate in the shaming and reintegration of the offender. In many instances it is the need to insist on the collective, community involvement of reintegration that becomes the most difficult aspect of Braithwaite's thesis (Moore, 1993). The community must express social disapproval and yet allow the offender the opportunity to join ranks with the conventional society. Western society has become too fractured, too independent, and has become too reliant on punishment.

The emergence of formal law in Western society followed the emergence of the state. Customary law, or two-party law, regulated societies for hundreds of years. When a dispute arose, the two parties involved in the dispute resolved their difficulties quickly, without the need for outside actors or agencies. Rules of custom dictated how these disputes were to be resolved, and preindustrial societies were relatively smooth-functioning and crime-free. However, with the advent of industrialization, the movement from a Durkheimian mechanical solidarity to organic solidarity, the advent of increasing wealth and concomitant poverty, the movement toward urbanization, and the loss of authority in industrial and postindustrial societies, the effectiveness of custom began to wane. What emerges is first the creation of the state, and then of mandates that are issued by this organizational entity, which are called law.

Nils Christie (1977) has argued that the modern state has usurped the role of the victim in Western society. Crime is defined as a violation of a code that offends all of society, and the state becomes the offended party. But Christie asserts that the state has "stolen" the conflict from the victim. Thus, the case is transformed into a dispute between the state and the offender, with the victim playing little or no role.

The victim is a particularly heavy loser in this situation. Not only has he suffered, lost materially or become hurt, physically or otherwise, and not only does the state take compensation, but above all he has lost participation in his own case. It is the Crown that comes into the spotlight, not the victim. It is the Crown that describes the losses, not the victim. It is the Crown that appears in the newspaper, very seldom the victim. It is the Crown that gets a chance to talk to the offender . . . . Something that belonged to him has been taken away from that victim. (Christie, 1977, pp. 7–8)

An integral part of Braithwaite's shaming and reintegration scheme is the role of the victim. It is the victim that shames and disapproves of the offender's actions. Sanctions that are imposed by family members, relatives, friends, or a personally relevant collectivity have more effect than sanctions imposed by a remote legal authority. "Repute in the eyes of close acquaintances matters more to people than the opinions or actions of criminal justice officials" (Braithwaite, 1989, p. 69). However, in most contemporary Western societies it is the state that takes action, the state that is the offended party; the victim plays a very minor role. In fact, concepts of victim compensation are rarely used. Justice is equated to the offender's being found guilty and punished. The victim may have suffered an egregious loss, but the criminal justice system does not incorporate victim compensation into the definition of justice.

SOCIAL CONTROL IN CHINA

China had never developed an extensive legal code or formal justice system (Troyer, 1989). Based on Confucian ideology, *li* (informal law and custom) was superior to *fa* (formal law). By establishing a strong set of moral codes and strong custom, Chinese social control sought to develop moral character, and rule by moral example and persuasion rather than by formal, external law. The essence of Chinese social control is seen in the neighborhood mediation committees. Virtually all conflicts were resolved in these committees, which were comprised of nonprofessionals, albeit "solid citizens" of China (Clark, 1989). This was grassroots social control in the extreme. It meant that the central government surrendered authority to local groups of citizens who attempted to resolve disputes of every sort quickly and efficiently. But there was no standardization of settlement procedures, no legal code, and no professional jurists. The objective was to solve problems before they escalated into major disputes. No lawyers were present, and the resolution would be quick and forthright. Often the mediation session would end with written agreements or stipulations. But the dispute was resolved quickly and formal legal procedures were not necessary. Again, a Confucian moral code became the bedrock of neighborhood mediation.

The essence of Chinese life is not "to lose face." Vagg (1998) states that concept of "face" entails two dimensions. The first is the notion of "face" being social success, high honor, or high accomplishment. The second sense of "face" is the notion of respect toward an individual, a moral standing or the judgment of a person regarding his observance of proper conduct. Hence, to lose "face" is to lose honor, respect, and self-worth. In the process of dispute settlement it is critical that one not lose "face." The adversary system that emerged with common law is based on the precept of winner-take-all. One party wins and the other party loses. In China, the adversary system would strip the loser of all dignity. Thus, the art of mediation and compromise is to make one's point, to present an argument, but surely not to crush the opponent. The loser always walks away with some dignity, and the winner never asserts that he or she is entitled to a total victory. Neighborhood mediation committees were steeped in the art of compromise. Each party is asked to yield on some points and yet recognize that dignity and honor are of central importance. In Western courts, this would imply that the winner relinquishes some rights because it is "the honorable thing to do."

The art of negotiation and compromise is practiced in China even in those instances when formal courts are invoked because serious transgressions of the code incurred. Though the defendant is represented by a lawyer, the court process is more akin to the defendant's throwing himself on the mercy of the court than trying to argue for his or her innocence (Rojek, 1985). Because the defendant was arrested, there is an assumption of guilt. Chinese law does not allow the defendant to remain silent. Article 64 of the Chinese Criminal Procedure states that "the defendant shall answer questions put by the investigation personnel according to the facts." Invariably the defendant pleads guilty to the offense but implores mercy of the court. Article 63 of the Criminal Code states that "those who voluntarily surrender after committing a crime may be given a lesser punishment." It would appear that built into the Criminal Code of contemporary China is the concept of "saving face," in that a good attitude and admission of guilt are important considerations. Despite the image of the Chinese courts as being harsh and punitive, many sentences are relatively mild, provided the victim is compensated.

China was an example par excellence of Braithwaite's image of a society that had low crime rates because of shaming and reintegration. The practice of "self-criticism" meant that it was perfectly acceptable for one member of the community to bring to the attention of another a fault or a failing. The community became responsible for itself, and open criticism at the grassroots level meant that minor issues never escalated to major disputes. The center of authority was focused within the family, and the family became inextricably woven into the neighborhood. Rather than wait for deviant behaviors to manifest themselves, crime control was prevention-oriented rather than rehabilitation-oriented. That is, rather than wait for acts of deviance to occur, bad attitudes were reacted to before they became bad behaviors. Deviant individuals were shamed before neighborhood mediation committees and given the opportunity to repent. A hallmark of Chinese society is the fact that offenders were given the chance to correct themselves and the community received offenders back into their midst. When deviance occurred, it was seen as the failure of the family or the community, and collectivized guilt complemented individual guilt. Because the offender, from the Confucian perspective, is correctable, the community participated in the rehabilitation process. Prison sentences, though strict and austere, were not lengthy, and the offender was released into the care of the community without any stigma. The Chinese rarely give up on an offender, but when they do, this means there is no hope of rehabilitation. Capital punishment is reserved for these "uncorrectables." The very essence of Chinese society is to belong, to participate, to be "thy brother's keeper." For generations, all aspects of shaming and reintegration were part and parcel of Chinese social control. However, contemporary China is beginning to experience serious fractures in its traditional social control practices, and crime, which was virtually nonexistent, is becoming a reality.

SOCIAL CHANGE IN CHINA

The genius of Chairman Mao was to recognize the compatibility of communism with the traditional Chinese social organization. Under Mao, allegiance to the Communist Party was substituted for the family (Rojek, 1989). Mao, while rejecting the prescripts of Confucianism, used Confucian ideology for his own purposes. Mao also believed that individuals were good and could be led to virtue. The famous "Mass Line," in which power flowed from the bottom up rather than the top down, was infused with Confucian thought. Mao's concept of the "dictatorship of the proletariat" was based on his vision of political leaders listening to the masses. Indeed, the ongoing struggle between Mao's understanding of Marx and the Soviet Union's interpretation of Marx evolved around the role of the peasant. In the Soviet Union power flowed from the top down, with a heavy emphasis on a top-heavy bureaucracy, but for Mao, power flowed from the bottom up. Chinese self-discipline and self-cultivation negated the need for a strong bureaucracy and a heavy-handed government.

With the death of Mao in 1976 and the emergence of Deng Xiaoping in 1977, China embarked on what became known as the "second revolution." Deng set out to modernize China and to spearhead an economic revolution. In order to accomplish this, he needed to bring about a "de-Maofication" of China. Deng's two famous slogans—"practice is the sole criterion of truth" and "seek truth from facts"—launched China on a pragmatic slide and a gradual dilution of Mao's legacy. Deng announced the "open door" policy, in which technology transfer became a major objective. The emergence of joint ventures permitted foreign corporations to establish themselves in China for "mutual benefit." Deng took pride in pointing to "one country, two systems" and to his constant refrain that "it does not matter whether the cat is white or black as long as it catches mice." Though China has made impressive economic strides, crime, which was unknown, has become a fact of life, and the very heart and soul of China have been bartered for economic progress.

According to Dutton (1997), China had exceptionally low crime rates from 1949 (the founding of the People's Republic of China) to 1979, when economic reforms began in earnest. Though official statistics can be sanitized and manipulated, from all indications, crime in China was extraordinarily low. Further, recidivism rates of 8 percent or less were quite common (Deng et al., 1998). Deng's open door policy led to the rapid transformation to a socialist market economy. These changes are so dramatic, complex, and far-reaching that the basic character of China has been permanently altered (Deng and Cordilia, 1999).

For the younger generation, the uniforms of socialism have transmuted themselves into jeans, tennis shoes, and miniskirts. Western jackets for men are now de rigueur articles, not only in cities but also in suburban and even rural locales. Chinese prefer foreign cigarettes, music, and films. MTV, CNN and videos, both legal and illegal, flourish on plentiful television screens, as do a barrage of commercials for eateries like McDonald's, Pizza Hut, and Kentucky Fried Chicken. Fueled by disposable income, urban shoppers flock to Wal-Mart, Sam's Club, and Pricemart. Nearly 10 million Chinese wield portable telephones on their outings. The ubiquitous bicycle, once dominating the thoroughfares, now competes with private automobiles, taxis, and mopeds—all oblivious to the hour of day or night. (Anderson and Gil, 1998, pp. 248–261)

What is astounding about the social change is the speed with which it occurred. Whereas the United States has espoused a capitalist economic system for more than two hundred years and gradually adjusted to the demands of urbanization and postindustrial development, China is going through the same metamorphosis in a matter of a few years. The traditions of thousands of years are being jettisoned, and Western ideology, practices, and values are being adopted en masse. The government is encouraging this race toward modernism despite the ramifications that this has for the very core of Chinese social life. In fact, as aptly stated by Orville Schell (1988), "to be rich is glorious." The "new" China seems to be predicated on an individualism that counters communalism, and on a frenzied striving for wealth and material goods that weakens, if not destroys, the very essence of interpersonal obligations.

Perhaps the most demonstrable change in Chinese social life is the advent of the "floating population," the movement of rural residents to the urban areas. This was initially caused by the dismantling of the collectives in the 1980s, the industrialization of the agricultural sector, and the grinding poverty of many peasant farmers. It is estimated that between 100 and 120 million rural workers have migrated to the urban areas in search of economic opportunities (Curran, 1998). The National People's Congress encouraged this movement of displaced rural peasants to the cities, but lacking skills and education, these workers are not readily employable. But a greater problem is that this transient population cripples one of the key elements of Chinese social control, the household registration system. From a social control perspective, the household registration system meant lifetime residency in a specific area and blocked migration from one area to another. Registration was controlled by the police; and residency, employment, medical care, education, and even food were contingent on a household registration card. Thus, internal migration was extremely rare, and towns and neighborhoods became extremely stable. Grassroots social control became greatly simplified in a society where strangers were easily identified and residents lived in the same domicile for generations. But the economic reforms of the 1980s led to a drastic alteration of the household registration system. "As a market-oriented economy has been gradually replacing the traditional state-planned economy, a labor market that requires free exchange of human resources has begun to form in China" (Situ and Liu, 1996). With hordes of agrarian laborers migrating to the cities in search of employment, problems escalate very quickly. This influx of rural peasants produces a shortage of living space, the disruption of stable neighborhoods, the presence of strangers in once intimate neighborhoods, and, above all, increasing crime rates. Burglary, robbery, drug trafficking, prostitution, and even violence increased significantly in China in the 1980s and 1990s.

The one-child policy was enacted in order to curb China's growing population. China currently has 1.2 billion people, 21 percent of the world's population (Population Reference Bureau, 1997). Further, China's current growth rate is 1.1 percent, which means that this current population will double in sixty-three years. Clearly, China cannot sustain any increase in its population, and a growth rate that will result in 2.4 billion by the year 2060 could be catastrophic. In order to address this problem, China adopted a one-child policy which permits each married couple to have one child. This program has had reasonably good success in the urban areas, where neighborhood volunteers informally maintain order and discipline, and vigorously enforce the one-child policy. Violation of the one-child policy can result in sterilization, abortion, loss of medical benefits, or, in some instances, imprisonment. However China is 22 percent urban and 78 percent rural. The one-child policy cannot be as rigorously enforced in the rural countryside and thus population in China continues to grow. But the one-child policy in the urban area is producing what is termed a "generation of princes or princesses," or "little emperors" because of the care and attention showered on these children. The danger is that the current generation of urban Chinese children is being pampered and spoiled by six doting adults: two excessively devoted parents and four overly solicitous grandparents. It has led to an overuse of medical care facilities by anxious parents or grandparents. It has also led to overweight children who are being fed by six caring adults. Previous generations of Chinese who were frugal, diligent, and self-sacrificing may be replaced by a new indulgent and selfish generation.

Though China had informal social control techniques for thousands of years that produced a very cohesive and well-disciplined society, the nation is moving rapidly in the direction of formal law. The current Criminal Code was enacted in 1980, and in 1987 the Civil Code was fully enacted (Rojek, 1996). Along with the promulgation of criminal and civil codes there were dramatic increases in legal training and the number of lawyers establishing private practices. It was the tradition that whatever lawyers existed in China were all employed by the government. Mao taught to "depend on the rule of man, not the rule of law." Clearly this is no longer the case. Similarly, it is apparent that neighborhood mediation may eventually be usurped by formal litigation in the courts. The advent of joint venture law implies a marked infusion of Western legal practice into China with the appearance of multinational corporations. The implication is that custom is giving way to formal law, and the common practice of settling disputes informally without the presence of formal court officials is beginning to wane.

The Communist Party is the dominant, all-powerful group in China. It is estimated that only 4 percent of all Chinese are actually members of the party. Government officials are referred to as cadres, but they are not automatically members of the party. Traditionally, to be invited to join the Communist Party was a mark of high honor. Indeed, it was important that as a young child, one begin to develop a dossier that would eventually permit that person to become a member of the party. All upward mobility is ultimately controlled by party officials. Thus, to progress to the upper ranks in government, industry, education, or the military, one had to be a member of the Communist Party. However, party membership is not held in high esteem by all Chinese, particularly young Chinese. Especially since "the event" of Tiananmen Square in 1989, there has emerged a pervasive cynicism with regard to the party among many young Chinese, and a marked aversion to party membership is not uncommon. The irony of this predicament is that the Communist Party controls all decision-making in China and if young Chinese, particularly young intellectuals, do not join the party and bring about change from within, then the party becomes dominated by the hard-liners. Indeed, it may be no accident that many in the Communist Party are from the old school and the party has become a haven for the octogenarians. There is also a critical "brain drain" occurring in China, with many of the brightest students leaving to study overseas but never returning. There have been numerous efforts to recruit "overseas Chinese" to return to China by offering incentives such as better housing or employment opportunities.

Undoubtedly the most remarkable change in China is the wholesale effort by its citizens to pursue wealth and material possessions. In the 1970s the government encouraged stories of the 1,000 yuan family; in the 1980s it was the 100,000 yuan family; in the 1990s it became the 1,000,000 yuan family. Indeed, the government is proud of the motto "to be rich is glorious." The commune system has long ended, even state socialism is weakening, and the open market economy is embraced wholeheartedly. China is second only to Japan as Asia's largest and fastest-growing market for products with a growth in gross domestic product averaging 10 percent in the 1990s (Kelley and Luo, 1999). By the year 2000 China's consumer market was expected to be larger than that of the United States or western Europe. Particularly with the advent of joint ventures between China and the major industrial powers, the old China is quickly fading into the past. In the 1980s and 1990s China has been the leading destination country in the world for direct foreign investment. China could boast of its low unemployment because of the "iron rice bowl" which implied that everyone was employed. Those who did not have a job were referred to as "waiting for employment." Unemployment is a new phenomenon in China and with the rapid infusion of Western economic strategies, workforces will inevitably be reduced.

Under a centrally controlled command economy in which the central leadership determined all economic policies, the Communist Party determined the country's goals. But with the introduction of forms of a capitalist laissez-faire economy, government control is shrinking and market forces of supply and demand are becoming the primary determinants of what is produced. The Chinese are beginning to experience unequal benefits, double-digit inflation, unstable prices in the agricultural sector, and economic corruption. China has been accused of mortgaging its future with the profit motive driving uncontrolled pollution, rampant growth of cities, destruction of forests and arable land, and increasing social inequality. The official poverty figure given by the Chinese government is 7 percent, but the World Bank estimates it to be 33 percent (Tan, 1999). There is also strong evidence that there is a widening gap in income between the rich and the poor. Whereas education had been a hallmark of Chinese society, there is evidence of increasing numbers of school dropouts because of the urge to "make money" rather than to continue one's education. It has also been alleged that the government has been underfunding public education in order to subsidize industrial growth.

All of this rapid change led to a pronounced increase in crime in the late 1980s. In the period from 1985 to 1995, crime rose more than 20 percent annually (Curran, 1998). Not surprisingly, property offenses surged in this time frame: robbery increased 1,768 percent, theft increased 1,090 percent, and counterfeiting increased 984 percent (*Press of Law Yearbook of China*, 1998). Despite these enormous increases, the minister of public security stated that the actual number of offenses was "several times more numerous" than officially reported (Dutton and Li, 1993). Unless China can take corrective measures immediately, it appears that crime in the coming years will dwarf the crime surge that the United States experienced in the 1960s. In many ways, the social underpinnings of Chinese society are being swept away by social change, and this society could be experiencing what Durkheim described as a state of anomie.

NEW STRATEGIES OF SOCIAL CONTROL

In an effort to deal with a rapidly growing crime problem, the central committee of the Chinese Communist Party has put forth a strategy of mobilizing and coordinating crime control for the whole society. The official title of the document was "Decision on Strengthening the Comprehensive Treatment of Social Order," but in reality it is simply a campaign for cracking down on crime. China has long used the campaign strategy for dealing with social problems. For example, in recent years there have been the "severe strike" campaign to curb street crime; the "six evils campaign" to attack fraud, drug production, gambling, kidnapping, pornography, and prostitution; the "strike hard campaign" attacking murder, robbery and rape; the "crack down on prostitution" campaign. Each of these campaigns represents a short-term, highly focused attack, with much fanfare and publicity, on a specific offense. It is questionable whether the goals are ever accomplished, but this has become a routinized dimension to policing activities in China. These campaigns do have ramifications in terms of police vigilance and activity, and often there is public notice of arrests, and at times quotas for arrests, in order to demonstrate that the social problem is being addressed (Leng and Chiu, 1985). Often the police will announce a period of leniency if offenders voluntarily turn themselves in. Citizens are admonished to report criminal violators and to help the police track down offenders. When arrests are made, there may be a public display of the criminal violators. Obviously it is a period of heightened police activity, and the enthusiasm and exuberance to carry out these campaigns can result in heavy-handed police tactics.

In addition to reacting to criminal behaviors, Chinese social control also encompasses what might be termed thought control. Citizens are encouraged to confess their own guilt, the guilt of others, to use self-criticism, and to eradicate deviant ideas. In many settings "study groups" are organized to discuss, inform, and mobilize local citizens to participate directly or indirectly in these campaigns. Chinese citizens will often refer to these study groups as "to wash brain," and attendance is mandated in many *danwei* or neighborhood settings. Individuals who come forth with information will often be rewarded with commendations by cadres. Even if the information proves to be false or of no consequence, the individual will be praised for coming forth. The zealousness of these campaigns can easily become highly suspect in terms of human rights.

The police have the power to give administrative punishments that include detention, and the types of sanctions that might be imposed. A wide range of offenses, referred to as "minor acts of law infringement" that are not considered criminal, can be handled exclusively by the police. Individuals can be detained for months, and through the use of "reeducation through labor" regulations, they may be institutionalized for up to four years (Curran, 1998). Thus, police discretion can be greatly expanded during these anticrime campaigns, and human rights are often subverted in the interest of eradicating crime. The time spent in detention or reeducation through labor camps can be extremely harsh. Most criminal institutions in China are akin to high-production factories where prisoners work six days a week in total silence. Corporal punishment is not uncommon, and prisoners are expected to acknowledge their guilt and display a contrite attitude. As China's crime rate continues to climb, it should be expected that anticrime campaigns will be used more regularly.

The Ministry of Public Security issued an administrative report on crime in China (Dutton, 1997). It states that China has experienced "four high tides" of criminal offending. The first tide was the postliberation period of the early 1950s, the second tide was the late 1950s, the third tide was the Cultural Revolution (1966–1976), and the fourth tide started around 1987 and still exists. The document singles out the "floating population," criminal gangs, and juvenile delinquents. The tone of this report is one of alarm and a literal call to arms. Implicit in the document are assertions that swifter and more certain punishment is the only answer. This seems to open the door for more vigorous policing, detention, and imprisonment, and the relaxation of procedures that safeguard human rights.

CONCLUSION

China is undergoing massive social changes. It seems to be eagerly racing toward modernization, in the process tossing overboard a long tradition of social organization and social control, and burying its Confucian heritage. China seems to have a fascination with Western ideas and lifestyles, and desperately wants to adopt a market economy. The difficulty with this transition is that it is happening so rapidly that the old is being discarded, and the new is being introduced, without any consideration of how this meshes with Chinese culture. For hundreds of years China had a unique system of social control that produced a highly advanced civilization and virtually mitigated all forms of criminal behavior. What was discovered by Braithwaite (1989) as new and innovative—shaming and reintegration—had been practiced in China for generations. But China may be spinning out of control with a government that is trying to encourage growth and modernization as quickly as possible while trying to keep a lid on a crime wave that is looming out of control. Corruption and the acquisition of wealth are rife at all levels of the Chinese government. It is ironic that China had been the paragon of a society that was nearly crime-free and highly interdependent, but is rapidly becoming wracked with materialism and crime.

REFERENCES

Anderson, Allen F., and Vincent E. Gil. 1998. "China's Modernization and the Decline of Communitarianism: The Control of Sex Crimes and Implications for the Fate of Informal Social Control." *Journal of Contemporary Criminal Justice* 14: 248–261.

Bellah, Robert N. 1970. *Beyond Belief.* New York: Harper & Row.

Braithwaite, John. 1989. *Crime, Shame, and Reintegration.* Cambridge: Cambridge University Press.

Braithwaite, John, and Stephen Mugford. 1994. "Conditions of Successful Reintegration Ceremonies." *British Journal of Criminology* 34: 139–171.

Brooks, E. Bruce, and A. Taeko Brooks. 1998. *The Original Analects: Sayings of Confucius and His Successors.* New York: Columbia University Press.

Butterfield, Fox. 1982 *China: Alive in the Bitter Sea.* New York: Times Books.

Christie, Nils. 1977. "Conflicts as Property." *British Journal of Criminology* 17: 1–14.

Clark, John. 1989. "Conflict Management Outside the Courtrooms of China." In *Social Control in the People's Republic of China*, pp. 57–69. Edited by Ronald J. Troyer, John P. Clark, and Dean G. Rojek. New York: Praeger.

Curran, Daniel. 1998. "Economic Reform, the Floating Population, and Crime." *Journal of Contemporary Criminal Justice* 14: 262–280.

Deng Xiaogang and Ann Cordilia. 1999. "To Get Rich Is Glorious: Rising Expectations, Declining Control, and Escalating Crime in Contemporary China." *International Journal of Offender Therapy and Comparative Criminology* 423: 211–229.

Deng, Xiaogang, Lening Zhang, and Ann Cordilia. 1998. "Social Control and Recidivism in China." *Journal of Contemporary Criminal Justice* 14: 281–295.

Dutton, Michael. 1997. "The Basic Character of Crime in Contemporary China." *China Quarterly* 149: 160–177.

Dutton, Michael, and Tianfu Lee. 1993. "Missing the Target? Policing Strategies in the Period of Economic Reform." *Crime & Delinquency* 39, no. 3: 316–336.

Garfinkel, Harold. 1956. "Conditions of Successful Degradation Ceremonies." *American Journal of Sociology* 61: 420–424.

Kelly, Lane, and Yadong Luo. 1999. "An Introduction to Emerging Business Issues for China 2000." In *China 2000: Emerging Business Issues,* pp. ix–xx. Edited by Lane Kelly and Yadong Luo. Thousand Oaks, CA: Sage.

Lagerwey, John. 1987. *Taoist Ritual in Chinese Society and History.* New York: Macmillan.

Leng, Shaochuan and Hungdah Chiu. 1985. *Criminal Justice in Post-Mao China: Analysis and Documents.* Albany: State University of New York Press.

Moore, David B. 1993. "Shame, Forgiveness, and Juvenile Justice." *Criminal Justice Ethics* 12: 3–25.

Population Reference Bureau. 1997. World Population and the Environment. Population Reference Bureau, Washington, D.C.

Press of Law Yearbook of China. 1998. *Law Yearbook of China.* Beijing: Press of Law Yearbook of China.

Rojek, Dean G. 1985. "The Criminal Process in the People's Republic of China." *Justice Quarterly* 2: 117–126.

———. 1989. "Confucianism, Maoism, and the Coming of Delinquency to China." In *Social Control in the People's Republic of China*, pp. 84–96. Edited by Ronald J. Troyer, John P. Clark, and Dean G. Rojek. New York: Praeger.

———. 1996. "Changing Directions of Chinese Social Control." In *Comparative Criminal Justice: Traditional and Nontraditional Systems of Law and Control,* pp. 234–249. Edited by Charles B. Fields and Richter H. Moore, Jr. Prospect Heights, IL: Waveland Press.

Schell, Orville. 1988. *Discos and Democracy.* New York: Pantheon.

Situ, Yingyi and Weizheng Liu. 1996. "Comprehensive Treatment to Social Order: A Chinese Approach Against Crime." *International Journal of Comparative and Applied Criminal Justice* 20: 96–115.

Tan, Kwong-leung. 1999. "Social Development in China: Progress and Problems." *Journal of Contemporary Asia* 29: 95–108.

Troyer, Ronald J. 1989. "Chinese Thinking About Crime and Social Control." In *Social Control in the People's Republic of China,* pp. 45–56. Edited by Ronald J. Troyer, John P. Clark, and Dean G. Rojek. New York: Praeger.

Vagg, Jon. 1998. "Delinquency and Shame." *British Journal of Criminology* 38: 247–264.

Whyte, Martin K., and William L. Parish. 1984. *Urban Life in Contemporary China.* Chicago: University of Chicago Press.

Zhang, Sheldon X. 1995. "Measuring Shaming in an Ethnic Context." *British Journal of Criminology* 35: 248–260.

CHAPTER 8

Community Integration and the Effectiveness of Social Control

Hong Lu and Terance D. Miethe

Social scientists have long been interested in the relationship between community organization and crime (Hope and Shaw, 1988; Rosenbaum, 1986, 1987, 1988). Western community policing and crime prevention literature suggests that high community disorganization tends to be associated with high crime rates and low effectiveness of formal (police) and informal (community) social control (Cao et al., 1996; Covinton and Taylor, 1991; Lewis and Salem, 1986; Sampson and Grove, 1989; Skogan, 1987; Wilson and Kelling, 1983).

As Westerners have observed, high community integration was responsible for the effective social control in China in the past (Li, 1978; Whyte and Parish, 1984). However, an unexpected consequence of Chinese economic reforms and the "open door" policy was the undermining of the high community integration. Hence, China provides a unique opportunity to examine the relationship between community integration and the effectiveness of social control in a changing social context.

This chapter explores the relationship between community integration and the effectiveness of social control in the Chinese urban context. It starts with a discussion of Western theory and research on community integration and social control. Issues of changing community integration and formal and informal responses to crimes in China are then discussed. After analyzing data on community integration and social control in two Shanghai neighborhoods, the chapter concludes with a discussion of the theoretical and policy implications of the findings.

WESTERN THEORY AND RESEARCH ON COMMUNITY INTEGRATION AND SOCIAL CONTROL

The primary theoretical perspective that guides research on community integration and social control is social disorganization, which was created by Shaw and McKay (1942), and developed by others, including Bursik (1984, 1988) and Sampson and Grove (1989). This theory essentially contends that disintegrated community diminishes informal social control capacities, which results in high crime rates in the community. Wilson and Kelling (1983) extended this intellectual heritage with their "broken windows" theory, which asserts that urban neighborhood decay, symbolized by broken windows, if left unchecked, will lead to further deterioration of neighborhood conditions. Such community disintegration will ultimately result in the ineffectiveness of social control mechanisms to thwart criminal motivations and opportunities. This theory underlies the community policing movement in the West, making community an integral part of the social control of crime.

A common research strategy for examining the effectiveness of formal social control in Western countries involves surveys of citizen attitudes and confidence in law enforcement agencies. A general finding from these studies is that minority neighborhoods with low community integration (high population turnover and heterogeneous population) have strained relations with the police, and consistently rate police less favorably than those in middle-class, white neighborhoods (Cao et al., 1996; Jesilow et al., 1995; Webb and Marshall, 1995). Although some studies observe that police actively support community crime prevention programs (e.g., neighborhood watch) in both minority and white neighborhoods (Garofalo and McLeod, 1986), other studies find that police provide more enduring support to middle-class, more integrated neighborhoods than to minority, disintegrated neighborhoods (Rosenbaum, 1988).

Previous studies have also examined the effectiveness of informal social control. For example, Rosenbaum (1987, 1988) reviewed community crime prevention programs across the United States and concluded that informal social control had achieved little success in reducing crime rates and recidivism rates, and yielded inconsistent results about reducing fear of crime. Factors related to community integration are often identified as the basis for the ineffectiveness of the programs or other types of informal social control. Specifically, previous studies report that communities characterized by poverty, high percentage of rental units, high turnover rates, large proportion of minority occupants, and high crime rates tend to have low community attachment, low organizational participation, and low capacities for informal social control. These findings are observed in both studies using the individual as the unit of analysis (Greenberg et al., 1982; Lavrakas and Herz, 1982; Podolefsky and Dubow, 1981; Schneider, 1986; Skogan and Maxfield, 1981) and the neighborhood as the unit of analysis (Garofalo and McLeod, 1988; Henig, 1978, 1982).

Western research on policing and crime prevention has yielded several general findings. First, community integration is largely affected by factors such as economic status, racial composition, and residential mobility. Second, community disintegration is indicative of the diminished capacities of informal social control mechanisms. Third, by attenuating bonds to social institutions, community disintegration weakens police and other formal social control mechanisms.

Although the relationship between community integration and social control has been substantially investigated in the West, the issue has rarely been explored in non-Western settings. Yet, it is the non-Western communities that are generally characterized by high integration and effective social control (Findlay and Zvekic, 1988). In addition, the proposition that community disintegration leads to ineffective social control has not been fully explored in sociocultural contexts where police and community may not have had strained relations, and race and class have not been prominent characteristics that divide communities. Using data gathered in Shanghai's neighborhoods, the current study offers such an opportunity by exploring the effect of community integration on social control in China.

CHANGING COMMUNITY INTEGRATION IN CHINA

Prior to the recent reform movement, Chinese neighborhoods had several important characteristics that inhibited crime. These characteristics included low geographic and residential mobility, high population density, and homogeneity. In addition, Chinese neighborhoods were controlled by both the formal social control agency (the local police station) and the informal social control agency (community organizations managed by the grassroots branch of the Chinese government, the City Street Office, through the residence committee). These dual social control forces managed and oversaw political, social, economic, and legal matters in the neighborhood. The household registration records maintained by the local police in controlling an individual's residency status were particularly significant in social control because they ensured the stability of the neighborhood, made it easy to identify outsiders, and hence enhanced conformity.

Urban neighborhoods have been undergoing dramatic changes since the economic reforms started in 1978. Under these reform efforts, many basic features of social institutions have been dramatically altered, including fundamental shifts in family patterns, the organization of work, school organizations, neighborhood patterns, leisure activities, and political education and organization (Fenwick, 1987). The restraints which once virtually guaranteed a fully registered population no longer operate in this changing environment (Potter, 1994).

Economic reforms also had profound effects on human relations and socialist ethics at the cultural level. The old comradeship has been replaced by the personal relationship based on exchange values, resulting in what Gold (1985) calls the commodification of the relationship. Popular participation, which had been the foundation for the collective spirit, is restricted to a secondary role as a result of the professionalization movement in major sociolegal and government institutions (Brady, 1982; Leng and Chiu, 1985). These changes have important implications on levels of community integration and, in turn, on the effectiveness of formal and informal social control.

Because the key to understanding Chinese society's low crime is the controls exerted over citizens at the grassroots level (Troyer et al., 1989; Whyte and Parish, 1984), any changes at this level would have substantial effects on Chinese social control. Accordingly, sociostructural changes experienced in urban neighborhoods seem especially important in understanding crime in China.

First, mobility has been greatly increased in several aspects—travel, job mobility, and residential mobility. In response to the demands of economic development and the free market economy, the Chinese leadership realized that the tight control of people's movement would hinder economic growth. The replacement of the old household registration book with the new residence card has greatly enhanced travel mobility (Dutton, 1992). The growing economic opportunities in large and coastal cities have attracted large numbers of temporary residents or transient persons working or looking for work (see chapter 5 in this volume). In addition, the market economy permits greater job mobility for urban workers. Private housing markets facilitate residential mobility, particularly in large cities where the housing shortage is most prominent. These changes of locale by urban residents for reasons of economics, city planning, and individual choice have affected patterns of social interactions among neighbors, resulting in a destabilization of urban neighborhoods.

Second, the housing type has changed dramatically since 1978. In most old neighborhoods, one-story attached single houses are dominant, particularly in Shanghai. Residents usually share public toilets and semiprivate kitchens. They carry out domestic labor in the semi-public area that several households share (Pellow, 1993). One consequence of such spontaneous interactions among neighbors is to impede the opportunity for potential deviant and criminal activities (Whyte and Parish, 1984). However, the intimate neighborhood relations have not been carried over to the new neighborhoods. This is the case in large part because of the housing type. The multiple-story apartment complexes have permitted greater anonymity and privacy, and have done little to assist unacquainted neighbors to know one another.

Third, household size has become smaller over time. Improved housing conditions have reduced the average size of the household, making a three-person household (two parents with a child) the norm rather than the exception. According to the routine activity theory (Cohen and Felson, 1979), the significance of this structural change for purposes of social control is that smaller households are more vulnerable to crime because less guardianship is placed on their property. In old neighborhoods, older people often serve as the eyes and ears of the family and the neighborhoods. The relatively high rate of bicycle theft in neighborhoods with multiple-story apartment complexes may be attributed to declining guardianship.

In fact, Shi (1996) attributes the high risk of theft in these areas to (1) the lack of neighborhood surveillance; (2) more temporary residents and transients in the neighborhood and adjacent areas, who are the typical suspects and arrestees in bike theft cases; and (3) inadequate housing management, indicated by inadequate lighting and unsecured parking garages.

Fourth, with more economic prosperity and opportunity, people's attitudes and activities have become more focused on financial profits. Community lives have become less important than economic activities. City dwellers have also had to deal with changes brought by economic reforms that have polarized the community. For example, a 1994 survey shows that people have almost evenly split opinions on important social and policy issues, from the future of economic reforms, to the relationship between spiritual civilization and material success, to the gap between the rich and the working class, and to their own future. More than half of the respondents agreed that "so long as I gain benefits, I will support whatever the policy may be" (Ding, 1994). This self-serving mentality never dominated mainstream thinking in China in the past.

Changes in the value systems and the lack of consensus on major issues concerning the society are important because they suggest that community organizing may be more difficult. In the past, community organization and residents' mobilization were largely based on party and political loyalty, community consensus and solidarity, and neighborhood stability. These characteristics and conditions of community have changed since economic reforms. How to effectively mobilize residents to take part in community activities and perform community services has become a serious challenge to many urban communities in the 1990s and beyond (Lu, 1998).

FORMAL AND INFORMAL RESPONSES TO CRIME

Since the economic reforms began in 1978, crime rates in China have soared. For example, the total crime rates doubled between 1981 and 1990. Violent crime and "crimes of greed" have become epidemic, as openly acknowledged by the Chinese government and various reports (Chen, 1997; *Law Yearbook of China*, 1986–1997; Wu, 1992). Fear of crime is on the rise as well. A 1988 survey of 15,000 persons from provinces indicates that over 49 percent of respondents were afraid of walking in the street alone at night (Dai, 1993). This may not come as a total surprise for Westerners. After all, crime is seen as a natural consequence, or more optimistically as an index, of modernization and urbanization (Adler, 1983; Clinard and Abbott, 1973; Shelley, 1981).

Nevertheless, the seriousness and the extent of crime have greatly concerned the Chinese leadership. New laws have been promulgated; and administrative roles have been refined to address increasing concerns of crime, especially economic crime. Studies on the causes of crime and delinquency reveal that a Western ideological influence, changes in family and neighborhood structure, temporary residents, and transients have all been blamed for most crimes committed in large cities (Chen, 1993; Xiang, 1994).

Urban residential communities have been hit hard by crime waves. To cope with the increasing crime and criminality, local social control agents have adopted a number of new strategies. Social control has become both more offensive and more defensive.

On the offensive side, more local police officers have been assigned to patrol duties than ever (see chapters 11 and 12 in this volume). Policing has become more punitive and more focused on particular places and special populations (Dutton and Lee, 1993). Local police stations have joined the "responsibility system," with station chiefs signing a "contract" with the police department promising to keep the area safe (Fu, 1990; also see chapter 9 in this volume). In addition, locally organized crime prevention teams are formed under the joint leadership of the local police and residence committees (Fu, 1990; Lu, 1998). Team members patrol the neighborhoods regularly to deter criminals. Moreover, residents are recruited to aggressively seek out information about other residents' deviant and criminal behaviors. For example, several neighborhoods in Shanghai used team members who worked at public telephone booths as informants on residents' illegal activities (Lu, 1998).

On the defensive side, strategies used to prevent crime and defend the neighborhood's safety very much resemble those in the West. These strategies include neighborhood watch, operation ID, community newsletter, and target-hardening activities, such as installing locks, bars, grills, markings on property, alarms, and other devices (Lu, 1998; Rosenbaum, 1987, 1988).

Despite these efforts, local social control agents in China are not too optimistic about the prospects of residents' mobilization in light of the changes in the neighborhood conditions. For example, Chan (1993) studied a southern city, Guangzhou—a front-runner in the market economy. She found the following change of patterns in the relation between residents and their community organizations. First, residents have increasingly withdrawn from community affairs. They are willing to pay others to perform their assigned neighborhood duties (e.g., cleaning public toilets and neighborhood patrol). Second, community organizations are nearly paralyzed because fewer people are willing to subject their private lives to local mediation. When disputes concern their economic rights, people are more likely to bring the matter to court rather than to seek local mediation. Third, some residents have little respect for community workers and show little interest in community affairs. Instead, they regard their business partners, customers, colleagues and friends as more important than their neighbors and community organizations. In addition, two traditional methods of community control, *bangjiao* (community correction) and *tiaojie* (mediation), have become less effective during the transitional era as the traditional structural conditions have changed in many urban neighborhood communities (Zhang et al., 1996).

The importance of changes in neighborhood structure and their implications for community integration and social control cannot be overestimated. Nonetheless, little research, particularly empirical research, has been done to explore such an important relationship. The current study uses survey data gathered from Shanghai's neighborhoods to explore the relationship between community integration and social control.

METHOD

This study of the relationship between community integration and social control involved data from a neighborhood survey conducted in Shanghai, China, in the spring of 1997. One of the authors had access to two large residential neighborhoods in Shanghai. One neighborhood is located in the old Shanghai district. It includes around 19,000 households and 78,000 residents. It is mainly a residential area with relatively more homogeneous residents. The housing type is primarily one- or two-story houses with public bathrooms and semiprivate kitchens shared by several households. The intimate housing setting allows, and indeed necessitates, frequent interactions among neighbors. This neighborhood with higher community integration is characterized as Old Shanghai.

The other neighborhood is in the newly developed, suburban area. It consists of about 22,000 households and 61,000 residents. It encompasses both residential and commercial areas with heterogeneous and mobile residents. Multiple-story apartment buildings are the dominant housing type. With separate units for each household, residents have little need to interact with their neighbors. This less integrated neighborhood is called New Shanghai.

A total of twenty survey interviewers were recruited with the help of residence committee members. Households were selected through a cluster sampling strategy. Each neighborhood area was broken into ten blocks so that each interviewer was able to work in, and had total control over, a specific block. Within each block, a systematic sampling strategy was used. In one area, for example, every fortieth household was sampled within each block, based on its household number and the targeted sample size. Once households were selected, respondents were systematically selected based on age and gender, to increase representativeness. We restricted participants to those eighteen years or older, to comply with an American university scholarship standard for research involving human subjects. The surveys yielded 477 returns. The overall response rate was about 48 percent.

Measures of Variables

Our dependent variables are effectiveness of formal social control (local police) and effectiveness of informal social control (community organizations). Each of these variables is measured by a three-item composite index. A composite index for the effectiveness of formal social control is based on responses to the following three items: (1) "How effective do you think your local police are in solving community problems?" (2) "Have you seen police officers in your neighborhood?" and (3) "Do you know one police officer by his/her name?" The response categories are "not effective" and "effective" for the first question, and "no" and "yes" for the latter two items. Observing police officers and knowing their names are measures of the effectiveness of social control because such activities signify an enmeshment of police in the neighborhood. A similar argument applies to observing committee members and knowing their names. Responses are summed to create an index with the following scores: 0 means low effectiveness and 3 means high effectiveness. The index for the effectiveness of informal social control is similarly constructed with the phrase "community organization" replacing "local police."

Two main independent variables are community attachment and organizational participation. Community attachment is measured by the frequency of residents' interactions with neighbors. Those who interact with neighbors less than once a month are coded 1, more than once a week are coded 3, and in-between are coded 2. Community attachment reflects the informal social networks in the neighborhood, depicted as "friendship ties" by Sampson and Groves (1989, p. 777) and "area cohesiveness" by Skogan (1987, p. 446).

Organizational participation is measured by a six-item composite index reflecting the level of residents' participation in community organization. This index is based on responses to the following six items: (1) "Have you participated in community activities?" (2) "Have you participated in community services?" (3) "Are you willing to participate in community activities?" (4) "Are you willing to participate in community services?" (5) "Are you willing to participate in crime prevention programs?" (6) "Have you ever reported problems to the authorities?" The response categories are "no" and "yes" for each item. Responses are summed to create an index with scores ranging from 0 to 6, where 0 means no participation and 6 means active participation.

We also include basic demographic information to serve as controls. Age is measured in years; gender, marital status, and employment status are treated as dummy variables where female, married, and employed are coded 1. Education is coded (1) junior high or less, (2) academic or senior high, and (3) college or advanced technical school. Occupational prestige is coded (1) blue-collar and service sector workers, (2) routine white-collar workers, (3) higher-status white-collar workers, and (4) cadres (government officials) at all levels. Household crowding is measured by the number of persons in a household. Finally, residential mobility is measured by the number of years a respondent has lived in the neighborhood.

We employed Ordinary Least Square (OLS) regression techniques to estimate the relationship between community integration and effectiveness of formal and informal social control. Mean comparisons are used to examine the bivariate relationship among the variables. Table 8.1 presents descriptive statistical information on the major dependent and independent variables for the two neighborhoods.

Results

As shown in table 8.1, community attachment and organizational participation vary significantly between the two neighborhoods. Residents of Old Shanghai report having both higher community attachment and organizational participation than residents of New Shanghai. This suggests that economic reforms have indeed brought consequential changes in community integration. The reforms have reduced the level of both community attachment and organizational participation in New Shanghai. In addition, the data show that organizational participation is higher than community attachment in both neighborhoods. This indicates that community organizations in China are quite effective in mobilizing residents to participate in communal affairs even in neighborhoods with lower opportunities for social integration.

The results in table 8.1 also indicate that residents in Old Shanghai perceive both formal and informal social control to be more effective than residents in New Shanghai. Informal social control is judged to be more effective than formal social control in both neighborhoods. This is largely consistent with Confucian ideology and Chinese crime control and prevention strategies. Historically, Chinese formal social control relied largely on informal social control of family and community. In the current context, urban residents still believe that community organizations play an important role in maintaining order and controlling crime.

Multiple regression analyses were conducted to assess the net impact of measures of community integration (community attachment and organizational participation) on residents' perceptions of the effectiveness of formal and informal social control. As shown in table 8.2, the effectiveness of formal and informal social control is significantly affected by both measures of community integration. After controlling for other variables, residents who have higher levels of community attachment and

Table 8.1
A Comparison of Mean Differences of Major Variables by Neighborhood

Variable	Old Shanghai		New Shanghai		
	Mean	SD	Mean	SD	tScore
Community integration					
Community attachment	2.39	.69	1.49	.52	15.69*
Organizational Participation	3.27	1.96	2.24	2.12	5.46*
Effectiveness of					
Formal Social Control	2.35	.93	1.33	.81	12.51*
Informal Social Control	2.61	.62	1.86	.94	10.45*
N	211		266		

$*p < -.01$

Table 8.2
OLS Regression Estimates of the Effects of Community Integration on the
Effectiveness of Formal and Informal Social Control

	Dependent Variables	
Independent Variables	Effectiveness of Formal Social Control	Effectiveness of Informal Social Control
Community attachment	.371	.337
	(7.59**)	(6.593**)
Organizational participation	.24	.283
	(6.136**)	(6.918**)
Age	-.219	-.036
	(-4.912**)	(-.783)
Gender	.054	-.037
	(1.379)	(-.898)
Marital status	.087	.056
	(2.334*)	(-1.426)
Education	-.148	-.026
	(-3.044**)	(-.509)
Employment status	-.075	-.118
	(-1.766)	(-2.651**)
Occupation	.091	.125
	(2.264*)	(2.976**)
Household crowding	-.040	-.060
	(-.919)	(-1.308)
Residential mobility	.163	.114
	(3.316**)	(2.222*)
R2	.411	.355

Note: Standardized OLS regression coefficients (betas) are reported. T ratios are given in parentheses.
  *$p < .05$
**$p < .01$
$N = 477$

organizational participation consider both informal and formal social control measures to be more effective. This confirms most Western research findings about the
correlation between the two variables. In addition, our data reveal that whereas community attachment has a slightly stronger effect on formal social control, organizational participation has a stronger effect on informal social control. This indicates
that people who have more interactions with neighbors tend to view formal social
control as more effective. Those who engage in more organizational activities tend to
regard informal social control as more effective.

Several control variables are also significant in the regression analysis. People
who have a better job and are long-term residents perceive formal and informal so-

cial control to be more effective. Those who are younger, married, and less educated tend to rate formal social control more effective. In contrast, only unemployment status has a significant effect on informal social control. Unemployed persons viewed informal social control as more effective than employed persons.

We also examined whether differences in the effectiveness of formal and informal social control between the two neighborhoods actually hold once other variables are introduced. We ran two OLS regression models with the same variables used in the models presented in Table 8.2, with an added dummy variable representing neighborhood (New Shanghai is coded 1). Our results reveal that the effectiveness of both formal and informal social control is significantly negatively related to the neighborhood variable, indicating that both formal and informal social control are more effective in Old Shanghai than in New Shanghai. This finding further confirms our hypothesis that community integration has a direct effect on social control even at the neighborhood level.

Finally, we considered the possibility that the effect of community integration on social control may vary by type of neighborhood. We thus ran four OLS regression models that estimated the neighborhood-specific effects of community integration on residents' assessments of the effectiveness of both formal and informal social control. As shown in table 8.3, our results indicate that the positive association between community integration and social control is generally consistent in these two communities. Nevertheless, the effect of community integration in New Shanghai differs by the type of social control. Whereas measures of community integration strongly affect judgments about informal control, their effect on formal control appears to be weak. Community attachment is significantly related to formal social control, but the level of organizational participation does not significantly influence ratings of formal social control in New Shanghai. This suggests that judgments about the effectiveness of formal social control are less strongly related to organizational participation among residents of less integrated communities.

DISCUSSION AND CONCLUSION

Our analysis of survey data from two of Shanghai's communities reveals several general conclusions. First, community integration strongly influences residents' ratings of the effectiveness of both formal and informal social control. This is consistent with our theoretical prediction and most Western research findings. As expected from Western research, long-term residents perceive social control to be more effective than do more recent migrants. However, residents' socioeconomic status (e.g., education, employment status, and occupational prestige) had diverse and contradictory relationships to social control. Contrary to Western findings, people who have lower socioeconomic status do not always place less faith in the effectiveness of social control.

Table 8.3
OLS Regression Estimates of the Effects of Community Integration on the
Effectiveness of Formal and Informal Social Control, by Neighborhood

| | Old Shanghai | | New Shanghai | |
Independent Variables	Formal	Informal	Formal	Informal
Community attachment	.328	.248	.196	.390
	(6.175**)	(4.110**)	(2.259*)	(5.109**)
Organizational participation	.396	.233	.037	.330
	(7.709**)	(4.009**)	(.538)	(5.475**)
Age	-.273	-.149	-.003	.125
	(-4.181**)	(-2.006*)	(-.032)	(1.418)
Gender	-.060	-.167	.015	.083
	(-1.168)	(-2.849**)	(.187)	(1.210)
Marital status	-.010	.006	.250	-.212
	(-.190)	(.095)	(3.368**)	(-3.242**)
Education	-.285	-.148	.059	.237
	(-4.739**)	(-2.172*)	(.626)	(3.279**)
Employment status	-.037	-.076	-.130	-.226
	(-.634)	(-1.141)	(-1.464)	(-2.881**)
Occupation	.086	.172	.137	.002
	(1.498)	(2.634**)	(1.783)	(.030)
Household crowding	-.037	-.162	-.162	-.073
	(-.768)	(-2.943**)	(-2.154*)	(-1.104)
Residential mobility	-.025	-.049	-.145	.221
	(-.437)	(-.765)	(-1.899)	(3.276**)
R2	.438	.277	.180	.365

Note: Standardized OLS regression coefficients (betas) are reported. T ratios are given in parentheses.
  *$p < .05$
**$p < .01$
$N = 477$

Second, our data suggest that major changes brought to the urban neighborhood community by the economic reforms include community disintegration with (1) less frequent interactions among neighbors and (2) reduced participation in community affairs by residents. This pattern is indicated by the fact that residents of New Shanghai exhibited significantly lower community integration than residents of Old Shanghai. In addition, there is a disparity in the ratings of the effectiveness of formal and informal social control in the two neighborhoods, with New Shanghai residents judging social control to be less effective. Particularly interesting is that the effect of community integration on social control differs across the types of neighborhoods. In Old Shanghai (where integration is high), its impact on social control is significant, but in New Shanghai (where integration is declining), only informal social control is substantially affected by community integration; the effect of community integration on formal social control is marginal in this neighborhood.

The results presented in this chapter must be viewed with caution because of several methodological limitations. Scholars engaging in studies of China are often confronted with such methodological problems as nonrandom sample, validity of survey responses, variable constructs, access, and political and organizational interference (Zhang and Messner, 1995).

In this study, the neighborhood survey was administered by cadres of residence committees in Shanghai. Involving government officials in this project poses a potential threat to confidentiality and reliability of the survey responses. Yet, in China, little research can be conducted without assistance or cooperation of government agencies. Cadres from residence committees are semigovernmental officials who are from the neighborhood and are more enmeshed with residents. Hence, their involvement should pose less threat than that of other governmental officials. In addition, with the help of residence committee cadres, we recruited twenty survey interviewers. They were trained in techniques of conducting face-to-face interviews and were asked to sign a confidentiality agreement. This minimizes interviewer biases. Nevertheless, because survey techniques are relatively new and more unfamiliar to Chinese people than to Western people, the extent of biases associated with involving governmental officials and different survey interviewers cannot be determined until research with more representative samples and better research design is conducted.

Regardless of the methodological limitations, our findings carry some important theoretical and practical implications. First, our results are consistent with Western theories of social disorganization and the "broken windows" theory. Specifically, community integration has a positive effect on both formal and informal social control, even in the Chinese context. More important, the effect of community integration on social control differs by type of neighborhood. In a more integrated community, the variables of community integration (community attachment and organizational participation) have a stronger effect on both formal and informal social control than in a less integrated community. This suggests the need for scholars to investigate more fully the context-specific effect of community integration on social control that may underlie these two Western theories.

Second, informal social control is crucial for the success of the overall social control scheme in an urban community context. As our data suggest, residents tend to perceive informal social control much more effective than formal social control, regardless of the type of neighborhood. According to Western literature, formal and informal social control tend to have an inverse relationship. Specifically, when formal social control increases, informal social control is expected to decrease. This dynamic relationship, however, does not appear to be the case in China (Troyer et al., 1989). Informal social control continues to assume its traditional roles in local arenas, such as mediation, order maintenance, and welfare services (Dutton, 1992), despite the legalization, professionalization, and formalization movement in policing and the criminal justice system in China.

Third, community integration is of primary importance for successful social control both at the formal and the informal level. Our data suggest that with urbanization and modernization, China's urban neighborhoods became less integrated. As found in New Shanghai, the reduced interactions among neighbors and participation in community affairs have jeopardized the effectiveness of both formal and informal social control. The implication for Chinese policy makers is that there should be a priority for the police and residence committee members to rebuild the sense of community by encouraging interactions among neighbors and mobilizing residents to participate in community affairs.

The policing history of some Western countries (e.g., the United States and England) teaches us about the importance of a partnership between a professional police force and involved citizens. The current community policing movement in the West demonstrates that regardless of how well equipped and trained they are, without the cooperation and active involvement of citizens, the police cannot be effective (Greene and Mastrofski, 1988). China has had a long history of community policing that relied on close-knit neighborhoods and volunteers who served as eyes and ears for the police. In the era of police professionalization and modernization in China, we should not forget a basic ingredient of effective social control—community integration.

REFERENCES

Adler, Freda. 1983. *Nations Not Obsessed with Crime.* Littleton, CO: F. B. Rothman.

Brady, James. 1982. *Justice and Politics in People's China.* London: Academic Press.

Bursik, Robert J. 1984. "Urban Dynamics and Ecological Studies of Delinquency." *Social Forces* 63: 393–431.

———. 1988. "Social Disorganization and Theories of Crime and Delinquency: Problems and Prospects." *Criminology* 26: 519–551.

Cao, Liqun et al. 1996. "Race, Community Context and Confidence in the Police." *American Journal of Police* 9, no. 1: 3–22

Chan, Celia L. 1993. *The Myth of Neighborhood Help: the Contemporary Chinese Community-Based Welfare System in Guangzhou.* Hong Kong: Hong Kong University Press.

Chen, Wenzhang. 1997. "An Investigation of the Current State of Social Security in Changzhou." *Chang an* 43: 15–16.

Chen, Yulong. 1993. "Analyses of Migrant Laborers." *City Reform and Development* 2: 43–45.

Clinard, Marshall B., and Daniel J. Abbott. 1973. *Crime in Developing Countries.* New York: Wiley.

Cohen, Lawrence E., and Marcus Felson. 1979. "Social Change and Crime Rate Trends: A Routine Activity Approach." *American Sociological Review* 44: 588–608.

Conklin, John E. 1975. *The Impact of Crime*. New York: Macmillan.

Convinton, Jeanette, and Ralph B. Taylor. 1991. "Fear of Crime in Urban Residential Neighborhoods: Implications of Between- and Within-Neighborhood Sources for Current Models." *Sociological Quarterly* 32: 231–249.

Crutchfield, Robert D., Michael R. Geerker, and Walter R. Gove. 1982. "Crime Rate and Social Integration: The Impact of Metropolitan Mobility." *Criminology* 20: 467–478.

Dai, Yisheng. 1993. "A Survey of 'Sense of Public Security'." *Criminal Justice International* 9: 6–9.

Ding, Shuimu. 1994. "A Public Opinions Survey in Shanghai and the Coping Strategies in the Transitional Era." *Sociological Studies* 3: 19–25.

Dutton, Michael. 1992. *Policing and Punishment in China: From Patriarchy to the "People."* Cambridge: Cambridge University Press.

Dutton, Michael, and Tianfu Lee. 1993. "Missing the Target? Policing Strategies in the Period of Economic Reform." *Crime and Delinquency* 39, no. 3 316–336.

Fenwick, Charles R. 1987. "Crime in Post-Mao China." *International Journal of Comparative and Applied Criminal Justice* 9, no. 1 (Spring): 67–81.

Findlay, Mark, and Ugliesa Zvekic, eds. 1988. *Informal Mechanisms of Crime Control: A Cross-Cultural Perspective*. Rome: United Nations Social Defense Research Institute.

Fu, Hualin. 1990. "Police Reform and Its Implication for Chinese Social Control." *International Journal of Comparative and Applied Criminal Justice* 14, no. 1/2: 41–48.

Garofalo, James, and Maureen McLeod. 1986. "Improving the Effectiveness and Utilization of Neighborhood Watch Programs." Unpublished report to the National Institute of Justice from the Hindelang Criminal Justice Research Center, State University of New York at Albany.

———. 1988. "Improving the Use and Effectiveness of Neighborhood Watch Programs." In *Research in Action*. Washington, DC: National Institute of Justice, U.S. Department of Justice.

Gold, Thomas B. 1985. "After Comradeship: Personal Relations in China Since the Cultural Revolution." *China Quarterly* 104: 657–675.

Greenberg, Stephanie W., et al. 1982. *Safe and Secure Neighborhoods: Physical Characteristics and Informal Territorial Control in High and Low Crime Neighborhoods*. Washington, DC: National Institute of Justice, U.S. Department of Justice.

Greenberg, Stephanie W., and William M. Rohe. 1986. "Informal Social Control and Crime Prevention in Modern Urban Neighborhoods." In *Urban Neighborhoods: Research and Policy*, pp. 79–118. Edited by Richard B. Taylor. New York: Praeger.

Greene, Jack R., and Steven D. Mastrofski. 1988. *Community Policing: Rhetoric or Reality*. New York: Praeger.

Henig, Jeffrey R. 1978. "Copping a Cop: Neighborhood Organizations and Police Patrol Allocation." *Journal of Voluntary Action Research* 7: 75–84.

———. 1982. *Neighborhood Mobilization*. New Brunswick, NJ: Rutgers University Press.

Hope, Tim, and Mary A. Shaw. 1988. *Communities and Crime Reduction.* London: Her Majesty's Stationery Office.

Jesilow, Paul, et al. 1995. "Public Attitudes Toward the Police." *American Journal of Police* 14: 67–88.

Lavrakas, Paul J., and Lisa Herz. 1982. "Citizen Participation in Neighborhood Crime Prevention." *Criminology* 20: 479–498.

Law Yearbook of China. 1986–1997. Beijing: Law Publishing House.

Leng, Shaochuan, and Hungdah Chiu. 1985. *Criminal Justice in Post-Mao China.* Albany: State University of New York Press.

Lewis, Dan A., and Greta Salem. 1986. *Fear of Crime: Incivility and the Production of a Social Problem.* New Brunswick, NJ: Transaction.

Li, Victor. 1978. *Law Without Lawyers: A Comparative View of Law in China and the United States.* Boulder, CO: Westview Press.

Lu Hong. 1998. "Community Policing—Rhetoric or Reality: The Contemporary Chinese Community-Based Policing System in Shanghai." Ph.D. Dissertation, Arizona State University.

Pellow, Deborah. 1993. "No Place to Live, No Place to Love: Coping in Shanghai." In *Urban Anthropology in China.* Edited by G. Guldin and A. Southall. Leiden: R. J. Brill.

Podolefsky, Aaron, and Fred Dubow. 1981. *Strategies for Community Crime Prevention.* Springfield, IL: Charles C. Thomas.

Potter, Pitman B. 1994. "Riding the Tiger: Legitimacy and Legal Culture in Post-Mao China." *The China Quarterly* 138: 325–358.

Rosenbaum, Dennis P. 1987. "The Theory and Research Behind Neighborhood Watch: Is It a Sound Fear and Crime Reduction Strategy?" *Crime and Delinquency* 33: 103–134.

——— . 1988. "Community Crime Prevention: A Review and Synthesis of the Literature." *Justice Quarterly* 5: 323–395.

——— , (ed.) 1986. *Community Crime Prevention: Does It Work?* Beverly Hills, CA: Sage.

Sampson, Robert, and W. Bryon Groves. 1989. "Community Structure and Crime: Testing Social-Disorganization Theory." *American Journal of Sociology* 94: 774–802.

Schneider, Ann L. 1986. "Neighborhood-Based Antiburglary Strategies: An Analysis of Public and Private Benefits from the Portland Program." In *Community Crime Prevention: Does it Work?*, pp. 68–86. Edited by D. Rosenbaum. Beverly Hills, CA: Sage.

Shaw, Clifford R., and Henry D. McKay. 1942. *Juvenile Delinquency and Urban Areas.* Chicago: University of Chicago Press.

Shelley, Louise I. 1981. *Crime and Modernization: The Impact of Industrialization and Urbanization on Crime.* Carbondale: Southern Illinois University Press.

Shi, Hong. 1996. "Characteristics, Reasons, and Countermeasures of Bicycle Theft." *Beijing Police Academy Gazette* 4: 29–32.

Skogan, Wesley. 1987. "Disorder and Community Decline." Grant report, Center for Urban Affairs and Policy Research, Northwestern University.

Skogan, Wesley, and Michael G. Maxfield. 1981. *Coping with Crime: Individual and Neighborhood Reactions.* Beverly Hills, CA: Sage.

Troyer, Ronald J., John P. Clark, and Dean G. Rojek, eds. 1989. *Social Control in the People's Republic of China.* New York: Praeger.

Webb, Vincent J., and Chris E. Marshall. 1995. "The Relative Importance of Race and Ethnicity on Citizen Attitudes Toward the Police." *American Journal of Police* 14: 45–66.

Whitaker, Catherine J. 1986. "Crime Prevention Measures." In *Bureau of Justice Statistics Special Report.* Washington, DC: Bureau of Justice Statistics, U.S. Department of Justice.

Whyte, Martin K., and W. L. Parish. 1984. *Urban Life in Contemporary China.* Chicago: University of Chicago Press.

Wilson, James Q., and George L. Kelling. 1983. "Broken Windows." *Atlantic Monthly* (March): 29–38.

Wu, Henry H. D. 1992. *Laogai: The Chinese Gulag.* Boulder, CO: Westview Press.

Xiang, Weimin. 1994. "Characteristics and Management of Shanghai's Temporary Population." *Social Sciences* 8: 59–66.

Zhang, Lening et al. 1996. Crime Prevention in a Communitarian Society: *Bang-Jiao* and *Tiao-Jie* in the People's Republic of China." *Justice Quarterly* 13: 199–222.

Zhang, Lening, and Steven Messner. 1995. "Family Deviance and Delinquency in China." *Criminology* 33: 359–387.

CHAPTER 9

Crime and Crime Control in a Changing China

Shuliang Feng

China has achieved world-renowned social and economic development since it initiated the economic reform and "open door" policy in 1978. However, along with the rapid change, the country is facing new problems. One of these problems is the rapidly rising crime rate. China has developed strategies and measures to combat the crime waves. The present study describes crime problems and discusses the strategies and measures adopted by the Chinese government for fighting crime.

CRIME IN A CHANGING CHINA

China had very low rates of crime and was a virtually crime-free society in the past. However, since the economic reform and open door policy were implemented, China has begun to experience rising crime rates. Table 9.1 shows the recorded criminal cases from 1979 to 1988.

The table shows a significant increase in recorded criminal cases from 63.6 per 10,000 in 1979 to 198.6 per 10,000 in 1998. The number of criminal cases dropped between 1982 and 1987. The decrease was thought to be the result of the nationwide crackdown on crime launched in 1983. In 1988, criminal cases began to rise again. The number of recorded criminal cases reached 2,000,000 or more annually during the period 1989–1991. The rising crime rates may be explained in different ways. One is that there was a real increase in the number of criminal cases, and the other is that it was the result of the official effort to correct inaccurate recording of criminal cases. The Ministry of Public Security launched a research project on the police practice of crime recording from 1985 to 1990. The study

Table 9.1
Recorded Criminal Cases, 1979–1998

Year	Recorded Criminal Cases (Unit = 10,000)
1979	63.6
1980	75.7
1981	89
1982	74.8
1983	61
1984	51.4
1985	54.2
1986	54.7
1987	57
1988	82.7
1989	197.1
1990	221.6
1991	236.5
1992	158.2
1993	161.6
1994	166
1995	169
1996	160
1997	161.3
1998	198.6

Note: It is necessary to note the changes in the methods of recording criminal cases. For example, the changes of the norms for some types of criminal cases are bound to affect the statistics (the bottom line set at 25 yuan for a theft case in rural China and 80 yuan in the cities before 1991, whereas after 1991, the floor for theft rose to 300 yuan in the countryside and 600 yuan in the cities).
Source: *China Legal Yearbook*, 1980–1989.

found that almost one-third of the criminal cases had not been reported or recorded. With the concerted efforts of investigators from the Public Security Ministry, the study served to correct the underrecording of criminal cases.

The crime rates are only one indicator of the crime problem. Other important indicators are the consequences of crime and crime types of different seriousness. The adverse consequences of crime have intensified, which can be measured by the rise of police casualties.

Police casualties have increased significantly due to the rise of criminal cases. More than 1,000 policemen were killed between 1979 and 1989. The figure rose to 3,589 from 1990 to 1998. During these twenty years, more than 100,000 policemen were wounded. Table 9.2 records police casualties since 1949.

Table 9.2
Chinese Policemen Killed and Wounded on Duty Since 1949

Year	Wounded	Killed
1949–1980	N.A.	1026
1981	639	70
1982	574	66
1983	875	87
1984	703	83
1985	519	103
1986	1037	144
1987	2197	168
1988	5691	203
1989	8294	254
1990	7193	304
1991	9106	308
1992	7153	300
1993	8851	359
1994	9759	379
1995	9677	460
1996	11681	515
1997	8142	522
1998	8177	442
Total	100268	5793

Source: Legal Journal, February 13, 1999.

The increase in violent crimes has posed a great threat to the public security. According to classified statistics of criminal cases compiled by the public security departments, there has been a dramatic increase in homicide, aggravated assault, robbery, kidnapping, and other violent crimes. A comparison between 1997 and 1998 shows that the number of aggravated assaults rose by 17 percent and robberies by 23.74 percent (see table 9.3).

Gang crime has become a major type of criminal activity among young people. The number of gang-related crimes rose from about 30,000 in 1986 to more than 200,000 in 1994. In the east coastal regions, 70–80 percent of serious criminal cases have been attributed to gangs. About 70 percent of juvenile offenses are gang-related. In China, gang-related crimes usually develop from a single criminal activity to multiple crimes and from misdemeanors to serious crimes. Gangs tend to develop with more and more people involved.

Juvenile delinquency constitutes a large proportion of crimes. It was 10–20 percent of total crimes in the 1950s, 30 percent in the 1960s, and 50–60 percent during and after the 1970s. Drug abuse is spreading among young people. A survey

Table 9.3
Classified Criminal Cases, 1997 and 1998

Types of Criminal Cases	Criminal Cases in 1997	Percentage of the Total	Criminal Cases in 1998	Percent of Total	Increase or decrease of 1998 over 1997
Total	1613629	100.00	1986068	100.00	23.08
Killings	26070	1.62	27670	1.39	6.14
Assault	69071	4.28	80862	4.07	17.07
Robbery	141514	8.77	175116	8.82	23.74
Rape	40699	2.52	40967	2.06	0.66
Kidnapping	6425	0.40	6513	0.33	1.37
Burglary	1058110	65.57	1296988	65.30	22.58
Serious cases	448917	N.A.	N.A.	N.A.	34.40
Bike theft	56607	N.A.	N.A.	N.A.	3.60
Swindling	78284	4.85	83080	4.18	6.13
Smuggling	1133	0.07	2301	0.12	103.09
Counterfeiting currency	5422	0.34	6654	0.34	22.72
Others	186901	11.58	265917	13.39	42.28

Source: *Public Security Studies* 3(1998) and (1999).

shows that by the end of 1997, the number of registered drug addicts reached 540,000 in China; 85.1 percent were under the age of thirty-five (*Guangming Daily*, May 30, 1998). In response to the rising delinquency, the Standing Committee of the National People's Congress passed the Law of Preventing Juvenile Delinquency in June 1999, which was China's first law on crime prevention (see chapter 13 in this volume).

Crimes committed by the migrant population have become a major concern for social stability (see chapter 5 in this volume). It is estimated that China's migrant population is 80 million, coming mainly from rural to urban areas. Though contributing to the country's urban prosperity, the migrant population is becoming a major source of crime due to the difficulty of social control. Table 9.4 shows the proportion of the total crimes committed by the migrant population in several major cities of China.

CHINA'S STRATEGY IN CRIME CONTROL

It is necessary to describe how the Chinese view crime problems in order to understand China's strategy of crime control. Chinese criminologists generally hold that crime has multiple causes at the social level. Crime control and prevention therefore call for a comprehensive and systematic strategy. The basic principle of a

Table 9.4
Proportion of Crimes Committed by the Migrant Population in Selected Chinese Cities, 1994

City	Proportion of Crimes Committed Migrant Population	City	Proportion of Crimes Committed by Migrant Population
Beijing	46.2%	Shenzhen	97%
Shanghai	53.6%	Dongguan	85.4%
Tianjin	30%	Hangzhou	50%
Guangzhou	69.2–70%	Wenzhou	48.6%
Ningbo	41.2%	Guiyang	30%
Xi'an	53%	Jinan	28%
Chongqing	53.9%	Harbin	19.6%
Urumqi	43.2%	Nanjing	47%

Source: Feng 1995.

comprehensive and systematic strategy is the integration of punishment and prevention with an emphasis on the latter. Prevention focuses on the grassroots levels of both the cities and the countryside to nip crime in the bud. The ultimate goal of crime prevention is to guard social stability in order to ensure the development of economic reform.

A comprehensive strategy basically means a concerted effort of various social sectors to prevent and control crimes under the unified leadership of the Chinese Communist Party and the government through political, economic, administrative, legal, cultural, and educational means (Zhang, 1995, pp. 27–28). Essentially, the strategy assigns priority to crime prevention rather than punishment. It has developed through three stages.

Exploration and preparation were the first stage (1979–1981). The strategy was initiated by the Central Committee of the Chinese Communist Party (CPC) on August 17, 1978. It was endorsed in the Report on Calling for Attention to Juvenile Delinquency proposed jointly by the Propaganda Department of the CPC Central Committee, the Ministry of Education, the Ministry of Culture, the Ministry of Public Security, the State Labor Administration, the China Federation of Trade Unions, the Central Committee of the Chinese Communist Youth League, and the China Women's Federation. The report holds that it is necessary to call for a concerted effort of various social sectors to resolve the problem of juvenile delinquency. A joint conference on public security was held in Beijing, Tianjin, Shanghai, Guangzhou, and Wuhan in June 1981. The conference further confirmed that it was necessary to develop a comprehensive and systematic strategy for a fundamental improvement of the country's public security. A circular of the CPC Central Committee in January 1982 emphasized the importance of establishing a responsibility system to assign tasks of public security to various departments and institutions.

The second stage was characterized by diverse experiments of the strategy during 1982–1990. At this stage, experiments were conducted and experience was gained. Implementation of the strategy was standardized, and ideological, political, economic, administrative, and legal measures for the strategy were formulated and defined. Some official committees and unofficial organizations were formed to implement the strategy at various levels.

The third stage started in 1991 and continues today. The strategy has spread nationwide. The starting point of this stage was the national conference on the comprehensive control of social order held in Yantai, Shandong province, in 1991. The CPC Central Committee, the State Council, and the NPC Standing Committee issued Resolutions on Strengthening the Comprehensive Control of Social Order in February and March 1991. These resolutions provide a policy and legal basis for the comprehensive control of social order. The fourteenth Convention of the Chinese Communist Party, held in October 1992, included the theme "strengthening the comprehensive control of social order to maintain social stability" in the Communist Party Constitution. Afterward, resolutions and regulations were formulated to strengthen the responsibility system for public education regarding laws and offenders' rehabilitation.

The main problem in the comprehensive control of social order lies in the incomplete implementation in some sectors and at grassroots levels due to the lack of powerful organizations. Another problem is insufficient funds for the implementation of the strategy. But Chinese experience has proved that a comprehensive control of social order is a fundamental way to solve the problem of public security (Xu, 1996, pp. 11–19).

The basic content of China's comprehensive control of social order may be summarized as crime crackdown and prevention. The term "crackdown" means swiftly and severely eliminating criminals and criminal activities in various phases from crime investigation to imprisonment. "Prevention" implies adopting measures aimed at preventing and reducing crimes. With respect to the relationship between crackdown and prevention, the emphasis is placed on prevention. This principle was clearly stated in a resolution adopted at the fifteenth Congress of the Chinese Communist Party (1997). Previously, although the idea of prevention was mentioned, crackdown was considered the most effective way of dealing with the problem of crime. The shift of emphasis from crackdown to prevention has been viewed as a turning point in implementing the comprehensive control of social order (Feng, 1998).

China's experience has proved that it is necessary to rely on social forces to combat crime in a systematic way. Preventive measures should form a network in all areas, ranging from a community to a city to a county. Crime prevention is a system consisting of interrelated social forces. The basic structure of such a system includes prevention by the mass movement, by professionals, and by technical measures. The targets of prevention are the general population, major types of crimes, and special populations at high crime risk. Prevention should be implemented in social institutions and organizations such as family, schools, community, and work units (Feng, 1994, p. 152).

The comprehensive control of social order represents China's approach to the war against crime. It has a unique ideological and philosophical background. The essence of the strategy lies in mobilizing all possible social forces to fight crime, which continues Mao's Mass Line. In combating all sorts of crimes, China has followed the fundamental principle of combining the Mass Line with the specialized departments.

After China initiated the policy of reform and the open door, Deng Xiaoping put forth a strategic policy metaphorically called "Grasping by both hands"—a balance between material civilization and spiritual civilization. Spiritual civilization here means developing and changing nonmaterial elements of culture so that they would match material civilization. This idea serves as a powerful ideological and philosophical basis of the comprehensive control of social order. The strategy is part of the national plan of social and economic development (Deng, 1993).

For the Chinese, it is important to deal successfully with the relationships among economic reform, socioeconomic development, and social stability. Social and economic development is the goal of the nation, economic reform is a major approach to achieving development, and social stability is the prerequisite for the development. Crime prevention is essential to ensure a stable social setting for reform and development. China's crime prevention strategy is vital to social stability (Deng, 1993, p. 284).

CONCLUSION AND DISCUSSION

China is engaging in social and economic reform in pursuit of modernization. One unanticipated consequence of the reform is increasing crime rates. Although the increasing crime rates are still lower than those in some developed countries, they have become a public concern in China. The initial reaction of the Chinese government to the rising crime rates and public concern was to crack down on crime through mass campaigns and severe punishment. Later, the Chinese adopted a comprehensive and systematic strategy of crime control by combining crime crackdown with an emphasis on prevention. The purpose of this strategy is to mobilize various social forces, organizations, and institutions to be involved in a social war against crime.

A prime basis of the strategy is still Mao's Mass Line. Crime control is not only the business of the criminal justice system, but also a matter of mass participation. To mobilize mass participation, social organizations and institutions are called and assigned certain responsibility for crime prevention and control through the unified leadership of the Communist Party. The strategy can be viewed as a continuation of the Chinese tradition of informal control of crime and deviance.

However, it is not simply continuation of the Chinese tradition. The Chinese began to be aware of the power of formal control by law since the "open door" policy was carried out. The strategy does not overlook the role of the criminal justice system in crime control and prevention. The Chinese still adhere to the deterrence philosophy. Various laws and regulations have been passed and revised in order to hand over legal power to the criminal justice system and the public. When the government sees fit, a crackdown campaign against crime may be launched.

REFERENCES

Deng Xiaoping. 1993. *Deng Xiaoping's Selected Works*. Beijing: People's Publishing House.

Feng, Shuliang. 1994. *China's Strategy of Crime Prevention*. Beijing: Legal Publishing House.

———. 1995. "A Public Security Strategy with Stability as the Central Task." *Journal of Studies of Crime and Reformation* no. 11: 10–15.

———. 1998. "The Five Characteristics of the Strategy of 'Combining Prevention with Striking, with Emphasis on Prevention.' " *Public Security Studies* no. 4: 13–18.

Guangming Daily. Unattributed news report. 1998. May 30.

Legal Journal. 1999. News report quoting statistics released by the Ministry of Public Security. February 13.

Ministry of Public Security. 1998. "Statistics from the Ministry of Public Security." *Public Security Studies* no. 3: 2.

———. 1999. "Statistics from the Ministry of Public Security." *Public Security Studies* no. 3: 2.

Press of Law Yearbook of China. 1987–1998. *Law Yearbook of China*. Beijing: Press of Law Yearbook of China.

Xu, Weihua. 1996. *An Initial Study on the Comprehensive Control of Social Order*. Beijing: People's Court Publishing House.

Zhang, Shuyuan. 1995. *600 Queries on Comprehensive Control of Social Security*. Beijing: Patent Publications Press.

PART IV

Social Transition and the Changing Criminal Justice System

CHAPTER 10

Mixing Inquisitorial and Adversarial Models: Changes in Criminal Procedure in a Changing China

Peter Liu and Yingyi Situ

The People's Republic of China (PRC) has adopted an open-door policy and experienced tremendous changes since the end of the 1970s. One of these remarkable changes is found in its justice system. In 1979, the National People's Congress enacted the PRC's first criminal law and the Criminal Procedure Law, which placed the criminal justice system on a legal footing for the first time in the regime's thirty years. Since then, a number of significant laws have been adopted. The Organic Law of the People's Courts (1980) and the Organic Law of People's Procuratorates (1980) legalized a court hierarchy and a system of prosecution. The Organic Law of the Local People's Congresses and Local People's Governments (1980) applied the principle of dual leadership. In 1997, the 1979 Criminal Procedure Law was revised (Wang and Zhang, 1997). Though all of this legislation indicates the important development of China's justice system, this article focuses on the revised Criminal Procedure Law. Special attention is directed to its impacts on the criminal trial, the rationales underlying the changes, and the analysis of such changes.

This study was conducted by combining the methods of secondary source analysis, interview, and field observation. On the one hand, the researchers systematically reviewed the Chinese literature with regard to the nature of the revised Criminal Procedure Law and its practices reported in a Chinese legal professional newspaper, *Legal Daily*. These studies provide a comprehensive view of the important transition in Chinese criminal procedure. On the other hand, one of the researchers traveled to China during the summer of 1997 to conduct field observations in courtrooms and to interview legal personnel concerned, such as judges, procurators, and defense attorneys. The data collected during this trip verified the changes brought about by the revised Criminal Procedure Law and helped the researcher better understand the social, cultural and political contexts in which the changes in the Chinese criminal procedure occurred.

THE INQUISITORIAL SYSTEM AND TRADITIONAL LEGAL CULTURE IN CHINA

The inquisitorial system originated in a continental European tradition, represented by civil law countries such as France and Germany. Historically, the term *inquisitorial* refers to the use of torture to compel cooperation in Catholic countries during the Middle Age. In modern times, the inquisitorial system represents one type of criminal procedure that underlines the importance of extensive pretrial investigation and interrogations in order to ensure that no innocent person is brought to trial (Fairchild, 1993, p. 125). Those who actually are brought to trial are believed most likely to be guilty. Furthermore, this procedure focuses on the dominant role of the judge during pretrial investigation and trial. During a pretrial investigation, the trial judge examines all evidence to determine probable cause and whether a trial is needed. During the trial, the presiding judge questions the defendant and witnesses, presents and investigates evidence, and gets involved in debates between the prosecution and the defense regarding the proceedings and punishment.

The inquisitorial system has often been compared with the adversarial system, the popular type of criminal procedure in Anglo-American countries. As opposed to the inquisitorial system, the adversarial system emphasizes the trial rather than the pretrial investigation. Because the information from investigation is not considered until presented in court, the search for truth begins at the trial stage. The accused is protected from interrogation and illegal search. And he is treated as innocent until proven guilty. The adversarial system grants equal status to the prosecution and the defense. Both are active in court: questioning witnesses, examining evidence, and debating with the opposite side—leading the court proceeding. The judge acts as an umpire, making sure all parties play by the rules and being relatively passive in the proceedings.

The contrasting features of the inquisitorial and adversarial systems are determined by their different fundamental premises. Whereas the adversarial system stresses protection of social equality or individual rights and controlling of the state's power, the inquisitorial system focuses on maintaining social order and punishing criminals. Thus, it is not surprising that under the inquisitorial system, little attention is given to the manner in which the criminal law is enforced; little protection from the justice system is enjoyed by the accused; and abuse of power by investigative judges is observable. As a result, the fairness of trials is often challenged.

China adopted an inquisitorial justice system when its first codified Criminal Procedure Law was enacted in 1979 (Davidson and Wang, 1996). It reflected

China's traditional legal culture. China is one of the oldest civilizations on earth with more than 4,000 years of written history. Its cultural traditions have had a profound impact on Chinese legal philosophy as well as its legal system (Bodde and Morris, 1967; Du and Zhang, 1990; Spence, 1981). In imperial China, the emperor was considered "the Son of Heaven," with unlimited power to determine all subject matters and with ultimate control over his people. He was not bound by any law. Instead, his words were considered laws, and he enjoyed the privilege of being above the law. Under this totalitarian system, the justice system was designed to assert the authority and power of the emperor by punishing people who violated the order of the state. Law was clearly lacking in prominence compared with the place of law in Western history. All district magistrates were appointed and promoted by the emperor himself. This made them all aware of their dependence upon the emperor and their duty of personal loyalty to him. Moreover, the concept of separate powers was absent. Magistrates were also the heads of the local government and had the responsibility of dispensing justice. They did this in their capacity as police chief, prosecutor, and judge.

This emperor-dominated legal tradition has been transferred into the Communist Party–controlled legal system since 1949, when the Communists came to the center of Chinese politics. Under a system of proletarian dictatorship and collectivism, individuals became "bolts and nuts" in the machine of the socialist state, having no rights to choose their personal lifestyle. Individuals' interests were always inferior to the state's and group's. When facing criminal charges, individuals were generally deprived of their rights of defense because the defendant was usually treated as a people's enemy—and therefore an object of the proletarian dictatorship. Equality before the law was never recognized as a critical legal principle. A separate legal profession was recognized, but court, procuratorate, and public security were all considered state organs, whereas the defendant was considered a "bad element" in society. The rule of Communist Party rather than the rule of law directed and controlled the justice system.

When the Communist Party established the People's Republic of China in 1949, China followed the Soviet Union in developing its socialist legal system (Fairbank, 1992; Leng, 1967). Although the Soviet model was greatly influenced by the inquisitorial system, it was unique in terms of its revolutionary nature and Marxist political doctrine. The functions of law were to preserve the security of the nation in a hostile world; to facilitate the economic development of the country along socialist lines; and to educate its citizens about Marxist thought. Obviously, such roles of law were substantially different from the roles of law in the Western world. Moreover, the Communist Party dominated the socialist legal system. Party-made law and the party's intervention in judges' decisions were acceptable. Mao Zedong, the late leader of the party (1949–1976), adopted the Soviet model and modified it according to the realities of the Chinese political and cultural environment. One of his emphases was upon the informal model over the formal model. As a result, he abolished or ignored law, and used party policy rather than law in regulating Chinese society and the Chinese legal system. Thus, after Mao's death, while the new Chinese leaders initiated a program to modernize China's agriculture, industry, science, and technology, legal reform to establish a more formal justice system was also placed on their agenda (Lo, 1995).

In addition to expressing the inquisitorial system, China's 1979 Criminal Procedure Law (CPL) was also designated to be a tool of class struggle and to protect the socialist state. The Communist ideology—Marxism, Leninism, and Mao Zedong's *Thoughts*—guides the process (CPL, art. 1). It also strikes the enemies of the Communist Party and the state, and protects the working classes (CPL, art. 1; see Yu, 1994). These political features of the 1979 Criminal Procedure Law further aggravated the weakness of the Chinese inquisitorial criminal procedure and led to some very problematic legal practices in China. First, the accused was often viewed as an enemy of society and the object of punishment. Therefore, many defendant's rights, such as the early involvement of a defense attorney, did not exist. On the other hand, those who were loyal to the party very often were exempted from the legal procedure and their law-violating behavior was dealt with within the party system. This practice seriously violates the legal principle of equality before the law. Second, the judge not only was responsible for reviewing the documents necessary for the opening of a trial, but was actually involved in the substantive fact-finding process. This all but resulted in the judge's determination on a given case prior to the trial. Third, during the trial, the judge usually was on the same side as the procurator, who often did not even appear in court to present evidence. The responsibility of presenting evidence and questioning the defendant and witnesses lay with the judge. This practice raised serious doubt as to the fairness of the trial. Fourth, because the presumption of innocence is foreign to the Chinese criminal justice system, the defendant was often considered guilty even if there was insufficient evidence to prove guilt. Fifth, although the presiding judge and the people's assessors could give their opinions, they often did not have the authority to decide the verdict, which usually had to be reviewed and approved by the chief judge, or higher court. And sixth, the victim was not considered a party (*dangshiren*) to criminal procedure, so his/her rights were not ensured. In summary, under the 1979 Criminal Procedure Law, many important legal principles, such as separation of judges and lawyers, independence of the judge, and equality before the law were not in place. As a result, the legal system did not guarantee the justice, fairness, and equality that are fundamental in a democratic society.

A MIXED MODEL: REFORM OF CHINESE CRIMINAL PROCEDURE

Since the 1980s, the primary goal of China has been transferred from class struggle to modernization (Benewick and Wingrove, 1995; Soled, 1995). The socialist state-run economy has given way to a capitalist market economy, which demands a more pragmatic, objective, and fair legal procedure. The open door policy also requires an open and fair legal system, including both civil and criminal procedures, in order to be able to handle legal disputes involving foreigners in an internationally accepted manner. Clearly, the consequences of economic reform and the open door policy made it necessary to reform the Chinese criminal procedure in the 1990s (Lubman, 1996).

To solve the problem of injustice associated with traditional practices and to improve the rights of the defendant and the victim, the Fourth Plenary Conference of the Eighth National People's Congress made major revisions to the 1979 Criminal Procedure Law on March 17, 1996. The revised version of the Criminal Procedure Law seems to have changed it from the inquisitorial tradition to a mixed model having characteristics of both inquisitorial and adversarial systems.

The changes can be found in the trial function, trial organization, trial process, and judicial personnel. For our purposes, the main concern is whether the Chinese inquisitorial process has been completely abandoned, partially modified, or remained the same. To answer this question, our examination focuses on the roles of judge, procurator, defendant and defense attorney, and victim in the criminal trial.

The Judge

Before the Criminal Procedure Law was revised, there were several problems that affected the fairness of the judge in a trial (Liu, 1994; Lu, 1994; Tang and Jie, 1994; Zhang and Luo, 1994; Pan, 1994; Suo and Han, 1997).

First, the pretrial investigation conducted by the judges was both procedural review and substantive examination. Though the procedural review is necessary for judges to decide if a case is ready for trial, the substantive examination is more problematic. Under the 1979 Criminal Procedure Law, the judge, after receiving a case from the procuratorate, had to determine that the facts of the case were "clear" and the evidence was "ample" (art. 108). During such substantive examination, the judge actually reached the guilty verdict and decided the sentence. Thus it was not surprising that 99.65 percent of the people tried for criminal offenses in the Chinese courts in 1995 were found guilty. The judge's substantive examination before trial had rendered criminal trials in China an empty formality.

Second, lower court judges often asked for instructions from higher courts when they were presiding over difficult or important cases. This practice impeded the two-level appellate system because the higher court, according to the Criminal Procedure Law, was a court of second instance that should not interfere with the trial of first instance. However, in reality, the higher courts viewed themselves as supervisory organs of the lower courts, and thus often gave instructions to the lower courts upon reviewing files, or even substituted their own verdicts. The jurisdiction of lower courts was inevitably interfered with.

Third, after the trial, the trial judge had to submit his opinion to the chief judge, or president of the court, or adjudication committee appointed by the president of the court. The latter reviewed the trial judge's report and gave the final decision on the trial. This practice caused disconnection between trial and determination of guilt and punishment, because those who tried the cases did not make the decisions and those who made the decisions did not try the cases. As a result, the ideas of legality and justice were seriously violated. For difficult or important cases, instructions might be sought from the committee before the parties even received notice of the trial. This practice, which was expressed as "decision first, trial later," has been criticized as a violation of "the principle of differentiation of function and, as a practical matter, burdened the courts with the cost of carrying out extensive pre-trial investigations" (Lawyers Committee for Human Rights, 1996, pp. 52, 53).

Fourth, in the past, the trial relied heavily on the defendant's confession and placed less emphasis on the witnesses. During the trial, the judge focused on interrogating the defendant. Witnesses usually did not appear before the court, but submitted written testimony. When they were physically present in court, they were rarely questioned or challenged by the defense.

Finally, after reviewing the evidence at the stage of pretrial investigation, for the cases with insufficient evidence, judges did not proceed with a trial or dismiss them, but returned them to the procuratorate for further investigation. Because the understanding of the degree of sufficient evidence was often different between the court and the procuratorate, they usually got into arguments over issues of sufficiency, which resulted in low efficiency. The defendant could be imprisoned for years without going to a trial.

The revised Criminal Procedure Law greatly alleviated the problems listed above. The substantial fact examination by the judge prior to trial has been eliminated. Under the 1997 Criminal Procedure Law, article 150, and the Supreme People's Court's Interpretation About Questions in Implementing the Criminal Procedure Law of the People's Republic of China (hereafter Supreme Court's Interpretation), article 117, now the trial judge(s) only needs to conduct a procedural review prior to trial. The requirement for examining the substance of the case is eliminated. Specifically, if the court determines that the indictment presents the facts of the crime charged and is accompanied by a list of the evidence and the witnesses and photocopies of the major evidence, then it should commence the trial. Thus, the truth-finding has switched from pretrial proceedings to the courtroom. The court must reach its conclusion based upon the evidence presented in the trial and the arguments made by the prosecution and the defense. The pretrial determination of guilt is effectively avoided.

Also, under the Criminal Procedure Law articles 149 and 162, and the Supreme Court's Interpretation, article 177, the trial judge(s) has the authority to determine the verdict and sentence by majority rule, except for the most difficult or important cases, which are decided by the adjudication committee. This, to a certain extent, reinforces the independent authority of the presiding judges. It is an important step in developing a necessary mechanism in a checks-and-balances political framework. However, it is important to point out that the use of the word "independent" should not be equated with a form of separation of powers. Article 3 of the Constitution of the People's Republic of China clearly states: "All administrative, judicial, and procuratorial organs of the state are created by the people's congresses, to which they are responsible and under whose supervision they operate." To maintain political control over the courts and judges, adjudication committees are given the authority not only to handle particularly difficult cases, but also to override the decision of a judge and direct the judge to decide a case in a particular manner.

Moreover, the judge's role as an inquirer in the trial has been partially changed. According to the Criminal Procedure Law, articles 155–160, and the Supreme Court's Interpretation, articles 134–141, questioning witnesses and presenting evidence are done mainly by the procurator, the defense attorney, and the victim's attorney. The trial judge(s) may question the defendant and witnesses, provide the court with evidence, and interrupt the trial to investigate when it is deemed necessary. This practice has transferred the inquisitorial type of trial, which focuses on the judge's role in the courtroom, to a semiadversarial one in which the judge(s) determines the case based upon the facts revealed in the contest between the prosecution and the defense.

With regard to the judge's decision making, it is important to notice that according to the CPL, article 162, and the Supreme Court's Interpretation, article 178, for those cases that do not have a preponderance of evidence to prove guilt of the defendant, a "not guilty" verdict should be given. This has, for the first time in China's Criminal Procedure Law, implied the principle of presumption of innocence. Given the fact that a suspect was assumed guilty in both the Chinese tradition and the inquisitorial system, the implication of the presumption of innocence is not to be ignored. However, as the law states, such presumption is applicable only to cases that do not seem to have sufficient evidence. As for the cases that have "sufficient" evidence, it is unclear if there is a presumption of innocence to begin with. This is because in neither the official legal documents nor the scholarly discussions reviewed could the researchers find this principle. Obviously, the Chinese criminal justice system has not accepted such presumption in general. Even for cases without enough evidence, it is still too early to determine if this principle will be taken seriously in practice.

Procuratorate

The procuratorate has been, and continues to be, one of the most powerful components within the criminal justice system of the People's Republic of China under the new Criminal Procedure Law. In general, the procuratorate plays a dual role in the criminal procedure. On the one hand, it is an organ of legal supervision of procedure. It not only supervises the pretrial investigations of public security (police) to ensure compliance with the law, but also supervises the judicial activities of the courts to determine the legitimacy and justice of the procedures, judgments, and orders. By the Constitution, the procuratorate performs all of these duties "independently and is not subject to interference by administrative organs, public organizations, or individuals." On the other hand, the procuratorate represents the state and acts as a state organ of prosecution. The revised Criminal Procedure Law does not view the procuratorate as an equal party in a lawsuit (the equal parties are the defendant and the victim), implying that the state organ (the procuratorate) has superior status to the individuals involved. This powerful role played by the procuratorate in the criminal trial reflects the traditional Chinese philosophy that the public's interests take precedent over the individual's interest (Hook, 1996). It also makes it impossible for the defense attorney to compete with the procuratorate on an equal basis, and difficult for the judge to make decisions independently.

With regard to the functions of the procuratorate, there are a few important changes in the revised Criminal Procedure Law. The most important change lies in the role the prosecutor plays in the trial. As discussed previously, under the 1979 Criminal Procedure Law, the judge acted as the procurator. Specifically, the judge conducted a pretrial investigation and made a decision on prosecution based upon the evidence prepared by the prosecutor. During the trial, the judge interrogated the accused, questioned witnesses, and provided the court with evidence. In line with these responsibilities of the judge, the prosecutor was placed in a position in which he helped and supported the judge in preparing the case and charging the accused. Sometimes the prosecutor did not even appear in court. All he needed to do was to send all prosecution materials to the court in order for the judge to try the case. The revised Criminal Procedure Law abandoned this traditional legal practice and redesigned the prosecutor's role in the trial. As a result, it is the sole responsibility of the prosecutor to bring charges against the accused and to prove guilt of the accused. The burden of proof requires the prosecutor to prepare the case carefully, present sufficient and correct evidence, and conduct skillful rebuttal with the defense attorney. This is the first time that the role of the prosecutor in the court has become similar to that in the Anglo-American adversary system.

Another change in the procuratorate is related to making decisions to prosecute. In the past, the procuratorate had the authority to exempt an assumed offender from prosecution. This decision implied an exemption from penalty for a guilty person. Thus, the procuratorate had the authority to determine guilt or innocence. This authority has been taken away; according to the revised Criminal Procedure Law, only the court can make a judgment on guilt or innocence. For the procuratorate, a principle of prosecution convenience has been adopted. With this principle, when there is a lack of confidence of conviction due to insufficient evidence, the procuratorate may decide not to prosecute. But it is not allowed to make a determination of guilt (Suo and Han, 1997).

Finally, according to the CPL, article 205, the procuratorate has the authority to oversee the process of the trial and protest the verdict if it finds a mistake in the trial. The protest is sent to the trial court. The higher-level procuratorate should examine the case and, if it agrees, protest to the court at the same level. The higher-level court, therefore, must retry the case. The procuratorate should continuously excise its right to supervise the retried case. It has the right to oversee the retried case and to protest again if faults still exist. The concept of double jeopardy is not applied in the Chinese system. The special authority of the procuratorate in overseeing judicial activities makes it a strong checks-and-balances organ to the court.

The Defendant and the Defense Attorney

Under the 1979 Criminal Procedure Law, the formal term used for the accused was the "defendant" throughout the stages of the procedure. The revised Criminal Procedure Law reserves the term only for those who are charged with committing crime and are formally prosecuted. Before formal prosecution but after arrest, the accused is referred to as the "suspect of criminal act." This differentiation is not a mere distinction in name, but implies substantial progress in the ways the justice system perceives and treats the accused. Because "defendant" and "suspect" have different positions during the procedure, they are given different rights and responsibilities. In general, the defendant has more rights and legal protection than the suspect does. For example, a defendant can have an attorney to defend his interests and rights in the entire procedure. The attorney is entitled to the right of discovery (having access to all evidence and documents that the procuratorate holds). However, a suspect can only receive legal advice from an attorney. In the revised CPL, defining the accused as either defendant or suspect reflects the substantial difference between the investigation stage and the prosecution stage, making it possible to accurately understand the various legal positions of the accused.

Furthermore, under the traditional inquisitorial system, the defendant was the object of prosecution, a passive object being interrogated. He or she barely had the right of defense; there were only seven days to seek counsel and build a case. The reformed system has greatly improved the status of the defendant in the procedure. Now the defendant has an equal status with the plaintiff (usually the victim) in the lawsuit, although an inferior one to the procuratorate. Generally, the revised Criminal Procedure Law has granted the defendant many rights (see appendix for some important rights).

Among all of these rights, the most important change is that the defendant now has early access to legal counsel or another defender, such as a relative, friend, or someone recommended by the defendant's work unit. The former Criminal Procedure Law allowed the court to notify the defendant seven days prior to the trial of the right to have a defender. This obviously did not leave sufficient time for the defender to know the case and prepare the defense. This provision caused much criticism of violation of human rights from abroad. The revised Criminal Procedure Law, article 33, has regulated two stages of involvement of legal counsel. First, after originally being questioned by a law enforcement agency or being arrested, the suspect has the right to a lawyer for legal assistance, but this assistance does not mean defense, so the lawyer cannot become involved in the investigation. Second, once the case has been sent to the procuratorate, the defendant has a right to obtain a defender who can access the documents of the prosecution and technical reports from the procuratorate to conduct an investigation. The change in the timing of the lawyer's involvement demonstrates an important improvement in protecting the defendant's right to legal counsel. If it is said that the defendant's right to a lawyer was only "window dressing" used to decorate the Chinese justice system in the past, the revised Criminal Procedure Law, to a certain extent, guarantees the exercise of such right in reality.

The revised Criminal Procedure Law not only advances the time frame in which a defendant may have access to a lawyer, but also extends the defense lawyer's rights in the process of case preparation. Article 37 states: "Defense lawyers may collect relevant materials from witnesses, other relevant entities or persons with their permission," and "may ask the people's procuratorate and court to collect and provide evidence, or ask the people's court to notify . . . witnesses to testify in court." These provisions, if actually implemented, could enhance the defense counsel's efforts and place a greater burden on the procurator to prove guilt. Thus, while some of these provisions remain the modern version of inquisitorial procedural methods, it has been suggested that some adversarial elements may be entering into the Chinese procedural system (Terrill, 1999). However, it is important to notice that the ability of the defense counsel to gather evidence from other parties is considerably more limited than that of the police and procuratorate. Though the new law requires the defender to obtain other parties' consent for collecting evidence from them, all persons and institutions have a duty to comply with requests from the police and procuratorate for evidence.

Along with the improvement of the defendant's rights, the requirements for the defender's trial activity are adjusted under the new Criminal Procedure Law. As in the adversary trial, now both prosecutor and defense attorney are advocates. The burden of proof rests with the prosecution, and the main task of the defense attorney is to present facts, question witnesses, and test the strength of the prosecutor's case in order to show the defendant's innocence, lower the charge against the defendant, or reduce the penalty. The philosophy behind this adversarial practice holds that truth will emerge when both sides are allowed to argue their cases effectively and vociferously. Therefore, the new law requires the advocates for both sides to do their utmost, within the boundaries set by law, to protect and advance the interests of their clients. Clearly, the revised Criminal Procedure Law has introduced some important features of the adversarial system into the Chinese trial.

Victim and Victim's Attorney

The role of the victim in the criminal procedure has been changed under the revised Criminal Procedure Law. Previously, a victim was considered neither a lawsuit subject nor a witness in both public and private prosecution. As a result, the victim's rights to make a complaint, expose the facts, and prove the guilt of the accused in a trial did not exist. The new Criminal Procedure Law addresses the belief that the victim, having suffered a criminal act, is directly relevant to the results of the trial; therefore, his or her rights must be guaranteed and his or her interests must be protected. The revised law allows the victim or the victim's close relatives to entrust an attorney to take part in the procedure as a lawsuit subject in both public and private prosecution. Thus the victim, along with the public prosecution, has the right to sue the defendant through an attorney for criminal matters as well as for civil damages. More specifically, according to the CPL, articles 154–160, the victim has many unprecedented rights, such as the right to participate in court investigation and court debates, including examining evidence, questioning the defendant, the witnesses, and the expert witnesses, giving opinions about the case, and debating with other participants; the right to call witnesses, present new evidence, and ask to reexamine the evidences presented; the right to ask the withdrawal of a party if conflict of interest exists; the right to review court proceedings (records, notes) and ask for correction if mistakes are found; the right to ask the procuratorate to protest the verdict; and the right to supplement a civil suit against the defendant for damages (Suo and Han, 1997).

Clearly, the new Chinese Criminal Procedure Law has given the victims some important rights in judicial procedures. Such rights not only enhance the position of the victims in a criminal trial, but also create some substantial differences between Chinese criminal procedure and Western criminal procedure. Considering the complaints and criticisms emerging from the victim's rights movement in Western countries like the United States, it is impressive to see the new position and the special functions of the victim in the Chinese criminal court. However, when we systematically examine the Chinese Criminal Procedure, some serious questions about the real motivation behind the changes in the victim's role arise. As discussed previously, the procuratorate is not an equal party in a lawsuit; it is superior to the individuals involved, both the defendant and the victim. Under such a structure, there would be no opposite, equal party competing with the defendant if the victim were not granted his or her position in the trial. Thus, one might suspect that the victim is granted more rights under the new law in order to set up a balance in the trial structure, with the goal of maintaining the superior status of the procurator in the trial. Thus, while the new Criminal Procedure Law has made clear progress in improving the victims' rights, our optimism over such improvement should be very guarded.

The revised CPL allows the victim, through an attorney, to initiate a private prosecution against a defendant (art. 170). Cases of private prosecution include the following: (1) a case that will be handled only if there is a complainant, including insult, slander, forced interference with the freedom of marriage, bigamy, damaging a member of the armed forces' marriage, abuse, and deserting a dependent; (2) minor criminal cases in which victims have evidence; and (3) cases in which the victim has evidence to prove that the defendant violated his personal or property rights and the defendant ought to be investigated for criminal responsibility, and where the public security agencies or the people's procuratorates do not investigate the defendant for criminal responsibility. After examining the case, the court may do one of the following: (1) conduct mediation; (2) try the case with a simple procedure; (3) send the case to the procuratorate for public prosecution; or (4) in the case of insufficient evidence, ask the plaintiff to withdraw, or dismiss the case. The defendant in a private prosecution may countersue the plaintiff. The court examines the facts and gives verdict(s) and sentence(s).

Witnesses

The revised Criminal Procedure Law clearly stipulates that witnesses must appear before the court to be questioned by the procurator, defense attorney, and victim's attorney. This has eliminated the practice in the past that witnesses gave only written testimony and did not necessarily show up in court. Such a change sets up an important premise necessary for an advocate trial.

DISCUSSION AND SUMMARY

Based upon the previous discussion, it is clear that the revised Criminal Procedure Law has brought four prominent changes in the Chinese criminal trial. First, the judge no longer reviews the substance of the evidence during pretrial examination. The only requirement for the judge is to have a procedural review, ensuring the completion of the file that is composed of the charges, the index of evidence, photocopies of main evidence, and a list of witnesses. This change implies a significant restriction on the judge's involvement in the preliminary investigation and effectively reduces the possibility of the judge's predetermination of guilt that was prevalent in the previous inquisitorial practice of substantive examination.

Second, the procurator, not the judge, brings the charges and presents the evidence against the defendant during the trial. The procurator, the victim's attorney, and the defense attorney become active parties during court investigation and court debate. They all have opportunities to present their arguments, question witnesses, examine evidence, and debate the issues. However, the judge, as in the inquisitorial system, remains active in the court and has the authority to control the proceeding, to conduct an investigation, and to act as a referee to determine justice.

Third, the defense attorney gets involved at an early stage of the procedure and is an active party at the trial. The early involvement can effectively limit the abuse of power by the procuratorate and the judge, and thus better protect the rights of the defendant. The change in the defense attorney's role as an advocate introduces one of the most important adversarial elements into the Chinese criminal trial. Last, the victim becomes a party in the court and has the same status as the defendant in the lawsuit. This change enhances the victim's rights and is unique to the Chinese criminal procedural system.

The revised Criminal Procedure Law has incorporated some cardinal principles of the adversarial system into the previous inquisitorial system. As a result of this new development, the present Chinese criminal procedure can be described as a mixture of adversarial and inquisitorial models in the socialist context. On the one hand, the functions of the judge, prosecutor, and defense attorney are to a certain extent similar to those found in the Anglo-American adversarial system. On the other hand, as in the inquisitorial trial, the judge continues to play an active role by interrogating the defendant and questioning witnesses. However, the current Chinese criminal procedure is not a simple combination of selected elements of both the adversarial and the inquisitorial system. Instead, the political ideology of the Communist Party guides the reform. And the Chinese legal culture, in which the state's interests outweigh the individual's interests, continues to play a significant role. As a result, the new criminal procedure is strongly influenced by socialist ideology and Chinese characteristics which are different from both adversarial and inquisitorial models.

The most unusual feature of the Chinese criminal procedure is the superior status of the procuratorate. As discussed previously, the procuratorate, as a state organ, is not a party to the trial, and therefore enjoys higher status than the defendant. Moreover, the procuratorate is a large, hierarchical bureaucracy whose various levels correspond to the People's Court and stand side by side with the People's Court. This structure clearly indicates that the procuratorate is not under the court, the representative of law. Instead, it is a bureaucracy paralleling the court according to the design of both the old and the new versions of the Criminal Procedure Law. It is interesting that when the 1979 CPL was under discussion for revision, many personnel in the procuratorate protested the proposals that the procurator should arrive at the courtroom earlier than the judge and rise when the judge appeared (Yang, 1997). The special status of the procuratorate highlights the important position of the state, which is superior to individuals and is not submissive to law. The idea of the state's interest taking precedent over the individual's interest has a long tradition in Chinese history. It is obviously still functioning in today's China.

Different from both Western adversarial and inquisitorial models, the present Chinese criminal justice system is still under the leadership and control of the

Communist Party. The best illustration of this feature is the existence and power of the adjudication committee. The People's Court Organic Law, article 11, states: "people's courts at all levels set up adjudication committees which practice democratic centralism." The committees have the authority to decide individual cases and are often given the responsibility of handling particularly difficult cases. They can override the decision of a judge and direct the judge to determine a case in a specific manner. Thus, adjudication committees are actually the most important decision-making authority within a court. It should be pointed out that the committee is composed mainly of the president and vice presidents of the court, and heads and deputy heads of various divisions, who are the party secretaries of the court and divisions. When discussing the leadership role of the Communist Party in the criminal court, Suo and Han (1997, p. 101) state: "The independent authority of the People's Court in trial must be placed under the leadership of the Party . . . The People's Court in doing all work, especially the trial, should actively and consciously accept and obey the leadership of the Party. It should actively request instructions from and report to the Party organizations . . . It must seriously listen to and carry out the Party organizations' opinions and decisions, and transform them into the People's Court's action through legal procedures."

Thus, separation of powers does not exist in the Chinese justice system. The independent judicial authority of the court is, to a great extent, under the supervision of the party and relies upon the approval of the party. This "democratic centralism" is actually party control, which reflects the influence of the traditional feudalistic legal system in which the emperor had ultimate power.

The reform of the defense attorney's rights is also limited compared with what we find in the adversarial system. Three limitations have been identified by law (Terrill, 1999). First, with regard to the defense counsel's access to clients, it is believed that such contact should occur before the first interrogation, rather than after it. Also, at this stage of the process, defense counsel does not have access to the information the investigators have collected. The only information source available for defense counsel at this stage is his/her client. As a result of this restriction, the defense counsel's ability to prepare the case is damaged. Second, indigent defendants are not assured assistance from defense counsel unless they have a specific physical disability (blind, deaf, or mute), are a minor, or are facing the death penalty. Thus, despite the improvement that has been made to protect indigent defendants' rights, many of them do not benefit from the expanded role of defense counsel. Third, in cases involving political dissidents or state secrets, the defendant's right to legal counsel is basically denied unless granted by the investigators. Given these concerns, there is a degree of skepticism about the actual exercise of a person's due process rights.

Besides the centralization and emperor control, another factor of the legal culture, the two models of social control, also has a direct impact on the reform of the criminal procedure. It is obvious that the reform itself indicates an effort to modernize criminal procedure in accordance with the formal model of law. The influence of the internal model of law is shown in many provisions of the revised Criminal Procedure Law. For example, both procurator and defense counsel are required to use the courtroom to publicize law to the audience and educate people about the justice system. This educational function is unique to the Chinese criminal procedure. Moreover, "defenders" refers not only to lawyers, but also to relatives as well as people from social organizations and work units. This definition highlights the informal nature of the Chinese criminal procedure.

In summary, the revised law has led to some important progress in the Chinese criminal procedure. As a result, the adversarial model has been incorporated with the inquisitorial model, producing a mixture of Chinese criminal procedures. Significantly, the mixed model reflects Chinese efforts to reach a good balance among the authority of the Communist Party over the legal system, the strong influence of the Western culture of individualism, and the Chinese traditional culture of collectivism.

APPENDIX: SOME IMPORTANT DEFENDANT RIGHTS UNDER THE 1997 CRIMINAL PROCEDURE LAW

Rights of Defense

- Right to use his/her own language in the procedure (through a court-provided interpreter)
- Right to be informed of the charges and rights
- Right to counsel or representation(a system of public defenders for indigent defendants is under construction)
- Right to monetary or guarantor-based bail (only for minor crime defendants, or those with insufficient evidence, or for humane reasons)
- Right to refuse to answer the questions irrelevant to the case (relevancy is determined by the judge)
- Right to receive a copy of the indictment ten days prior to trial
- Right to participate in trial investigation, including testifying, questioning witnesses, and bringing in defense witnesses and evidence
- Right to debate the evidence and the case
- Right to give closing statement
- Right to countersue the plaintiff (in the case of private prosecution)

Constructive Rights

- Right not to be viewed as guilty before the verdict is reached
- Right to public trial (except when juveniles or state secrets are involved)
- Right to an independent and fair trial

- Right not to be tortured, threatened, lured, deceived, and treated in other illegal ways during interrogation
- Right not to be illegally searched, to have possessions seized, to be arrested, detained, or house-arrested

Rights of Remedy

- Right to request any person in law enforcement, procuratorate, or court to withdraw from the case
- Right to charge law enforcement, procuratorate, or court personnel who violate the defender's or suspect's rights during the procedure
- Right not to be detained longer than the legal period (maximum fourteen days for an ordinary criminal suspect; thirty-seven days for a most serious criminal suspect; fifteen days for administrative punishment; and fifteen days for a party in a civil case)
- Right to appeal without incurring additional penalty

Accompanying the Rights, the Defendant Must Take Responsibilities

- He/she shall accept measures of deprivation of freedom provided for by law, such as arrest, detention, or house arrest
- He/she shall answer questions from law enforcement, procuratorate, and court. There is no right against self-incrimination. This is a sign of the inquisitorial system
- He/she shall accept prosecution and appear in court
- He/she shall accept the verdict

REFERENCES

Benewick, Robert, and Paul Wingrove, eds. 1995. *China in the 1990s.* Vancouver, BC: University of British Columbia Press.

Bodde, Derk, and Clarence Morris. 1967. *Law in Imperial China.* Philadelphia: University of Pennsylvania Press.

Davidson, Rorber, and Wang Zheng 1996. "The Court System in the People's Republic of China with a Case Study of a Criminal Trial." In *Comparative and International Criminal Justice Systems.* Edited by Obi Ebbe. Boston: Butterworth-Heinemann.

Du Xichuan and Zhang Lingyuan. 1990. *China's Legal System: A General Survey.* Beijing: New World Press.

Fairbank, John K. 1992. *China: A New History.* Cambridge, MA: Harvard University Press.

Fairchild, Erika. 1993. *Comparative Criminal Justice Systems.* Belmont, CA: Wadsworth.

Fan Chongyi, ed. 1997. *Zhongguo Xingshi Susongfa* (Chinese criminal procedure law). Beijing: Chinese University of Political Science and Law Publishing House.

Hook, Brian, ed. 1996. *The Individual and the State in China*. Oxford: Clarendon Press.

Lawyers Committee for Human Rights. 1996. *Opening to Reform? An Analysis of China's Revised Criminal Procedure Law*. New York: Lawyers Committee for Human Rights.

Leng Shao-chuan. 1967. *Justice in Communist China*. Dobbs Ferry, NY: Oceana Publications.

Liu Xiucheng. 1994. "Xingsufa yi fanzui shishi qingcu zhengju chongfen wei tingshen qianti de guiding yingdang xiugai" ("The Contents of Clear Criminal Acts and Sufficient Evidence as the Prerequisite of a Trial in the CPL Should Be Revised"). In *Tingshen He Mianyu Qisu Zhidou De Guaige Yu Wanshan* (Trial and the System of Exempt from Prosecution: Reform and Perfection), pp. 117–122. Edited by Weimin Xie, Weihong Xue, and Meng Tao. Beijing: China's Legal System Publishing House.

Lo, Carlos Wing-hung. 1995. *China's Legal Awakening: Legal Theory and Criminal Justice in Deng's Era*. Hong Kong: Hong Kong University Press.

Lu Qinzhong. 1994. "Guanyu xingshi gongsu anjian tingshen moshi gaige de sikao" ("Thought on Reforming the Trial of Public Prosecution"). In *Tingshen He Mianyu Qisu Zhidou De Guaige Yu Wanshan* (Trial and the System of Exempt from Prosecution: Reform and Perfection), pp. 62–68. Edited by Weimin Xie, Weihong Xue, and Meng Tao. Beijing: China's Legal System Publishing House.

Lubman, Stanley B., ed. 1996. *China's Legal Reforms*. Oxford: Oxford University Press.

McKnight, Brian E. 1981. *The Quality of Mercy: Amnesties and Traditional Chinese Justice*. Honolulu: University of Hawaii Press.

Pan Jiayong. 1994. "Shilun tingshen fangshi gaige yu bianhu zhidu wanshan" ("On Reform and Trial Mode and Perfection of Defense System"). In *Tingshen He Mianyu Qisu Zhidou De Guaige Yu Wanshan* (Trial and the System of Exempt from Prosecution: Reform and Perfection), pp. 87–95. Edited by Weimin Xie, Weihong Xue, and Meng Tao. Beijing: China's Legal System Publishing House.

Soled, Debra E., ed. 1995. *China: A Nation in Transition*. Washington, DC: Congressional Quarterly.

Spence, Jonathan D. 1981. The Gate of Heavenly Peace: The Chinese and Their Revolution, 1895–1980. Harmondsworth, UK: Penguin Books.

Suo Weidong and Han Yong, eds. 1997. *Xinshi xingshi tingshen susong shiyong shouce* (Handbook of New Criminal Trial Procedure). Beijing: China's Procuratorate Publishing House.

Tang Youhong and Ping Jie. 1994. "Xingshi anjian tingshen fangshi gaige cuyi" ("On Reform in Criminal Trial"). In *Tingshen He Mianyu Qisu Zhidou De Guaige Yu Wanshan* (Trial and the System of Exempt from Prosecution: Reform and Perfection), pp. 46–52. Edited by Weimin Xie, Weihong Xue, and Meng Tao. Beijing: China's Legal System Publishing House.

Terrill, Richard J. 1999. *World Criminal Justice Systems: A Survey*. 4th ed. Cincinnati, OH: Anderson.

Troyer, Ronald J., John P. Clark, and Dean G. Rojek, eds. 1989. *Social Control in the People's Republic of China*. New York: Praeger.

Wang Chenguang and Zhang Xianchu. 1997. *Introduction to Chinese Law*. Hong Kong: Sweet & Maxwell Asia.

Yang Fuguo. 1997. "Tingshen fangshi gaibian hou ruogan wenti de tantao" (Issues After the Reform of Criminal Trial). In *Xinshi xingshi tingshen susong shiyong shouce* (Handbook of New Criminal Trial Procedure). Edited by Weidong Suo and Han Yong. Beijing: China's Procuratorate Publishing House.

Yu Shoyuan, ed. 1994. *Zhongguo susongfa xue* (Chinese Procedure Law). Beijing: Chinese Legal System Publishing House.

Zhang Biyou and Shuping Luo. 1994. "Gongsuren juzheng tansuo" ("Discussion on Procurator's Giving Evidence"). In *Tingshen He Mianyu Qisu Zhidou De Guaige Yu Wanshan* (Trial and the System of Exempt from Prosecution: Reform and Perfection), pp. 96–104. Edited by Weimin Xie, Weihong Xue, and Meng Tao. Beijing: China's Legal System Publishing House.

CHAPTER 11

New Directions of Chinese Policing in the Reform Era

Yisheng Dai

Since China adopted economic reform and the "open door" policy in the late 1970s, the establishment and development of a market economy with multiple forms of ownership have brought about huge infrastructural changes in Chinese society. This has also induced necessary reforms in political and legal aspects in response to rising crime rates and increased public concerns about safety and security. One such reform is the significant change in China's policing (see chapter 12 in this volume). This chapter describes briefly the changing directions of China's policing, which started in the late 1970s and has developed rapidly in recent years.

CHANGES IN THE FUNCTIONS AND ROLES OF THE POLICE

Since its founding, the Communist Party of China (CPC) has adhered to the doctrine of Marxism-Leninism. One of the core tenets of this doctrine is class struggle and the dictatorship of the proletariat (Mao referred to it as the people's democratic dictatorship). According to this theory, the police are an important instrument of the state which serves the will of the ruling class and is designated to thwart the revolt of the bourgeoisie and other exploiting classes. "The state apparatus, including the army, the police and courts, is the instrument for the oppression of antagonistic classes, it is violence and not 'benevolence' " (Mao, 1961, p. 418).

Governed by this principle, the police, in the early years of the People's Republic of China, served political goals such as suppressing counterrevolutionaries, and safeguarding and facilitating political movements with legal means. The tasks of maintaining public order and combating crimes usually took second place. In part, this was because the crime rates were low during the 1950s and 1960s, only five–eight cases per 10,000 population annually. This made crime control a rather easy task for the Chinese police.

After Deng Xiaoping assumed power in 1979, the CPC adopted new interpretations of the doctrine. The decision of the third plenary session of the eleventh CPC Central Committee in 1978 held that "At the present stage, class struggle will not remain a major contradiction in society" (Hu, 1991, p. 630). Later, the Constitution of the PRC, adopted in 1982, confirmed that "the exploiting classes as such have been abolished in our country" (Legislative Affairs Commission, 1987, p. 4), and that although "class struggle will continue to exist within certain dimensions for a long time, . . . the basic task of the nation in coming years is to build up socialist modernization" (Legislative Affairs Commission, 1987, p. 4).

In reaction to this substantial change of ideology, reform in policing functions and roles began to take place. In 1995, China adopted a new People's Police Act which replaced the old one of 1957. It affirms in legal form the changes that had taken place in the functions and roles of the police. In the 1957 act, the first article defined the nature of the People's Police as follows: "The police force of the People's Republic of China acts as an agent of the public. It is one of the important instruments of the people's democratic dictatorship and an armed administrative force of the state for the public order" (National People's Congress, 1998a, p. 161). Article 1 of the 1995 act shows certain changes. It stipulates what the police really are by listing the specific goals of policing: "This act is formulated according to the Constitution for the purpose of safeguarding state security and maintaining public order, protecting the legal rights of citizens, building the police force, improving the quality of the police, ensuring the legal power of the police for the socialist modernization" (National People's Congress, 1998b, p. 169).

The functions and roles of the People's Police were stipulated in article 2 of the 1957 act as follows: "The roles of the People's Police are: punishing counterrevolutionaries according to law, preventing and stopping other illegal activities, maintaining public order and social security, protecting public property, protecting legal rights and interests of citizens for the socialist construction" (National People's Congress, 1998a, p. 161). In contrast, the 1995 act defines the roles of the police in a more modernized, more citizen-oriented, more realistic, and less ideological way. Article 2 of the act stipulates that "The roles of the People's Police are: safeguarding state security, maintaining social order, protecting personal safety, personal freedom and property, protecting public property, deterring criminal activities" (National People's Congress, 1998b, p. 169).

Adoption of "Policing on Beat"

The adoption of police patrol in Chinese cities can be seen as a significant reform in China's policing. In contrast with Western countries, where modern policing dates back to the London city patrol of 1829, China has a different history in social control: the establishment of a *baojia* system—a system of localized self-government with the family at its center (Dutton, 1992, p. 88). The policing of the People's Republic of China inherits this tradition. The principle of policing is reliance on the masses and related informal organizations. "There are 1.2 million public security committees throughout the country with more than 5.8 million members. There are also 2.6 million public security groups, with 6.3 million members. Totally, there are more than 3.8 million public security organizations with about 12 million people. It is through this vast mass network that the police fulfill their task of maintaining public order and security" (Dai and Huang, 1993, p. 137).

Since the early 1980s, a rapid expansion of the market economy and the increasing mobility of population and employment have significantly weakened this mass basis of social control (see chapter 5 in this volume). Social control at the grassroots level has become more difficult than ever. As a result, the crime rate has increased drastically, from 8 cases per 10,000 in the early 1980s to nearly 40 cases per 10,000 in the 1990s (Dai, 1995; Guo, 1999). In reaction to the weakening of social control and increasing crime rates, the Chinese police have begun to adopt new strategies.

After experiments in several large cities such as Shanghai, Beijing, and Tianjin, a national conference of police in 1991 confirmed that a system of policing on the beat is one of the new strategies to solve public security problems in urban areas (Han, 1993). At present, a patrol system with a "110" calling center has been established in every city of China. Such a system is believed to be an effective means to guard community security.

Reform of Household Registration (*Hukou*)

In China, household registration is a traditional instrument of political and social control at the grassroots level. "The household register system was a mechanism by which the Emperor extended his governance and control of all facets of life in feudal society" (Dutton 1992, p. 191)After the 1911 revolution, the Republic of China inherited this system. The Chinese Communist Party also adopted this tradition after it gained power. The registration system has served as an important basis for policing. "Because police have responsibility for keeping the census, known as 'household or residence registration,' there is an officer assigned to keep track of anywhere from 400 to 800 families; individuals must get permission to leave a city or move into it" (Ward, 1997, p. 4). This system has been challenged politically and economically in recent years. Politically, more and more Chinese people have become aware of individual freedom of residence. The laissez-faire policy of a market economy promotes freedom of residence and employment. The old registration system is no longer an effective means of social control. Consequently, the

Chinese police began to reform the system by adopting a personal identification card system to parallel the family-based household registration system, allowing peasants to move into cities by giving them a temporary residence permit; a blue paper of residence that encourages professionals, technicians, and businessmen to move into cities for economic development; and giving priority for a residential permit in cities to people seeking to reunite their family. Currently, China has a large floating population, and many offenders come from this population group (see chapter 5 in this volume).

Professionalization of the Police Force

Traditionally, the Chinese police have recruited officers according to political loyalty and class origin, and have disregarded professional capability and education. On-the-job professional training was inadequate. Recently, there has been a trend to professionalizing the police force. The first aspect of this trend is the rise in the educational level of police officers. In 1980, less than 10 percent of police officers were college graduates or postgraduates. The proportion increased to 37.6 percent in 1997. Seventeen police academies and colleges and eighty-one police training schools across the country had been established by 1997 (Policing in China 1997).

Another aspect is the adoption of modern science and technology. Nine institutes of science and technology with a total staff of 3,000 have been established under the leadership of the Ministry of Public Security (MPS), and 140 similar institutes with a total staff members have been established by local police departments since 1979. The revised Criminal Procedure Law of 1996 calls for further efforts in the research and development of police science and technology. Article 46 of the law stipulates that "a defendant cannot be found guilty and sentenced if only his statement, but no evidence, is available; the defendant may be found guilty and sentenced if evidence is sufficient and reliable, even without his statement" (National People's Congress, 1997, p. 23). In order to collect adequate, effective, and reliable evidence, the Chinese police are developing advanced forensic science.

The trend is also reflected in the strengthening of an effective management of internal affairs to increase police integrity. Since 1990, the rapid economic development has brought increasing police corruption in China. The 1995 Transparency International Survey indicated that China was ranked as the second most corrupt of all the nations polled. By 1996, the same poll placed China as the fifth most corrupted nation and by 1997 China was ranked in eleventh place (Levi, 1997, p. 4). It seems that corruption occurs in every sector of Chinese government, but instances occurring in the criminal justice system are believed to be most dangerous and detrimental (see chapter 2 of this volume). An anticorruption drive was launched in all police departments of the country in 1998; 11,000 police officers were disciplined, and 1,380 received criminal punishment for corrupt acts ("Achievements . . .," 1999, p. 1).

The reform of criminal investigation divisions is also a significant step toward police professionalization. Before, Chinese police adopted the line of "relying on the masses." A large part of criminal investigation relied on neighborhood police stations with a mass-based information network. Because police officers in the grassroots units were not professionals, abuses of power often occurred. In 1998, it was decided by the MPS that all criminal investigation was assigned to special units of the police force. This reform also accords with the new Criminal Procedure Law, which stipulates in article 18 that "investigation of criminal cases shall be conducted by the public security organs." The grassroots security units cannot be regarded as an integral part of the public security organs (of the criminal justice system). They do not have the legal power.

Private Sectors Join in Security Work

Because state ownership was predominant in China in the past, all internal security affairs were under the jurisdiction of the state police. As China has formed an economic system of multiple ownership—joint ventures, solely foreign-owned firms, collective investments, individual proprietorships, and others—it has become very difficult for the state police to do security work in these entities. For example, police cannot enter a private company without the permission of its owner unless they have a lawful warrant. Even state-owned enterprises now refuse to let police interfere in their internal affairs because the economic reform has separated enterprises from the government and turned many of them into state holding companies. As a result, private police forces have emerged. More than 1,500 private security companies nationwide are engaging in various kinds of security work ranging from guarding hotels, banks, supermarkets, airports, and railway stations to electronic surveillance and escorting the transport of currency. Some foreign firms have entered this field, providing advanced techniques and equipment.

PROGRESS IN POLICE LEGAL REFORM

For thirty years, China's policing depended not on law but on the policies and directives of the Communist Party. The first Criminal Law and Criminal Procedure Law, passed in 1979, laid down some fundamental principles of "rule of law." For the police it was the first time the principle of habeas corpus was really established in China. This marked the beginning of a legal reform of police in China. In 1996, the revised Criminal Procedure Law was enacted. It made a number of changes in the criminal justice system. According to the law, the defense is allowed a greater role in processing a criminal. The defense lawyer is able to give advice to the suspect after the first interrogation (it may occur before detention). The defense counsel, as well as relatives of a suspect, may apply for the cancellation of any compulsory measures, such as detention or arrest, if the time limit prescribed by law is exceeded. To regulate the power and discretion of public security personnel, the new Police Act issued in 1995 clearly defines the obligations and power of the police. In addition, the Law of Administrative Punishment, enacted in 1996, confirms that victims of police power abuse can initiate a lawsuit against the police department for compensation. In March 1999, an amendment to the Constitution was adopted by the National People's Congress, in which the "rule of law" is set as a basic principle of the People's Republic of China.

SUMMARY AND DISCUSSION

Since 1979, China's policing has undergone tremendous changes in response to economic reform and crime problems. The present study reviewed several major dimensions of these changes in the functions and roles of Chinese police. These changes are consistent with the recent emphasis on formal control of crime and related problems in China. Earlier, China relied heavily on mass movement and informal control to deal with criminal and deviant behaviors. Since the economic reform of the late 1970s, an unanticipated consequence has been rising crime rates and related public concern about safety and security. To meet these legal and social challenges, the Chinese police began to adopt reforms in functions and roles. Although it seems that the reform models Western police patterns, such as policing on the beat, the social and cultural foundation is different.

Mao's Mass Line still plays an important role in the operation of policing. The emphasis is still on mass involvement in policing because the Chinese believe that policing would be fruitless without mass and community involvement. Crime and related problems are matters not only for the police but also for the community and public business. Only when common people are involved in policing does policing work.

In addition, some mass organizations, such as neighborhood committees, constitute the organizational basis for policing at the grassroots level. Any policing needs to let these mass organizations be involved. A neighborhood police station in China has a variety of connections and associations with the community where it is institutionalized. In sum, when the reform of Chinese police is observed and studied, the cultural tradition, the political system, and the social context of China should be fully taken into account. Otherwise, any explanation may be misleading.

REFERENCES

"Achievements Gained in Anti-Corruption Drive." 1999. *China Police Daily,* January 7, p. 1.
Dai, Yisheng. 1995. "Expanding Economy and Growing Crime." *CJ International* 11, no. 2: 9–16.

Dai Yisheng and Huang Zu Yuan. 1993. "Organization and Functions of Public Security Agencies of the People's Republic of China." *Euro Criminology* 5–6: 137–143.

Dutton, Michael R. 1992. *Policing and Punishment in China*. Cambridge: Cambridge University Press.

Guo Xiang. 1999. "Delinquency and Its Prevention in China." *International Journal of Offender Therapy and Comparative Criminology* 43, no. 1: 61–70.

Han Qinzhang. 1993. "Chinese Cities Adopt Police Patrol System." *China Policing Studies*, trial issue: 54–56.

Hu Sheng. 1991. *Zhong guo gong can dang qi shi Nian* (Seventy Years of the CPC). Beijing: History Press of CPC.

Legislative Affairs Commission of the National People's Congress of the People's Republic of China. 1987. *Laws of the People's Republic of China*. Vol. 1. Beijing: Foreign Languages Press.

Levi, Michael. 1997. "Stealing from the People." *China Review* 8: 4–9.

Mao Zedong. 1961. "On the People's Democratic Dictatorship." In *Selected Works of Mao Tse-Tung*. Vol. 4, pp. 411–424. Beijing: Foreign Languages Press.

Ministry of Public Security. 1998. *Yearbook of the Ministry of Public Security, 1997*. Beijing: Ministry of Public Security.

National People's Congress of the People's Republic of China. 1997. Criminal Procedure Law of the People's Republic of China. Beijing: China Procuratorial Press.

National People's Congress of the People's Republic of China. 1998a. "1957 People's Police Act." In *Ren Ming Jing Cha Fa Ruo Gan Wen Ti Yan Jiu* (Study on the Problems of People's Police Act), pp. 161–169. Edited by Lee Zhong Xing. Beijing: Qunzhong Publishing.

———. 1998b. "1995 People's Police Act." In *Ren Ming Jing Cha Fa Ruo Gan Wen Ti Yan Jiu* (Study on the Problems of People's Police Act), pp. 150–160. Edited by Lee Zhong Xing. Beijing: Qunzhong Publishing.

Ward, Dick. 1997. "Public Security in Modern China." *Crime and Justice International* 13, no. 3: 4–8.

CHAPTER 12

Traditions and Changes of Police Culture: Organization, Operation, and Behavior of the Chinese Police

Allan Y. Jiao

Police culture has been studied both as an independent phenomenon and as a dependent circumstance of the society. As an independent phenomenon, "police culture" refers to police behaviors and values developed informally on the job and resulting from the bureaucratic police organizational environment (Cain, 1973; Manning, 1977; Holdaway, 1983). According to Manning (1977), for example, it refers to the essential techniques, knowledge, rationales, and beliefs that define good police work. Skolnick (1966) discusses the personal character of a police officer as influenced by the features of the police occupation. As a dependent circumstance of the society, police culture is viewed as being derived from its larger social environment and directly resulting from an interaction between the field of policing and the various dimensions of police knowledge. A broader and more comprehensive theory of culture as suggested by Chan should "situate culture in the political and social context of policing, recognize the interpretive and active role of officers in structuring their understanding of the organization and its environment, and allow for the possibility of change as well as resistance to change" (1996, p.112).

Informed by the perspective that broader social processes and larger societal patterns influence police culture, this chapter will examine the organizations, operations, and behaviors of the Chinese police as influenced by the traditions and changes of Chinese culture. Also viewing police culture as characteristics of a unique occupation, this chapter will discuss the distinctiveness of routine police working situations and their effects on Chinese police behaviors. Because the cultural perspective not only enables us to better understand various police issues but also helps police executives improve their management practices, this chapter will conclude with a brief discussion of some policy implications of culture and cultural change for policing in China. Information and analyses used in this chapter are based on the author's personal interviews of police officers and observations of police practices in Beijing, Shijiazhuang, Handan, Changsha, and Guangzhou, China, in recent years, supplemented by relevant documents and literature review.

TRADITIONS OF CHINESE POLICE CULTURE

Influenced by traditional Chinese culture, the police organization in China features a hierarchical structure: the Party Line, the Mass Line, and the Prevention Line. These consolidate different elements of the police organization, and provide meaning, direction, and mobilization to the police force (Kilmann et al., 1985).

A hierarchical relationship exists among police agencies that runs from the Ministry of Public Security at the national level, to provincial departments of public security, and to county and local public security bureaus. The organization of Chinese police in a uniform manner at all levels of government, as well as the standardized police training, reflect the homogeneity of Chinese culture. Historically, Chinese society had a very low level of geographical mobility, although this has begun to change with the economic reforms. Chinese communities are typically populated by residents with similar ethnic backgrounds. Apart from several minority autonomous regions, the Han race accounts for over 95 percent of the population in all the provinces. Such homogeneity is conducive to widely shared values and common definitions of social problems and solutions (Zhang et al., 1996), resulting in a common interest in maintaining uniformity in police organization.

The Party Line represents the Chinese Communist Party's direct involvement in organizing the Chinese police. The traditional belief in the functions of ethics and morality in social control has directly influenced this involvement, which is represented in a Confucian ideology of moral order. This ideology emphasizes collective interests and administrative ethics; Confucius did not believe that people should be directed by laws and regulated by punishment. The rule of law, Confucius believed, would push people to pursue their individual interests at the cost of larger social justice and fairness. Instead, people should be directed by virtue and regulated by moral principles, which will enable them to develop a sense of shame and have concern for others, resulting in a moral order in the society. The role of the police, therefore, should not be based on laws, but on ethics and moral principles; and a good police agency should be able to lead, shape, and teach. The rejection of codified and publicly promulgated laws for centuries also served a practical purpose—to enable the police and the people to create new and mutually acceptable solutions to conflicts without their hands being tied.

Consistent with this tradition of moral order, the Chinese police have been organized first and foremost following the Communist Party directives, which are believed to represent the highest ethical and moral standards in government administration. A "Political Section" was established in all police departments in 1952, and the position of "political director" was created to organize and lead activities within the police. The main responsibilities of the Political Section are disseminating party policies, engaging in ideological/political work, instructing police officers on their morality and professional ethics, and monitoring police corruption and misconduct. High moral standards, often equated with good political consciousness, are emphasized because the party believes that only moral police officers will have a sense of discipline, a sense of responsibility, and the commitment to serving the public.

The Party Line is closely related to the Mass Line, another major characteristic of Chinese police organization influenced by traditional Chinese culture. The Mass Line combines traditional Chinese egalitarianism with modern Marxist communism, both founded on the ideal of equality of people and elimination of social classes. To fulfill this ideal, the Communist Party, as a party that represents the ordinary people, advocates a strong and close relationship between the police and the community. The police must truly belong to the people and view themselves as public servants. The police, therefore, are functionally and structurally integrated into the community, and police officers are required to cultivate the spirit of serving the people and involve the public in their daily work. And so goes the analogy commonly used by the Chinese police that describes the relationship between the police and people as that between fish and water.

The police have practiced several principles that address the methods of police work and characters of police officers in implementing the Mass Line. These principles require that the police serve the mass interests whenever possible, differentiate law-abiding citizens from law violators, combine severe punishment and lenient treatment, emphasize investigation and research, make judgments and seek truth according to facts, work within the law and policy, and fight against police brutality. As individual officers they must be firm in character and maintain a clear mind, have both courage and wisdom, be morally clean and free of corruption, love the people, and have a sense of discipline.

To carry out the Party and Mass Lines, the Chinese police have borrowed the disciplines and standards originally used by the Chinese People's Liberation Army and proven successful during the Communist Revolution in winning over the Chinese masses. These are the famous "Eight Major Disciplines and Ten Points for Attention" familiar to every police officer in China. The Eight Major Disciplines are (1) following leaders and commanding officers; (2) abiding by policies and laws; (3) no leaking of secrets affecting national security; (4) no violation of mass interests; (5) no corruption and bribery; (6) no obtaining of confessions by torture; (7) no harboring of evildoers; and (8) no framing of innocent people. The Ten Points for Attention are that police officers should (1) have a strong standing and be able to differentiate the innocent from the guilty; (2) be firm, brave, calm, and wise; (3) do good deeds and serve the people; (4) speak politely and handle matters fairly; (5) honor the old, love the small, and respect women; (6) show courtesy and be disciplined; (7) revere the customs of the masses; (8) correct violations without creating difficulties; (9) practice and publicize policies; and (10) work hard, study hard, and keep fit.

The Mass Line not only emphasizes building better police-community relations but also stresses the police role in mobilizing community resources for the purpose of crime prevention. It is, therefore, closely related to another organizational principle of the Chinese police: the Prevention Line. The Prevention Line reflects the Chinese cultural emphasis on early intervention and education. A striking feature of the Chinese police in crime prevention is their role as public security organizers, through which they are actively involved in organizing community crime prevention organizations such as neighborhood public security committees, specialized public order organizations, people's mediation committees, and police-community joint defense programs. Public security committees made up of local civilian residents are the core of social control in China. They can be found in all organizations, enterprises, and institutions in urban and rural areas. Specialized public order organizations are often responsible for order on the streets, especially in busy sections of cities and towns, fairs, and markets; they are also organized to ensure the safety of trade outlets, such as hotels and taxis. People's mediation committees, which are responsible for mediating millions of domestic disputes and interpersonal conflicts every year, are located in the streets, residential quarters, factories, mines, and rural areas (He, 1991). Throughout the country police-community joint defense programs have also been established that work as guards in factories and villages. The Prevention Line, as a part of "the total society strategy," aims to "mobilize a wide range of social forces—political, economic, cultural, judicial, educational, and organizational—to combat crime" (Zhang et al., 1996, p. 206).

Police Operations

Like the way police are organized, Chinese police operations have been influenced by traditions of moral order, collective responsibility, and early intervention. Chinese police officers are inclined to understand the meanings of power and authority as derived from one's ethics and morality, not from legal, procedural, or democratic processes. They frequently use moral reasoning and emotional appeals to help juvenile delinquents and adult offenders return to law-abiding life. In dispute mediation, they often rely on a neutral community member who determines what is appropriate in a particular case according to ethical considerations. This practice reinforces the tradition that police should act in accordance with what they think is right, not with what the law dictates (Peerenboom, 1993).

Recognizing that order is inherent in the process of existence itself—that which causes and that which is caused are not finally distinguishable (Hall and Ames,

1995)—the police integrate education and reindoctrination of the offender into the sanctioning phase (Ingraham, 1987). In the process of doing this, the police, as mandated by the culture of collective responsibility, work with as many people as possible. They involve community groups, for example, in reintegrating offenders into the community, often including people from an offender's life, such as his family, school, neighborhood, and workplace (Zhang et al., 1996). Chinese police typically rely on offenders' families for support and emphasize relationship over legal right and duty (Dellapenna, 1997).

The police operations specifically intended to carry out the early intervention and crime prevention policy mainly involve police work with the public security committees and criminal case investigation. Because the Chinese police are not separated from the rhythms of community life, the relatively few formal and informal control agents are able to effectively conduct police work and avoid impediments to effective neighborhood watching (Johnson, 1986). Assisted by public security committees in urban and rural areas, which bear the responsibility for crime prevention, the police frequently inspect crime-prone public places such as railway stations, ports, wharves, hotels, hostels, markets, cinemas, theaters, and stadia to ensure security and reinforce administrative control. They are particularly interested in investigation of crime-inducing factors or causes of social disorder. With information developed from such investigation, they develop plans and strategies to eliminate the causes of crimes.

As part of their effort to prevent crime, the police are actively engaged in management of what the Chinese call the "cultural" market, which usually includes recreational and sport centers and shopping and commercial districts. In this respect, the Chinese police often work closely with the municipal Department of Culture to maintain order and security in these areas. Together, they inspect and stop illegal business activities involving obscene articles, illegal computer and video games, gambling, and superstition. The Chinese police and the public believe that these businesses have a negative influence on primary and secondary school children because they promote violence, distract students from their studies, and create disorder in the cultural market.

Although crime prevention makes sense to people in a society indoctrinated with the Confucian philosophy of early intervention and education, not all crimes can be prevented. In responding to crimes that have already occurred, the Chinese police emphasize persistent follow-up investigation of most crimes, work closely with business and community organizations to develop leads, and are often able to gather valuable information because of their closeness to the community. They emphasize fact-finding rather than interrogation of suspects. They take crime clearance rates very seriously because their performance is often measured by the percentage of crimes solved, and a high clearance rate is believed to deter future crimes and help gain public support for the police.

The Chinese police have developed strategies to target different crimes with different approaches. They rely on local public security organizations and the masses to solve most of the ordinary criminal cases. They often combine cases and have joint operations with other police agencies to deal with transient criminals. Police agencies from different locations and levels of government are easily coordinated, due to the hierarchical police structure, to assist each other in criminal investigations, making arrests, and recovering property. Some regions that share similar crime problems have institutionalized this type of cooperative program. For accumulated cases that create social disorder in specific areas, the police organize special squads and concentrate their efforts on targeting these problems. To deal with economic crimes committed by those who violate Chinese economic laws, the police have set up a new unit called the Economic Police Unit.

Police Behaviors

Due to the heavy cultural emphasis on ethical and moral forces in the society for purposes of social control, police officers in China are traditionally expected to function as role models and moral authorities in the community. Such social expectations put great pressure on the police officers to conduct themselves properly and maintain a positive image in public. One aspect of Chinese officers' practices that project this positive image is the role they play as public educators. They teach teenagers about the importance of morality and discipline, educate the public against moral decay, and resort to ethics and reason to resolve disputes between citizens.

In their interactions with the public, police officers control their emotions, behave modestly, and demonstrate a neutral attitude. They look reserved, speak politely, and handle matters as fairly as possible. Influenced by the Chinese culture, the police officers believe that harmonious community relations rely on the management of officers' emotions. To avoid disharmony in the group and circumvent potentially disruptive behavior, the police believe that they should monitor the expression of extreme emotions that might threaten, offend, and disrupt the stability of existing relationships (Bond and Hwang, 1986; Chiu and Kosinski, 1994; Markus and Kitayama, 1994). The importance of emotional moderation in Chinese culture can be traced back to Confucian teachings, in which the fundamental moral idea of moderation, balance, and subtlety is emphasized (deBary et al., 1960).

In Chinese culture, the emphasis on emotional moderation ranges from individuals' indirectness, subtlety, and simplicity to governments' inclusive, nonaggressive forms of security and disesteem for war. On an individual level, a lack of emotional moderation is believed to have dire consequences for the individual's mental and physical health (Koo, 1976; Tsai and Levenson, 1997). From birth, children raised in Chinese culture are socialized to control their emotional impulses and maintain a modest attitude (Ho, 1994). Such emphasis is evident in a study by Lee et al. (1997) indicating the emphasis on self-effacement and modesty among Chinese children. This cultural orientation toward emotional moderation is also reflected in Chinese poetry, which portrays love as friendship, and describes nature as consisting of delicate and pragmatic humanistic systems (Zhu, 1995). The Chinese emphasis on emotional moderation and social harmony has been extended even to the realm of state relations, where China has strong traditions of inclusive, nonaggressive forms of security (Ferguson, 1998).

The Chinese police officers' concern for manners and attitudes during their interactions with the public is also influenced by their strong collective values and orientations. The concept of community interests is germane to them not only because of the primacy of the state, but also because the legal and political systems center on the principle of collective responsibility. Chinese officers' decisions are, therefore, mostly made according to what is best for the social functioning of the group (Dellapenna, 1997). As Zhang and Jin (1998) found in their study, making and maintaining friendships and having positive, warm relationships seem more important for the Chinese because interpersonal conflict and difficulty are more significantly related to suicide ideation among Chinese.

Primarily socialized in a collectivistic culture and egalitarian value system, police officers lean toward the left politically and ideologically. They advocate the importance of putting individual self-interests subordinate to serving the common good. They believe in collective duties and responsibilities, the role of the community, and the significant part government plays in a civil society. Because of this liberal orientation, police officers do not find it difficult to identify with the Party Line, the Mass Line, and the related socialist moral standards.

The liberal orientation among Chinese police officers is cultivated in part by the strong communitarian spirit in the community and the relatively peaceful working environment officers find themselves in. The community residents have traditionally been supportive of police being stationed in their neighborhood. Individual civilians are not allowed to possess any weapons due to strict government gun-control policy, so the danger or threat of guns is almost nonexistent in the minds of individual officers. There are also community security programs that police officers can rely on in conducting their daily activities. Without the feeling of danger and isolation from the community, they tend to think of themselves as a part of the community or of a social war against crime. Due to the homogeneity of the culture, they are able to socialize with members of their neighborhood with relative ease, understand and respect customs of the masses, and often see eye to eye with the community on law-and-order issues. There is generally emotional cohesion and mutual support between the police and the community. In this type of working environment, many police officers have developed a social work mentality, directing them to do good deeds for the public, which in return gives them a sense of fulfillment. Public appreciation of police services reinforces the police officers' status as role models and moral authorities, and increases their cohesion with the community.

The emphasis on police-community cohesiveness reflects fundamental Chinese cultural values such as collectivism, community mutuality, and group functioning. These values legitimize mutual dependency between the police and the community, promote personal sacrifices for the common good, and require individual officers to be cooperative with each other and work as a team. These values reduce community members' resistance to individual police officers' intervention, especially when the officers are viewed as moral authorities. The values of collective interest, teamwork, and mutual dependency also reduce individual officers' resistance to police administration's effort to bring about changes, and discourage individual officers' own initiatives for changes in police organization and operations.

CHANGES OF CHINESE POLICE CULTURE

Police Organization

Although the three traditional features of police organization—the Party Line, the Mass Line, and the Prevention Line—remain with the Chinese police, their effects on the police organization have been significantly reduced due to rapid economic and social changes in the Chinese society since the late 1970s. The economic development in China since then has created vast social dislocation and income inequality, which have frequently disturbed the social fabric and been blamed as the major causes of crimes and social problems (see chapter 6 in this volume). In the meantime, the reduced influence of the Maoist ideology in Chinese political life and public disenchantment with Communist ideals have led to a spiritual vacuum in the Chinese society, especially among the postwar generation.

The Party Line and traditional reliance on moral order are currently being supplemented by an emerging legal order and professional orientation (see chapter 11 in this volume). Today the police are organized not only to carry out the Communist Party policies but also to uphold the laws passed by the National People's Congress, the legislative body of the Chinese government. Police officers are trained in both substantive and procedural criminal law, as well as special laws and regulations that govern police activities. More and more police recruits have received college-level education and are bringing a strong professional orientation to the police organization as they replace many of the "old guards" and increasingly assume leadership positions in major police agencies across the country.

The professional orientation in the police agency imbued with this "new breed" of police managers has had a visible effect on police organization, especially in the area of police-community relations. Traditionally the police have been organized under the Mass Line principle, which requires that they seek input and ideas directly from the public. Today, police officials have demonstrated a strong interest in learning police organization and management from academicians and Western nations. The police have thus put greater emphasis on organizational efficiency and effectiveness in controlling crimes and maintaining public order. A clear division of labor for the purpose of increasing police efficiency, for example, has been established within municipal police bureaus that separate the Criminal Investigation Division from the Patrol Division, the Neighborhood Police, and the Traffic

Division. The Patrol Division is divided into mobile patrol and foot patrol (see chapter 11 in this volume).

The Prevention Line, another traditional police organizational principle, has occasionally given way to a method called "severe attacks." Unlike crime prevention, "severe attacks" focus on deterrence by attacking crime problems that have already occurred. This occasional shift from a proactive to a reactive approach can be attributed to at least two external factors. First, rapid social and economic changes in Chinese society have led to rampant crimes, especially prostitution, gambling, and sale of drugs and guns. In the face of the rising crime rates, public opinion quickly changes to support crime control, law enforcement, and harsh penalties. In response to the public demand, the police have sometimes been mobilized to "severely attack" the crime problems. Second, increased social mobility in Chinese society has increased the transient population and reduced the traditional sense of community. In addition, there has been a growing distrust of government in general due to serious official corruption. The reduced community consciousness and increased public dissatisfaction with the government have resulted in less voluntary participation in community crime prevention programs. The functions of the traditional neighborhood police and the public security committees based on the Prevention Line have therefore been reduced to a less significant level, sometimes even considered out-of-date.

Police Operations

Along with the changes in Chinese police organization have come modifications of traditional police activities or operations. Chinese police operations today feature new policing programs in response to changes that have been taking place in Chinese society and in the crime situation. One of the most visible changes has occurred in police patrol: a new mobile patrol program has been created to complement the neighborhood police and foot patrol programs. Marked patrol vehicles have become a part of the patrol force in many large and medium-size cities in China, and are used to conduct Western-style routine patrol on the street. The sudden appearance of these police vehicles has created some excitement and a fresh sense of security among the Chinese public, and is widely supported. Both police officials and the public believe that these vehicles have a strong deterrent effect on would-be offenders.

The mobile patrol program and some other new police programs are more reactive than proactive, and more punitive than rehabilitative in nature. With the availability of police patrol vehicles, the police have adopted a rapid response system with modern communication and dispatching techniques. Major police agencies have purchased advanced information and computer network systems to help them process criminal data and fight crime more efficiently. According to Dutton and Lee (1993), the Chinese police have launched periodic campaigns against crime since the late 1970s. Although one of the purposes of these campaigns is to deter crime, they are a departure in the most dramatic fashion from the traditional crime prevention program.

The Chinese police have also established a legal education program to train police officers in law and the legal system. The police officers are expected to develop a stronger legalistic orientation in their daily work. In addition, this program serves to enhance general legal education because properly trained police officers are often assigned to provide legal education in schools and civic organizations. This program is a deviation from the more traditional educational campaign that emphasizes moral, ethical, and ideological instruction.

The symbolic changes in Chinese police operations to a stronger legalistic orientation are also reflected in the enactment of new police regulations. The most significant legislation has been the Police Law of 1995, which may eventually replace the Security Administration and Punishment Act (SAPA) of 1957, 1986, and 1994. SAPA can be considered the "traditional" Chinese police law, which details routine police activities for the purpose of maintaining public order. It includes rules and procedures for dealing with minors, the mentally ill, and the disabled; working with institutions such as government agencies, corporate organizations, and commercial businesses; and educating the public regarding public order management. The police implement these regulations with a focus on prevention and education by warning, mediation, and giving fines. They may also respond to certain minor unlawful acts with administratively punitive measures. These unlawful acts include those that cannot be resolved by ordinary criticism-education measures, create public disorder, endanger public safety, breach community moral standards, violate citizen rights, encroach on public and private property, and obstruct residential registration and identification management. These unlawful behaviors have been easily reconciled as administrative problems that are not subject to criminal sanctions; nevertheless, the police are authorized to give penalties in the form of administrative detention of from one to fourteen days when necessary.

The Police Law of 1995 embodies a new law enforcement and professional orientation in response to the changes that have taken place in Chinese society (see chapter 11 in this volume). In contrast to SAPA, this law contains no specific administrative sanctions, and it requires that the police impose administratively coercive and punitive measures in accordance with relevant laws and regulations. This law, as well as the new programs and operations created by the Chinese police, creates an impression that traditional Chinese police cultures, guided by the Party Line, the Mass Line, and the Prevention Line, are being replaced by a more aggressive law enforcement orientation. But upon closer examination, changes in Chinese police law and practices are not so dramatic.

The seeming orientation to law enforcement of the new police law does not contravene the fact that the Chinese police remain primarily a crime prevention force. Among the specific police activities stipulated in the Police Law of 1995, for example, the majority are still concerned with crime prevention and order mainte-nance. These activities include preventing and stopping criminal activities; main-taining public order and preventing problems that endanger social order; organizing and administering fire prevention; controlling firearms, ammunition, knives, and flammable, explosive, and radioactive materials; supervising the oper-ation of certain types of professions and industries; managing the household regis-tration system; supervising offenders sentenced to control, detention, deprivation of political rights, probation, and parole; supervising and administering computer information network security and protection; guiding and supervising security work in government offices, social organizations, and enterprises; and guiding crime prevention and security activities of community public security organiza-tions. Although the police are required to follow laws and procedures more closely according to this new law, they are allowed to continue to use administrative sanc-tions such as detention for investigation.

It may be more accurate to say at this point that there has been more window dressing and rhetoric to placate the public than substantive cultural transforma-tions within the police force. Interviews with Chinese police officials indicate that they continue to embrace traditional crime prevention activities as the most effec-tive measure to accomplish the goal of crime control. Meanwhile, they do not see severe punishment and stern crackdowns as contradictory to traditional crime pre-vention because they believe that these more punitive measures are necessary un-der unusual circumstances, and will ultimately return police operations to a traditional prevention mode.

Police Behaviors

Various social and cultural factors influence individual police officers, their pri-mary socialization, the police organization, and individual officers' particular working situations. In recent years, Chinese families have grown less attached, compared to the nuclear family structure that used to dominate this most impor-tant part of the social fabric. Police management, as discussed previously, has be-come more professionalized, although symbolically. And the immediate police working environment has apparently become more commercialized and material-istic. These changes naturally have an effect on Chinese police behaviors.

Although Chinese police officers continue to be assigned to work within the community and to collaborate with public security groups, the traditional emo-tional cohesion and support between the police and the community are barely maintained in some neighborhoods. Voluntary participation by members of the community in public security activities has dwindled in many areas. More crimes that are reported to the police, especially property crimes, remain unsolved, creat-ing dissatisfaction among crime victims. Consequently, Chinese police officers do not enjoy as much support as they used to, and have grown less interested in community service. In the same vein, Chinese officers have lost some of the moral authority they used to possess which would allow them to play the role of teachers and leaders in the community.

The working behaviors of police officers, influenced by this social environment, have changed in both positive and negative ways. On the positive side, individual police officers have become more active in making suggestions and initiating changes in police organization and operations, and in dealing with new challenges in crime and in the community. Encouraged by more professionally oriented police managers, they have become more involved in the decision-making process. Some officers are also more open in their questioning of new policies or changes introduced by police administration.

On the negative side, there seems to be more police corruption and abuse of power among individual officers (see chapter 11 in this volume). This has been largely caused by the lessened moral authority police officers have in the community and the continued authoritarian mentality of some officers. These negative behaviors should be viewed in the context of China's change from a largely agricultural society into an emerging free-market economy (see chapter 2 in this volume). Although the idea of moral authority might have had a positive influence on the community when China was largely a rural society, it contributes more easily to police corruption and abuse of power during the current economic transition.

As the country experiences dramatic economic and social changes, the police face more crimes and public order violations, and are pressured by the public to be more efficient in dealing with them. Yet the Chinese legal system remains in the embryonic stage and cannot supersede the traditional value system in guiding individual police behaviors. At this particular time in Chinese history, police officers have not internalized the legalistic values and due process concepts. They often believe that it is more important to follow ethical and moral principles shared in the community. The continued political involvement of the Communist Party in police work reinforces this idea among many individual officers.

Consequently, Chinese police officers may be involved in corrupt behaviors and violate individual rights in the name of protecting collective interests and the public good. Not indoctrinated with a rule-of-law tradition, most Chinese police officers also believe that it is of utmost importance for them to enjoy a certain level of flexibility in law enforcement. The Chinese police regulations, including the Security Administration and Penalty Act (SAPA) and the Police Law of 1995, provide officers with this flexibility. They do not always have to follow the court-sanctioned criminal procedures, which impose more stringent requirements on arrest and detention, when they are dealing with public order violations, thus resulting in many abusive behaviors.

When asked about the causes of increased police corruption, Chinese police officials often cite bad social influences; poor working habits, such as emphasis on word of mouth rather than facts; and lack of education and training. It is believed that officers involved in corruption and misconduct usually do not possess the generally recognized socialist moral standards and values. Tolerant police leaders and police organizational culture are also blamed as causes of abusive police behaviors. Police administrators who ignore, tolerate, or even take the lead in forced confessions create an organizational atmosphere where police abuse of power is considered acceptable. The police have also attributed police misbehavior to individual officers' personality, their temperament, and suspects' attitudes. Individual officers involved in abuse of power are often believed to be younger, less educated, hot-tempered, unstable, and to have a strong ego and a privileged mentality (see chapter 2 in this volume).

When asked about how to reduce police corruption and misconduct, police officers often cite the importance of prevention rather than disciplinary measures. And the best preventive measure, according to Chinese police officials, is raising individual officers' ethical standards and strengthening their moral character. Some reform programs have been introduced in recent years to encourage good police behaviors and reduce police corruption and misconduct. The Police Law of 1995 stipulates that police are now subject to four types of supervision: procuratorate, administrative, internal, and citizen. As a result, police officers have been put under greater scrutiny and are expected to become more professionalized in the process. Police professionalism, however, represents a culture that is essentially alien to the Chinese police tradition. As Reenen (1997) observes, Western legalistic values have been imported into police forces in many countries in the world under the disguise of police professionalism. The incorporation of legal notions in the police system directly challenges the traditional Chinese cultural expectations of their police as moral authorities and public educators in the community. Because the society continues to be directed by ethics and collective responsibility, the creation and maintenance of a set of legal values within the police is a slow and difficult process.

CONCLUSIONS

Overall, police culture is similar because police officers everywhere play the same roles and operate in the same criminal justice system (Skolnick and Fyfe, 1993; Crank, 1998). In addition, police officers work in similar social, economic, and political environments, which provide similar clienteles and create similar social expectations. The cultural environment for the Chinese police, characterized by a hierarchical social structure, moral order, and group functioning, has led to a more cohesive and, in a sense, dutiful community (Hsu, 1991) that has worked closely with the police everywhere in China. As China changes to a more open and freer society, the police are searching for new approaches to deal with the strife associated with rampant crime and less community participation in public security work.

This chapter mainly describes the influence of the cultural contexts on police organization, operations, and individual officer behaviors in China. There are multiple layers or sources of cultural influences on police, ranging from the larger political, social, and economic contexts to community characteristics, to police organizational environment, and finally to commonly shared individual officers' routine work experiences. Police practices in China can be better understood when all these cultural elements are carefully examined. Sometimes the values of individual officers and the culture of a police organization may seem unique due to the distinctive nature of police organization and particular officer working situations; but when examined closely, they do not escape the influence of the larger culture. The Chinese police culture, therefore, must be understood as being dependent upon the social, political, and economic conditions of policing. The general social values and beliefs that inform the society are believed also to inform the decisions of street-level police officers (Lipsky, 1980).

Understanding the social processes forming the police culture also has practical implications, because it helps police leaders understand the difficulties in creating a new police culture or improving an old police culture (Greene et al., 1992). A policing style or culture cannot deviate significantly from the commonly shared values and beliefs in a particular community or society if it is to be sustained. If the larger cultural characteristics are gemeinschaft, for instance, the police culture should not be based on features of a gesellschaft society (Tonnies, 1963).

Since the society has a great influence on policing styles or orientations, fundamental cultural transformations in a society should lead to changes in the police. Police cultural changes consistent with the change occurring in the larger society should have a long-term effect on police practices. In recent years the Chinese police have implemented some newly developed programs aimed at upgrading the police system and inculcating a legalistic orientation. Although these programs seem to be purely police-initiated reforms, they reflect social cultural changes in China. Like many cultures in the world, the Chinese people are searching for practical ideas and programs beyond their own culture. As a result, many changes have taken place in business organizations, community life, and family structures. These changes in turn have influenced the change of police practices in China.

The Chinese police are making some progress in developing a law enforcement approach, albeit symbolically, and in modernizing themselves with advanced Western management and response technology. The emphasis on legal and procedural knowledge, requirement of higher education, and the establishment of a mobile patrol force are just a few examples of the Chinese effort to change from community-based policing to professional policing. To a certain extent, these developments reflect the erosion of the collective spirit and lack of voluntary participation in community policing in contemporary Chinese society. The problem of public indifference to community affairs has emerged in

China at a time of rapid economic growth and social changes (Jiao, 1995). This change in Chinese society presents the police with an immediate policy issue: Should the police adapt to this change by adopting a more professional police management orientation?

The issue here is, again, cultural. A policing style based on a culture of police professionalism cannot be developed in a short time in China because, in China today, psychological and emotional ties to the family, the work group, and the society remain strong; and the Chinese police executives have hardly changed their traditional philosophy of policing, continuing to view their officers as public servants and protectors. As Guyot (1991) states, unless police officers are treated as professionals, they will not act as professionals. The Chinese police, therefore, should respond to Chinese social ties and dominant ideas of policing, and continue their community orientation at the major policing approach, but supplement it with some new initiatives that reflect current changes in Chinese society.

On the other hand, genuine police cultural changes in China could happen if Chinese culture could be reconciled to a legalistic culture. The decline of Christianity in China during the early 1700s can be attributed to the conflicts it created in the Chinese culture. Since Christianity's philosophical and religious elements could not be reconciled with Chinese culture, its practice deteriorated (Zurcher, 1997). The key to changing the Chinese police system is to examine it to see if there is goal fit, goal clarity, and goal agreement in this change process. Because the answer to this question seems negative, it is perhaps safer to say at this point that the Chinese police will continue to preserve what they consider the virtues of the Chinese culture while at the same time assimilating the knowledge and experiences of policing in other countries.

Nevertheless, police executives are often able to forge ahead with new police programs aimed at changing traditional police cultures and to demonstrate certain effects of their reform efforts even though changes in a society, theoretically speaking, must occur before a new policing culture takes root. The strength and persistence of this effect, however, depend on whether the contextual and cultural constraints police encounter in developing a new culture have been reduced, and whether the police have organizational and managerial control over the traditional culture they intend to change. Police executives must also have a high level of commitment to maintain the new culture and establish new sets of expectations and norms that promote the new police behavior and reduce reliance on traditional police strategies and organizational values. Due to the power of the field (i.e., the social, economic, legal, and political sites in which policing takes place), changing police culture requires changes in the field at both the management and the street level. The new expectations, norms, values, and administrative behaviors should contribute to the creation of a new organizational culture, and acculturate police officers to new ideas of policing.

REFERENCES

Bond, Michael H., and K. K. Hwang. 1986. "The Social Psychology of the Chinese People." In *The Psychology of the Chinese People*, pp. 265–317. Edited by Michael H. Bond. New York: Oxford University Press.

Cain, Maureen E. 1973. *Society and the Policeman's Role*. London: Routledge and Kegan Paul.

Chan, Janet. 1996. "Changing Police Culture." *British Journal of Criminology* 36: 109–134.

Chiu, Randy K., and Frederick A. Kosinski. 1994. "Is Chinese Conflict-Handling Behavior Influenced by Chinese Values?" *Social Behavior and Personality* 22: 81–90.

Crank, John P. 1998. *Understanding Police Culture*. Cincinnati, OH: Anderson.

deBary, William T., Wing-tsit Chan, and Burton Watson. 1960. "The Mean." In *Introduction to Oriental Civilizations: Sources of Chinese Tradition*, pp. 117–121. Edited by W. T. deBary. New York: Columbia University Press.

Dellapenna, Joseph W. 1997. "The Lesson of the Triple Twisted Pine: Plum Blossoms on Mountain Peaks and the Future of the Rule of Law in Hong Kong." *Vanderbilt Journal of Transnational Laws* 30: 637–673.

Dutton, Michael, and Tianfu Lee. 1993. "Missing the Target? Policing Strategies in the Period of Economic Reform." *Crime and Delinquency* 39, no. 3: 316–336.

Ferguson, R. James. 1998. "Inclusive Strategies for Restraining Aggression: Lessons from Classical Chinese Culture." *Asian Philosophy* 8, no. 1: 31–46.

Greene, Jack R., Geoffrey P. Alpert, and Paul Styles. 1992. "Values and Culture in Two American Police Departments: Lessons from King Arthur." *Journal of Contemporary Criminal Justice* 8, no. 3: 183–207.

Guyot, Dorothy. 1991. *Policing as Though People Matter*. Philadelphia: Temple University Press.

Hall, David L., and Roger T. Ames. 1995. *Anticipating China: Thinking Through the Narratives of Chinese and Western Culture*. Albany: State University of New York Press.

He Bingsong. 1991. "Crime and Control in China." In *Crime and Control in Comparative Perspective*, pp. 241–257. Edited by Hans-Gunther Heiland, Louise I. Shelley, and Hisao Katoh. New York: Walter de Gruyter.

Ho, David Y. F. 1994. "Cognitive Socialization in Confucian Cultures." In *Cross-Cultural Roots of Minority Child Development*, pp. 285–313. Edited by Patricia M. Greenfield and Rodney R. Cocking. Hillsdale, NJ: Lawrence Erlbaum.

Holdaway, Simon. 1983. *Inside British Police: A Force at Work*. Oxford: Basil Blackwell.

Hsu Cho-yun. 1991. "Applying Confucian Ethics to International Relations." *Ethics and International Affairs* 5: 15–31.

Ingraham, Barton L. 1987. *The Structure of Criminal Procedure: Laws and Practice of France, the Soviet Union, China, and the United States*. New York: Greenwood Press.

Jiao, Allan Y. 1995. "Community Policing and Community Mutuality." *Police Studies* 18: 69–91.

Johnson, Elmer H. 1986. "Neighborhood Police in the People's Republic of China." *Police Studies* 9: 8–12.

Kilmann, Ralph H., Mary J. Saxton, and Roy Serpa. 1985. *Gaining Control of the Corporate Culture*. San Francisco: Jossey Bass.

Koo, Linda Chih-ling. 1976. "Nourishment of Life: The Culture of Health in Traditional Chinese Society." Ph.D. dissertation, University of California, Berkeley.

Lee, Kang, Catherine Ann Cameron, Genyao Fu, Fen Xu, and Julie Board. 1997. "Chinese and Canadian Children's Evaluations of Lying and Truth Telling: Similarities and Differences in the Context of Pro- and Antisocial Behaviors." *Child Development* 68: 924–936.

Lipsky, Michael. 1980. *Street-Level Bureaucracy: Dilemmas of the Individual in Public Services*. New York: Russell Sage Foundation.

Manning, Peter. 1977. *Police Work*. Cambridge, MA: MIT Press.

Markus, Hazel R., and Shinobu Kitayama. 1994. "The Cultural Construction of Self and Emotion: Implications for Social Behavior." In *Emotion and Culture: Empirical Studies of Mutual Influence*, pp. 89–132. Edited by Shinobu Kitayama and Hazel R. Markus. Washington, DC: American Psychological Association.

Peerenboom, Randall P. 1993. *Law and Morality in Ancient China: The Silk Manuscripts of Huang-lao*. Albany: State University of New York Press.

Reenen, P. Van. 1997. "Police Integrity and Police Loyalty: The Stalker Dilemma." *Policing and Society* 8: 1–45.

Skolnick, Jerome H. 1966. *Justice Without Trial*. New York: John Wiley and Sons.

Skolnick, Jerome H., and James J. Fyfe. 1993. *Above the Law: Police and the Excessive Use of Force*. New York: Free Press.

Tonnies, Ferdinand. 1963. *Community and Society*. East Lansing: Michigan State University Press.

Tsai, Jeanne L., and Robert W. Levenson. 1997. "Cultural Influences on Emotional Responding: Chinese American and European American Dating Couples During Interpersonal Conflict." *Journal of Cross-Cultural Psychology* 28: 600–626.

Zhang Jie and Jin Shenghua. 1998. "Interpersonal Relations and Suicide Ideation in China." *Genetic, Social, and General Psychology Monographs* 124, no. 1: 79–94.

Zhang Lening, Dengke Zhou, Steven F. Messner, Allen E. Liska, Marvin D. Krohn, Jianhong Liu, and Zhou Lu. 1996. "Crime Prevention in a Communitarian Society: *Bang-Jiao* and *Tiao-Jie* in the People's Republic of China." *Justice Quarterly* 13: 199–222.

Zhu Guangqian. 1995. "Comparing Chinese and Western Poetry." In *Asian Thought and Culture: Contemporary Chinese Aesthetics*, pp. 95–121. Edited by Liyuan Zhu and Gene Blocker. New York: Peter Lang.

Zurcher, Erik. 1997. "Confucian and Christian Religiosity in Late Ming China." *Catholic Historical Review* 83, no. 4: 614–654.

CHAPTER 13

The Recent Development of Juvenile Justice in China

Guoling Zhao

Juvenile delinquency and juvenile justice are a major concern in the field of justice worldwide. China is a developing country with a large number of juveniles (360 million) and increasing juvenile problems. During the past few decades, juvenile justice in China has had a significant development in response to ongoing economic reform and increasing rates of delinquency. This chapter will explore the recent development of juvenile justice by focusing on judicial protection of minors and juvenile courts in China.

THE DEVELOPMENT OF JUDICIAL PROTECTION OF MINORS

Before exploring the recent development of judicial protection of minors, it is useful to briefly review the history of legal protection of minors in China. China has a long legal history of protecting minors. There were many stipulations on protection of minors in ancient Chinese laws. For example, during the Zhou Dynasty (1066 B.C.–221 B.C.), it was stipulated that a person who committed a crime and was under the age of seven or above eighty might be exempted from punishment (Kang, 1996, p. 388). During the Han Dynasty (206 B.C.–220 A.D.), a person who committed a crime and was under the age of eight or above eighty might be exempted from punishment (except for murder). In addition, a person who committed a crime and was under the age of ten or above seventy, might be exempted from corporal punishment (Kang, 1996, p. 388). The rules alleviating and lessening criminal responsibility in Chinese history were not limited to the imposition of punishment but also applied to the specific nature of punishment. For instance, the Han Dynasty prescribed that a convicted criminal under the age of eight or above eighty might not wear instruments of punishment (Kang, 1996, p. 389).

The law of the Qin Dynasty (221 B.C.–206 B.C.) written on the bamboo books found in Qin tombs prescribed that "if A instigated B to kill someone for money and the height of B is less than six chi (about 4.53 feet), it means B is a child. A rather than B should have his or her body torn apart by carriages." These bamboo books involve twelve fields of the juvenile protection, including family education, infant protection, social protection, legal protection, and labor protection, etc. For example, the chapter "Jiuye" states that young males should not be dispatched to jobs outside the area where they live and should not be recruited to do unsuitable or heavy jobs. It also prohibits selling juveniles alcohol or inducing them to drink heavily. The bamboo books also have rules of interrogation. For example, torture during interrogation is prohibited for juveniles. The law of the Tang Dynasty (618–907) is more specific about age and criminal accountability. It prescribes that a juvenile under the age of seven is exempt from the death penalty; under age ten, can appeal to higher officers if convicted of rebellion or murder; under fifteen, might surrender property for offenses rather than be exiled.

The next several dynasties—Yuan, Ming, and Qing—generally followed the law of Tang Dynasty. For example, the criminal law of the Yuan Dynasty (1206–1368) stated that a juvenile under the age of fifteen who committed murder or homicide should pay retribution to the victim's family rather than be put to death. The Qing Dynasty (616–1911) prescribed that punishment for offenses should be lenient for a convicted person under the age of fifteen or above eighty (Kang, 1996, p. 392).

All these examples indicate that early in their history, the Chinese were concerned with people's age and their accountability for criminal behavior when punishment was imposed. Although there was no separate justice system for juveniles, many criminal laws during different periods of ancient China showed attempts and tendencies to treat juveniles and adults differently through the criminal justice system.

During the twentieth century, the Chinese government adopted the Provisional Regulations of Marriage (1931), which provided special protections for minors. The Constitution Outline of 1934 contains a reference to "protecting the rights of the young workers" (Constitutional Law Section of the People's University of China, 1955, p. 77) The Labor Law and other laws also had regulations protecting minors' rights in regard to life and work. Since the founding of the People's Republic of China, especially since China implemented the open-door and reform policies in 1978, protection of minors and related juvenile legal rights have developed significantly. The Constitution of the People's Republic of China (1982) solemnly proclaims that children should be protected by the state under the fundamental law and the supreme law. Article 46 of the Constitution provides that the state will foster development of children's moral characters, their intellects, their health, and more. Article 49 further states that children are protected by the state (National People's Congress, 1982, pp. 30–31). These regulations lay a constitutional foundation and offer the guiding principles for protecting minors.

The National People's Congress and its standing committee drafted 253 laws and 106 legal resolutions between 1979 and 1999 (Qiao, 1999, p. 11). Many of these laws and regulations are related to juvenile legal rights. For example, the Principles of Civil Law sets out a system of guardianship to guarantee minors' legal rights and interests (National People's Congress, 1986, pp. 5–6, 19). The Marriage Law of the People's Republic of China provides that when the People's Court handles a divorce case, the rights and interests of children must be taken into account (National People's Congress, 1980, pp. 60–61). The Criminal Law of the People's Republic of China stipulates that anyone who violates the legal rights of minors will be severely punished. For example, severe punishment must be imposed for abuse, abandonment, murder, abduction, kidnapping, and rape of children. The Criminal Law also establishes the age of eighteen as a standard for full legal accountability of a convicted offender (National People's Congress, 1997, pp. 142, 181–185). Both the Civil Procedure Law and the Criminal Procedure Law of the People's Republic of China establish special measures to guarantee the rights and interests of minors with respect to litigation procedures. For example, a legal representative should be present in the litigation process; the court should appoint a defense lawyer for a juvenile offender; a juvenile case should not be tried in public (National People's Congress, 1996, pp. 54, 72). Other laws, such as the Labor Law and the Law of Compulsory Education, also set up legal guards for juvenile rights and protection.

In addition to these laws and regulations addressing the protection of juvenile legal rights and interests, there are two special laws that target juvenile protection—the Law of the People's Republic of China on the Protection of Minors and the Law of the People's Republic of China on the Prevention of Juvenile Delinquency. In addition, the Chinese government has signed international conventions on children's rights. For example, the Chinese government signed the United Nations Convention on the Rights of the Child; the World Declaration on the Survival, the Protection and Development of Children; and the Action Plan for Implementing the World Declaration on the Survival, and the Protection and Development of Children.

THE LAW OF THE PEOPLE'S REPUBLIC OF CHINA ON THE PROTECTION OF MINORS

The Law of the People's Republic of China on the Protection of Minors (Standing Committee of the National People's Congress, 1991, pp. 24–31) is the first comprehensive law in China to provide systematic and overall protection of minors' rights and interests. It was adopted at the twenty-first meeting of the Standing Committee of the Seventh National People's Congress on September 4, 1991, and became effective on January 1, 1992. Following the passage of the protection law, twenty-eight provinces, autonomous regions, and municipalities have established local regulations for the protection of the rights of minors.

The protection law has seven chapters with fifty-six articles covering various aspects of minors' protection. The law is divided into five parts. Part I addresses the general provisions in seven articles, such as the legislative purpose, the guiding philosophy, and the legal foundation. Part II consists of four chapters with thirty-eight articles. It stipulates that various social institutions are responsible for the protection of minors, including family, school, other social organizations, and judicial institutions. It also defines missions and methods of protection. Part III includes nine articles addressing legal responsibility and accountability if the protection law is violated. Part IV is supplementary provisions with two articles. These provisions stipulate the procedures and related rules for the enforcement of the law.

The guiding philosophy is protecting the physical and mental health of minors; safeguarding their legal rights and interests; promoting their moral, intellectual, and physical development, and training them to become law-abiding citizens of a socialist society with well-developed morality, social skills, and qualified education.

The protected subjects stipulated by the law can generally be divided into two types: general and special subjects. The general subjects are minors under the age of eighteen. They should be protected equally regardless of gender, nationality, class, ethnicity, and race. The special subjects are minors in special circumstances: orphans; minors from broken families; minors of illegitimate birth; disabled minors; and minors who engage in delinquent behaviors. For delinquent minors, the guiding principle is education and persuasion with love and reintegration.

The law stipulates minors' self-protection and grants a minor the legal right to report any abuse and harm to his or her physical and mental health. It also stipulates that the protection of minors is a responsibility of various social organizations and institutions. Especially, the Communist Youth League, women's federations, labor unions, youth federations, students' federations, and Young Pioneers shall assist governments at various levels to enforce the law.

The protections include the following:

1. Protecting juveniles' economic, political, or social rights. For example, the law stipulates that the state shall encourage social organizations, enterprises, institutions, and citizens to sponsor social activities and events that are helpful and valuable to the development of minors; and that people's governments at various levels shall establish and improve places and facilities suited to the need of minors for their development.

2. Protecting juveniles from being victimized by parents or other people. For example, the law stipulates that the parents or other guardians of minors shall fulfill their responsibility of guardianship and their obligations to bring up the minors. They shall neither maltreat or abandon the minors nor discriminate against female or handicapped minors.

Infanticide and infant abandonment are forbidden; parents or other guardians of minors shall respect the minors' rights to receive education.

3. Protecting juveniles from the possible abuse of power. For example, it stipulates that for delinquent juveniles, the guiding policy should be education and persuasion with love and redemption, and the principle should rely mainly on education while making punishment subsidiary; public security organs, people's procuratorates, and courts guard minors in custody pending trial, and separate them from adults. Trials of juveniles over fourteen years but under sixteen shall be closed to the public.

The law also stipulates measures for its implementation. Governments at various levels should establish a reward system for organizations or individuals achieving successes in protecting minors; conditions should be made for minors to attain compulsory education (nine-year education, including elementary and middle school); the guardianship of a minor should be changed if his or her parents or guardians interfere with or harm the minor's rights and interests seriously; runaway children and begging minors should be sent back to their parents or guardians by civil administrations; abandoned minors should be sent to citizens who would be able to adopt them or to child welfare organizations; those minors who break laws or commit minor offenses should be sent to work-study school for rehabilitation if their schools and families are not able to discipline them; minors who have committed crimes but do not receive a criminal penalty should be educated and disciplined by their parents or guardians; minors over sixteen years old should be sent to a rehabilitation center; people will be punished if they sell or supply books, newspapers, magazines, or video/audio products with obscene, violent, murder, and terror contents to minors; behaviors which harm minors' physical and mental health and legal rights and interests should be reported.

THE LAW OF THE PEOPLE'S REPUBLIC OF CHINA ON PREVENTION OF JUVENILE DELINQUENCY

It is believed that the law (Standing Committee of the National People's Congress, 1999, pp. 276–285) is the first one that stipulates the prevention of juvenile delinquency in China. The law was adopted at the tenth meeting of the Standing Committee of the Ninth National People's Congress on June 28, 1999, and became effective on November 1, 1999. The law has eight chapters with fifty-seven articles. Chapter I contains the General Provisions. It stipulates the legislative purpose—safeguarding juveniles' physical and mental health, developing socially desirable behavior, and preventing juvenile delinquency. It also defines the fundamental guideline—preventing juvenile delinquency on the basis of education and protection. The basic method of delinquency prevention is comprehensive treatment under the administration of governments at all levels. Governments should formulate plans for delinquency prevention, organize and coordinate prevention programs involving different government departments, and monitor and assess the implementation of the law and related activities.

Chapter II focuses on education as a measure of delinquency prevention. It stipulates that juveniles shall be educated in Communist ideology, morality, legal knowledge, patriotism, and collectivism. Juveniles who reach the age of compulsory education shall be educated in delinquency prevention. The purpose of such education is to enhance their awareness of laws and delinquency. Educational programs of delinquency prevention shall be incorporated into school curriculums. The justice and education departments of governments at all levels, the Youth League of Communism, and the Youth Pioneers shall organize and carry out legal education in various forms. Parents and other guardians of juveniles shall take direct responsibility for legal education of juveniles and be actively involved in school programs on delinquency prevention.

Chapter III defines offenses that should be prevented by parents and schools: truancy, running away from home, carrying weapons, gang fights, begging, theft, destroying public property, gambling, pornography, and other illegal acts. The law provides that parents, other guardians, and schools shall educate juveniles not to smoke or drink. It is illegal to sell cigarettes or alcoholic beverages to juveniles. This chapter also defines responsibilities of parents, guardians, schools, law enforcement agencies, and other social organizations in preventing these offenses. For example, the law stipulates that the neighborhood committee shall assist law enforcement agencies to strengthen the security around elementary and middle schools.

Chapter IV addresses corrections of serious juvenile offenses that do not warrant criminal punishment. These serious offenses include: instigating gang fights, recidivism in carrying controlled weapons, aggravated assault, robbery, disseminating pornographic materials and products, engaging in prostitution, recidivism in theft-larceny; recidivism in gambling, drug abuse, and other highly harmful offenses. The law stipulates that when a juvenile commits any of these serious offenses, his or her parents or guardians shall take strong measures to control and educate in collaboration with school, or may send the juvenile to a work-study school for rehabilitation. A work-study school should have the same curricula as those in a normal school, and focus on legal education and treatment rather than punishment for the juvenile offender. For a juvenile offender under the age of sixteen who does not deserve criminal punishment, his or her parents or guardians shall be required to take strict control and provide education. Whenever it is necessary, the juvenile may also be sheltered and rehabilitated by a social welfare agency. During rehabilitation, the social welfare agency should ensure that the juvenile offender receives the same education as that given to nondelinquent juveniles. A juvenile who has completed a rehabilitation term shall enjoy the same rights in education and employment, and should not be discriminated against.

Chapter V concerns self-prevention of delinquency. The law stipulates that juveniles shall conform to a variety of laws and regulations; develop self-respect, self-discipline, and self-improvement; strengthen identification with law-abiding behaviors and self-protection; and enhance awareness in resisting crime instigation and inducement. Judicial administrations, schools, and the society shall protect juveniles who report and fight against crimes from retaliation and revenge.

Chapter VI addresses the prevention of recidivism. The law rules that for juveniles who have been held legally responsible for offenses, education, persuasion, and redemption are the principal correctional measures. Legal punishment is a complementary measure. Juvenile legal rights, such as legal assistance, should be ensured in the justice processing. The trial of a juvenile criminal case shall be held in a juvenile court consisting of a judge and personnel who have special knowledge of physical and psychological characteristics of juveniles. The trial and the juvenile case should be closed to the public and mass media. Juvenile offenders should be separated from adult offenders. While serving a term of punishment, legal education, vocational education, and compulsory education (if not finished) should be given to a juvenile offender. For juveniles who do not deserve criminal punishment because of their age or the nature of their offending, because they are parolees, or because they are on probation, their parents, schools, and communities should actively participate in rehabilitation and education.

Chapter VII defines legal responsibility in preventing delinquency. The law stipulates that if parents or guardians fail to perform their defined roles in preventing delinquency, law enforcement agencies can warn and educate them. Any member of law enforcement who fails to legally handle a reported juvenile case should be given administrative sanctions. Legal responsibility can be pursued if such a failure leads to serious consequences. Whoever instigates, forces, or induces a juvenile to engage in delinquency shall be given administrative or legal penalties in accordance with the nature of the behavior.

The law of delinquency prevention is a legal reaction to the rising number of juvenile offenses and related public concerns in China. The broad content of the law reflects the basic strategy of crime control—a social war against crime. This social war is a mass movement to suppress crime during the economic reform and open door policy. The war is a combination of informal and formal control, although the emphasis placed on formal control has increased recently; in the past there were few legal measures.

THE DEVELOPMENT OF THE JUVENILE COURT

Since economic reform and open door policy have been implemented in China, the nation has been facing dramatically rising crime rates, especially delinquency rates. In recent years, juvenile cases have increased every year, and juvenile legal rights and interests have been repeatedly violated. It is essential to establish a juvenile justice system. In late 1984, the grassroots People's Court of Changing District of Shanghai city set up a collegial panel to hear juvenile cases, the first special juvenile court in the country. Since then, more than 3,300 juvenile courts have been established in China (Ren, 1998, p. 43).

The age range for a juvenile who can be referred to a juvenile court is fourteen to eighteen. There is no waiver procedure by which a juvenile can be transferred to adult criminal court for trial except in some regions without a juvenile court. Roughly, there are three stages in the development of juvenile court in China. Preliminary establishment and experiment were the first stage (1984–1988). In the second stage (1988–1990) juvenile courts spread nationwide. Evaluation and improvement is the last stage (since 1990). There are several major features of juvenile court in China.

First, "double protections" are a foundation of the juvenile court. Double protections imply a balance between protections of juveniles and the community. On the one hand, juvenile offenders should be given adequate punishment in order to protect the security of society and the community. Too lenient punishment would have no deterrent effect. On the other hand, too severe punishment would harm juvenile legal rights and juveniles' development due to the adverse consequences of the punishment.

Second, the judicial process of juvenile court should be a legal and educational process. Legal judgment and education should be combined in the processing of a juvenile offender. The trial in juvenile court is not only a process of legal judgment about the fact and causes of an offense, but also a process of protecting juvenile legal rights and educating the juvenile offender.

Third, special procedures are provided for juvenile processing that are different from those for adults. Juvenile courts provide juvenile offenders with a more informal atmosphere, and the trial is closed to the public. An educational stage is added to the court trial and the court acts as a "parent."

Fourth, education is the major purpose of juvenile processing; punishment takes a back seat. Lenient punishment should be given to the extent possible, in order to provide protection of the juvenile's legal rights and reputation. Although anyone who has committed a crime must be guilty of an offense, including juveniles, the Criminal Law of the People's Republic of China prescribes that a juvenile offender above age fourteen but under eighteen shall be given a lighter or mitigated punishment. No death penalty is imposed on a juvenile offender. The Criminal Law divides criminal responsibility of a juvenile delinquent into three types.

1. A juvenile under the age of fourteen shall not bear any criminal responsibility, but when necessary, he or she can be disciplined by parents or guardians, or may be taken by a government agency for rehabilitation.

2. A juvenile older than fourteen and younger than sixteen shall bear certain criminal responsibility if he or she commits homicide, aggravated assault, rape, robbery, drug-trafficking, arson, explosion, or poisoning.

3. A juvenile above the age of sixteen shall bear complete criminal responsibility. If he or she is under the age of eighteen, he or she shall be exempt from the death penalty (National People's Congress, 1997, pp. 142, 147).

The juvenile justice system in China consists of four major subsystems: police, the people's procuratorate, the juvenile court, and corrections. When a juvenile case is handled by any of these four, the principle of "education first and penalty second" should be followed. The police are responsible for filing a juvenile case. The people's procuratorate examines and approves an arrest. The procuratorate appears in the court for prosecution and provides protection of juvenile legal rights. At present there are over 3,000 people's procuratorates and about 6,000 procurators who work on juvenile cases (Office of the Central Committee of Social Public Security, 2000, p. 31). There are more than 3,000 juvenile courts and over 15,000 judges (Office of the Central Committee of Social Public Security, 2000, p. 32).

In addition to the juvenile justice system, informal control is available for juvenile offenders who are not subjected to court trial and criminal penalty. The emphasis in this case is on education and persuasion. There are diverse nonjudicial measures for juvenile rehabilitation, such as *bangjiao* (help and education) and work-study schools. *Bangjiao* can be performed by an informal group in the community or a work unit. Such a group may consist of parents, relatives, and selected neighbors who are influential and close to the juvenile. A *bangjiao* group may be formed by staff members of a work unit. Work-study education is an important measure of preventing and reducing delinquency. Work-study schools were initiated in 1955, and eighty-eight such schools have been established (Office of the Central Committee of Social Public Security, 2000, p. 35). A work-study school is a special program of education for nine years. Students in a work-study school enjoy the same rights as those in general schools in terms of education and employment. The principle for a work-study school is rehabilitation through education and discipline.

SUMMARY AND DISCUSSION

Since China implemented the open-door and reform policies in the late 1970s and early 1980s, the juvenile justice system has developed significantly in response to the rising rates of delinquency and the awareness of juvenile protection. Laws and regulations for juveniles have been promulgated. Examples of those laws and regulations are the Law of the People's Republic of China on the Protection of Minors and the Law of the People's Republic of China on Prevention of Juvenile Delinquency. These laws address the relationship between juveniles and the community, juvenile legal rights and interests, and prevention and control of juvenile delinquency. These laws reflect Chinese philosophy and traditions that emphasize collective interests, state intervention, delinquency prevention rather than control, and mass involvement. Although these laws have been adopted formally, law enforcement and the effectiveness of these laws are an open question because of the lack of a legal tradition in China.

The development of juvenile courts in China represents efforts to enforce laws concerning juveniles. The characteristics and principles of the juvenile court are quite comparable with those in Western nations. However, the operation of the juvenile court in China may be different in certain ways due to the unique features of China's social, cultural, and political systems. For instance, processing in the juvenile court may be greatly affected by the power of the juvenile's relatives or other personal networks. Any observation and assessment of China's juvenile courts should be made in the context of the nation's social, cultural, and political systems.

REFERENCES

Constitutional Law Section of the People's University of China. 1955. *Reference Material on the Constitution Law of the People's Republic of China.* Beijing: Publishing House of the People's University of China.

Kang Shuhua. 1996. *New Theory on Juvenile Legal Science.* Beijing: Higher Education Publishing House.

National People's Congress. 1980. "The Marriage Law of the People's Republic of China." *Gazette of the Standing Committee of the National People's Congress of the People's Republic of China* no. 5.

———. 1982. "The Constitutional Law of the People's Republic of China." *Gazette of the Standing Committee of the National People's Congress of the People's Republic of China* no. 5.

———. 1986. "The Principles of Civil Law of the People's Republic of China." *Gazette of the Standing Committee of the National People's Congress of the People's Republic of China* no. 4.

———. 1996. "The Criminal Procedure Law of the People's Republic of China." *Gazette of the Standing Committee of the National People's Congress of the People's Republic of China* no. 3.

———. 1997. "The Criminal Law of the People's Republic of China." *Gazette of the Standing Committee of the National People's Congress of the People's Republic of China* no. 2.

Office of the Central Committee of Social Public Security. 2000. *For Tomorrow: Editing and Rearrangement of Materials of Exhibition of Preventing Juvenile Delinquency.* Beijing: Legal Publishing House.

Qiao Xiaoyang. 1999. "Legislation: Pillar of Administering a Country According to Law." *People's Daily*, September 15, p. 11.

Ren Jianxin. 1998. "Report of the Supreme Court." *Gazette of the Supreme People's Court of the People's Republic of China* no. 2: 42–48.

Standing Committee of the National People's Congress. 1991. "The Law of the People's Republic of China on the Protection of Minors." *Gazette of the Standing Committee of the National People's Congress of the People's Republic of China* no. 5.

———— . 1999. "The Law of the People's Republic of China on Prevention of Juvenile Delinquency." *Gazette of the Standing Committee of the National People's Congress of the People's Republic of China* no. 4.

Index

Dispute settlement: concept of face in, 94; Confucian moral code in, 94; negotiation and compromise in, 94; in neighborhood mediation, 93–94, 95, 110; shaming and reintegration in, 94–95

Drug crimes, 62; causes of, 43–46; characteristics of, 40–41; death penalty and, 47–48; and drug control agreements, 46; economic reform movement and, 43–45; legal system and, 45, 46–47; motivation and opportunity in, 43–44; neighborhood contract system and, 48; official control strategies and, 46–51; official statistics on, 38; publicity as deterrent against, 47–48; recent increase in, 37, 39; shame and, 45; severe strikes against, 47–48; and social control mechanisms, 44–46

Drug use, 61; and crime, 42; health impacts, 42; history of, 37, 38; juvenile, 125–126; mandatory treatment of, 48–49; public campaign against, 40; regulations on, 48; social norms and, 45; social order impacted by, 42; stigma of, 39; of youth, 41–42; war on, China vs. United States, 50–51

Durkheim, Emile, 4, 6, 8, 18, 74

Economic growth, and rise in crime, 78

Economic reform movement: bribery and corruption and, 23, 26, 29–31; crime increase and, 3, 5; and criminal procedure, 137; and cultural change, 107–109; drug crime and, 43–45; "getting rich is glorious" slogan and, 43–44; and rural-urban inequality, 79–81; and urban neighborhoods, 107–109; and violent crime, 5–6

Economy, Chinese, 82, 98–99

"Eight Major Disciplines and Ten Points for Attention," 161–162

Engels, Friedrich, 74

Gang crime, 59, 68, 125

"Getting rich is glorious" slogan, 7, 26, 29–30, 33–34, 43–44, 83, 96, 98

Government officials: bribery and corruption of, 25–29; traditional dual image of, 25–26

Hobbes, Thomas, 90

Homicide, 5, 6

Household registration (hukou), 97, 107, 118; reform of, 153–154

Household size, urban, 108–109

Hu Changquing, 27

Income distribution, China vs. United States, 78

Income inequality, 99; and ascribed status, 81, 82, 83; as cause of crime, 78; and crime increase in China, 77–83; and Chinese economic reform, 79–80; Gini coefficient measure of, 68–69, 78; and relative deprivation theory, 68–69; rural versus urban, 78–79; and Western theories of crime, 74

Jiang Zeming, 81

Juvenile delinquency: and age of accountability, 177–178, 179; causes of, 61; drug-related, 125–126; classification of, 59; rate of, 125; research, 58; recidivism and, 183; and serious offenses, 182

Juvenile justice, 177–183; criminal responsibility and age in, 184–185; history and development of, 177–179; and juvenile court, 183–185; legal responsibilities in, 183; prevention in, 181–183; punishment in, 186; regulations and laws, 126, 127–128, 178–183; rights and protection in, 179–181

Labor camps, 100

Larceny, changing definition of, 75

Law, Anglo-American, 92

About the Editors and Contributors

Liqun Cao, Ph.D., is Associate Professor of Sociology and Criminology at Eastern Michigan University. His research has been published in *Justice Quarterly, Criminology, Journal of Criminal Justice, American Behavioral Scientist*, and *American Journal of Police*. Currently, his research interests are in the areas of social control, criminological theory, crime prevention, and comparative criminology.

Mei Cong is an Assistant Professor at the Institute of Law Sciences, Tianjing Academy of Social Sciences. Her research has been focused on criminal motivation and criminality of differing age groups.

Yisheng Dai is the former Director of the Research Institute of Public Security; Minister of Public Security, PRC; Vice President of the Chinese Society for Juvenile Delinquency Studies; Visiting Professor at the University of Illinois at Chicago; correspondent for *Crime and Justice International*, and Assistant Editor of *International Journal of Offender Therapy and Comparative Criminology*.

Shuliang Feng is Professor and former Deputy Director of the Institute for Crime Prevention, Ministry of Justice, PRC. He is currently Vice President of the Chinese Society of Criminology. He is the author and coeditor of several books and numerous articles. His major research interests are crime prevention and criminal justice.

Allan Y. Jiao is an Associate Professor at Rowan University in New Jersey. He earned his Ph.D. in criminal justice from Rutgers University. He has published extensively in the field of policing. Recent articles have appeared in *Police Studies, International*

Journal of Comparative and Applied Criminal Justice, Policing: An International Journal of Police Strategies and Management, Journal of Crime and Justice, Journal of Criminal Justice, Police Practice and Research: An International Journal, and *Practical Applications for Criminal Justice Statistics.* His book *Police Auditing: Theories and Practices* was published in 2000. Jiao's primary research interests involve police organizational diagnoses and police performance evaluations.

Jianhong Liu is an Associate Professor at Rhode Island College. He earned his Ph.D. from the State University of New York at Albany. His work has appeared in *Justice Quarterly* and *Criminology.* His research interests include Chinese crime, social control, and Chinese criminal justice. He is currently examining social capital and subcultural values for Chinese offenders and also examining economically motivated crimes in China.

Peter Liu is an Assistant Professor at Monmouth University in New Jersey. He earned his Ph.D. at Indiana University of Pennsylvania. His areas of interest include research methods, criminology, comparative criminal justice systems, and administration and judgment of criminal justice systems.

Hong Lu is an Assistant Professor of Criminal Justice at the University of Nevada, Las Vegas. Her research interests include social control, sociology of law, and comparative criminology. Her current research focuses on the comparative study of crime and criminal justice in the United States and China. Her work has appeared in *Crime and Delinquency, Social Science Journal,* and *International Journal of Comparative and Applied Criminal Justice.* She has written several book chapters on crime control and the police.

Guoan Ma is currently a Professor at Shanghai Law University. He earned his Ph.D. in Law from Peking University and Master of Law from China University of Political Science and Law. He is the author of *Migration and Crime in China,* and coauthor of *Highlights in Criminal Sciences—Review and Prospects at the Turn of the Century.* He was Young Asian Scholar at Melbourne University, Australia, in 1997.

Steven F. Messner is Professor of Sociology and Chair of the Department of Sociology at the State University of New York at Albany. He earned his B.A. from Columbia University and his Ph.D. in sociology from Princeton University. His research has focused on the relationship between features of social organizations and crime rates, using data for neighborhoods, metropolitan communities, and nation-states. He has been involved in studies of crime in China and the situational dynamics of violence. Currently, he is conducting research on the spatiotemporal variation in violent crime across U.S. counties and on the relationship between social capital and homicide. He has published extensively in professional journals and is coauthor, with Richard Rosenfeld, of *Crime and the American Dream;* coauthor, with Allen E. Liska, of *Perspectives on Crime and Deviance*; and coauthor, with Rodney Stark, of *Criminology: An Introduction Using ExplorIt.*

Terance D. Miethe is a Professor of Criminal Justice at the University of Nevada, Las Vegas. He is the author of four books and numerous articles in the areas of criminology and legal studies. His most recent book is *Whistle Blowing at Work: Tough Choices in Exposing Fraud, Waste, and Abuse on the Job* (1999). His current research involves the historical examination of homicide situations in Western societies.

Dean G. Rojek is a Professor at the University of Georgia. His special interests are juvenile delinquency and the sociology of law. He is the author of two books and numerous articles; and is a coeditor of *Social Control in the People's Republic of China* (1989).

Yingyi Situ is an Associate Professor at Richard Stockton College of New Jersey. She earned her Ph.D. at Indiana University of Pennsylvania. Her areas of interest include environmental crime, comparative criminal justice, quantitative and qualitative research methods, criminology, crime control, and social control.

Lening Zhang is Assistant Professor of Sociology and Criminology at Saint Francis University (PA). He has published numerous articles in the fields of crime, criminal justice, and substance abuse. His current research focuses on the relationship of substance abuse and crime and the comparative study of crime and criminal justice in the United States and China.

Guoling Zhao is a Professor at Beijing University. She is Vice President and Secretary-General of the Chinese Society of Criminology. She is the author of numerous articles, and was a visiting professor at Hong Kong University. Her major research interests are criminal law, criminal justice, juvenile justice, and children's rights and protection.

Lu Zhou is the Vice President of the China Society of Juvenile Delinquency Research, and the Director of the China Research Association of Criminology. He is also Director of the Institute of Law Sciences at Tianjing Academy of Social Sciences. He has published books on positivist criminology and crime control policy in China.